90 0716556 6

WITHDRAWN
FROM
UNIVERSITY OF PLYMOUTH
LIBRARY

2|11|07
9|11|07

University of Plymouth Library

Subject to status this item may be renewed
via your Voyager account

http://voyager.plymouth.ac.uk

Exeter tel: (01392) 475049
Exmouth tel: (01395) 255331
Plymouth tel: (01752) 232323

Flexibility and Lifelong Learning

What can the politics of discourse tell us about the discourse of politics?

How are flexibility and lifelong learning positioned within policy?

Flexibility and lifelong learning have become key aspects of education policy in nation-states and bodies such as the European Union and Organisation of Economic Cooperation and Development in recent years. They are positioned as necessary for the knowledge economy and social inclusion. The failure to adapt by becoming more flexible and participating in lifelong learning is held up as a failure at individual, organizational and national levels.

But how has that narrative come to be constructed? In what ways is it persuasive? And what forms of political action are possible and necessary? These are the questions addressed in this text. Drawing upon the work of Michel Foucault and on the notion of rhetoric, this book forensically explores examples of the work of policy texts in the discourses of education, lifelong learning and flexibility that they construct. In so doing, it argues the need to take policy discourse seriously and not simply dismiss it as 'spin'.

Through a detailed examination of policy texts from primarily Australia, the United Kingdom and the European Union, this text provides insights into the strategies through which flexibility and lifelong learning are realized as part of the common sense of educational discourse. Rather than simply rejecting these ideas, or suggesting that they are merely the window dressing for the more malign interests of the knowledge economy or globalization, it suggests a politics of the wedge and possibilities for the insertion of different meanings. Central to the claims of this text is the fact that we need to engage closely with the discursive and rhetorical strategies of policy, in order that we understand both how it is constructed and thus how it can be deconstructed.

Katherine Nicoll is Lecturer in Education at the Institute of Education, University of Stirling, UK.

Flexibility and Lifelong Learning

Policy, discourse and politics

Katherine Nicoll

Routledge
Taylor & Francis Group

LONDON AND NEW YORK

UNIVERSITY OF PLYMOUTH

9007165566

First published 2006
by Routledge
2 Park Square, Milton Park, Abingdon, Oxon OX14 4RN

Simultaneously published in the USA and Canada
by Routledge
270 Madison Ave, New York, NY 10016

*Routledge is an imprint of the Taylor & Francis Group,
an informa business*

© 2006 Katherine Nicoll

Typeset in Galliard by
Newgen Imaging Systems (P) Ltd, Chennai, India
Printed and bound in Great Britain by
Biddles Digital, King's Lynn

All rights reserved. No part of this book may be reprinted or
reproduced or utilised in any form or by any electronic,
mechanical, or other means, now known or hereafter
invented, including photocopying and recording, or in any
information storage or retrieval system, without permission in
writing from the publishers.

British Library Cataloguing in Publication Data
A catalogue record for this book is available from the British Library

Library of Congress Cataloging in Publication Data
A catalog record for this book has been requested

ISBN10: 0–415–37283–6 (hbk)
ISBN10: 0–203–96944–8 (ebk)

ISBN13: 978–0–415–37283–1 (hbk)
ISBN13: 978–0–203–96944–1 (ebk)

Contents

Preface

A preface is a convention of writing, which offers the author a space to comment or reflect on a completed text and to mention circumstances outside the text and of its writing which are not mentioned within it. This includes an acknowledgement of influences upon the production of this text, those who are responsible but are not to blame! I want therefore to make a few comments of this kind. This book is the outcome of many years of work during my travels as an academic in Australia and the United Kingdom. Many people have contributed to my writing over the years and have supported my efforts to formulate a textual politics and politicization of texts, when examining education policy. Key here are Nicky Solomon and Clive Chappell, good friends as well as colleagues.

I would also like to acknowledge colleagues within the Institute of Education, University of Stirling for enabling me to take research leave to complete this text, and the Organizational, Vocational and Adult Learning Research Centre at the University of Technology, Sydney for providing me with a temporary home while on leave. I would also like to acknowledge financial support from the Carnegie Trust for the Universities of Scotland, which enabled me to undertake research contributing to this text.

Many of the ideas in this text I have rehearsed at conferences and in publications. I have benefited from the many engagements that has entailed. Some of that work has been with my partner and colleague Richard Edwards. He has lived with this text almost as long as I have. Without his support and guidance, it may never have been completed.

In the end, this text is mine in the making and yours in the taking...

1 Departures and beginnings

Political analysis and criticism have in a large measure still to be invented – so too have the strategies that will make it possible to modify the relations of force, to co-ordinate them in such a way that such a modification is possible and can be inscribed in reality. That is to say the problem is not so much that of defining a political 'position' (which is to choose from a pre-existing set of possibilities) but to imagine and to bring into being new schemas of politicization. If 'politicization' means falling back on ready-made choices and institutions, then the effort of analysis involved in uncovering the relations of force and mechanisms of power is not worthwhile. To the vast new techniques of power correlated with multinational economies and bureaucratic States, one must oppose a politicization, which will take new forms.

(Foucault 1980: 190)

Post-compulsory education policies and politicians tell us that we must become more flexible as individuals, whether we are learners or workers. Our institutions must be more responsive to demand. As our future environment is no longer certain, all must become flexible. As learners, we must take on new skills in contexts of change. As individuals, we must ensure that we equip ourselves to be employed or to maintain our employment. As educators, we must be flexible at work, be prepared to take on new ways of doing our jobs and new ways of thinking if the needs of our students and societies are to be met. Educational institutions must be flexible if they are to equip populations with the attributes that our corporations and economies will need for the future. We are incited by politicians to become lifelong learners, to learn continuously so that we might better contribute to work and societies. Organizations, we are told, need to become learning organizations and societies learning societies.

These themes of flexibility and lifelong learning have been around for some time now. They emerge and are repeated over and over within policy discourses, within education institutions in conversations over what should best be done within teaching programmes, within the media and elsewhere. They are, for many, signs of the new times in education – whether this is considered good or bad.

There is no doubt that it is in part through the themes of flexibility and lifelong learning that governments and intra-national policy organizations have argued for quite radical change within education systems and societies over the last years. They are embedded within wider arguments for the marketization of systems of education, and for economic and social reform. They are not just talk, even though they are often represented as such within the media and by policy analysts. They do things; they take effect. Their effects are of course quite difficult to pin down. They are not uniform but fragmented and what appears as an effect within one context may emerge quite differently elsewhere. To some extent what can be identified as effect depends upon the analytic resources that one brings to bear. However, they do appear to be bound up in complex ways with moves away from welfare state forms of governance towards those that are identified as post-welfare within some nations. In some national contexts they are argued to work in support of a reconfiguration of previous relations between state and civil society. They seem to help reconfigure education and training systems; as they enter into our schools, colleges and universities as themes for change, they support reconfigurations of curricula, alter the relationship between the teacher and learner, revise assessment practices, and inscribe an ethic and value of learning where education and training was previously considered a social rather than economic good. They are argued by some to be themes that support the reconfiguration of the political field and moves towards post-modern forms of economies and societies. They are thus powerful and political in the work that they do. In part, this is through policy strategies that are deployed in their name – for example, the policy theme of flexibility is often accompanied by financial strategies to increase intra-institutional competition. The themes of flexibility and lifelong learning become embedded within institutional and other discourses and are taken up in sites of education and elsewhere as local themes for the reconfiguration of practices of teaching and learning.

They are then themes and arguments of policy that appear to have the capacity to rework relations that have previously been relatively stable – between governments, education and training institutions, students and teachers, and workplaces – and shape them into new forms. Such relations have always been in some sense relations of force or power, which attempt to be productive and mold our societies in ways that we take to be useful. Education and training systems are productive of particular kinds of people and societies; they help produce us and the worlds that we live in. Themes of flexibility and lifelong learning thus act in the reconfiguration and co-ordination of those relations of force that have previously been stabilized in a particular way, the workings and detail of which are thus important to understand further.

Some within the fields of education and policy studies appear relatively content with these themes and arguments. They have adopted them as truths and visions guiding their work of teaching or policy analysis. They have conducted research to see how they might be best realized. Others, however, have been much more troubled by and concerned about them and have sought ways to oppose them or at least to expose the work they do. This book joins this latter group, as it takes flexibility and lifelong learning as discourses of policy that are to some degree problematic. Flexibility and lifelong learning take on different signification, different meanings, within different locations and discourses. They are slippery, and, in themselves, hard to pin down. Within institutions of education and training and by people more widely they are quite commonly taken to signify what is 'good' and perhaps progressive about courses, institutions and learning. For example, increasing the flexibility of courses is thought to be useful to people, because it can signify an improvement of access to learning and may afford a widening of choice in the kinds of courses and topics available. Lifelong learning is often taken to denote a beneficial opening of learning to individuals across their lifespan. And there are few who would refuse the possibility of learning being open to them whatever their age. However, there is more to flexibility and lifelong learning than such local discourses imply. They are not just these things. When one raises one's head out of the immediate context one begins to see their correlation with the vast new techniques of power of which Michael Foucault speaks. Although meanings of flexibility and lifelong learning are not usually linked up directly with those of an increasing power of multinational economies or bureaucratic States, the increasing economization of education, training and learning and its enmeshment with policy arguments for flexibility and lifelong learning certainly points strongly in this direction. The question is how could this be considered and theorized? This book thus looks to invent strategies that may help find ways to articulate such a correlation. But it is a contribution that goes further than this. It considers possibilities from its articulation, for the modification of the relations that have been forged so powerfully through these themes. To this extent it is concerned with the politics of flexibility and lifelong learning as policy themes and with their politicization.

Distrust of policy making and policy makers has become more common as politics has become positioned as more concerned with the spin of media presentation than with substance. Of course, this is a powerful rhetorical achievement. To position a political party or interest group as engaged in spin is to attempt to undermine and delegitimize their position, and to position audiences as needing to distrust what is written/said. In some ways, this might appear to be fair. To suggest that an increase in funding is sufficient to achieve the policy goals set, when, in real terms, it signifies a decrease in funding, is rightly challenged. Or, as Fairclough (2000) does in his analysis of the language of the 1997 New Labour government in the United Kingdom, to suggest that new and old labour reflect different ideological positions is to manipulate language in the attempt to control public perception.

A contemporary concern over 'spin' and the more general undecidability associated with the proliferation of media and messages is nowhere more pronounced than in the world of policy. Thus, as Fairclough (2000: 3) suggests,

> language has . . . always been a relevant consideration in political analysis. But language has become significantly more important over the past few decades because of social changes which have transformed politics and government. An important part of these changes is a new relationship between politics, government and mass media – a new synthesis which means that many significant political events are now in fact media events.

Indeed, the mediatization of those events point to the rhetorical strategies engaged in not only by politicians but also by the media, as they attempt to engage in political struggle and mobilize their own audiences in the name of reporting (Macmillan 2002). Listen to the radio news and the struggles that take place between reporters and politicians over whether or not the chosen topic, for example, funding or student debt, does or does not represent a 'crisis'. Crisis narratives provide an imperative for policy action and, therefore, invest situations with political importance, almost regardless of the relative weight of evidence and analysis by all concerned. They engender a certain policy hysteria (Stronach and MacLure 1997). Within policy arguments, increasing flexibility and lifelong learning are represented as the solutions to the crises that we face.

While studies that point to a lack of substance in flexibility and lifelong learning policy are important, they may devalue or misunderstand the role and purpose of discourse in general and rhetoric in particular. This is, despite the importance of discourse and rhetorical analysis to be found in areas such as deconstruction (Parker 1997), genre studies (Freedman and Medway 1994), and the representation of research (Nelson *et al.* 1987; Atkinson 1996). Implicit within many studies that deploy the argument of rhetoric – like the term 'spin' – to criticize and denigrate certain communicative practices are forms of ideology critique. This is to construe certain representations in texts as mystifications of the material world by those who exercise power. Here, the notion of rhetoric is collapsed into ideology, and a transparent view of reality, clear of rhetorical traces, is implicitly posited as possible. By contrast, the argument of this book is that the study of policy in general and lifelong learning policy and themes of lifelong learning and flexibility within policy in particular precisely as rhetoric can illuminate our understanding in slightly different ways. These point to the very real and powerful rhetorical practices that are in play both in policy representations and within our own. The significance of this work is in that 'part of the job of the rhetorical analyst is to determine how constructions of "the real" are made persuasive' (Simons 1990: 11). The question is not so much about whether reality matches rhetoric or not but which rhetorical performance is more persuasive, how, why and with what effects. Here presentation and representation are taken to be substantial actions in their own right.

Flexibility and lifelong learning are important contemporary themes of post-compulsory education policies within many post-industrial countries. They are presented within policies as solutions to the particular challenges of the contemporary world that must be overcome. They are crisis narratives. Over the years, there has been quite a significant analysis of them within the policy studies and post-compulsory education literature (e.g. Field 2000b; Coffield 2002; Edwards *et al.* 2002). Certain theoretical approaches have dominated this work with resulting productivity but also specific forms of constraint. These latter produce particular discursive relations – relations of power – within and between the domains of study and policy and thereby limit the meanings of flexibility and lifelong learning that emerge. In the process, specific questions of the discursive and rhetorical construction of flexibility and lifelong learning and the power and politics involved in this have been marginalized. This book takes these constraints as its point of departure in three trails of exploration and theorization. It identifies a different beginning for the politicization of flexibility and lifelong learning within policy studies and alternative resources for their analysis.

This book then explores the potential for different forms of discourse analysis as a means to examine flexibility and lifelong learning, to theorize them and furnish new avenues for politicization. It brings together a range of theoretical resources, beginning with aspects of the poststructuralist work of Michel Foucault (1972, 1996) and the rhetorical analysis of Jonathan Potter (1996). It takes specific formal and national policy documents as the site for the analysis of discourses and themes. At first glance, these forms of analysis might be considered by some to be more akin to literary criticism than to any kind of critical policy analysis. However, to take this view would be to overlook their productivity and misunderstand the kind of work that they do. They are selected, as they make it possible to identify and expose the politics involved in constituting, maintaining and dispersing flexibility and lifelong learning as themes within policy discourses. To make these analyses possible it is necessary to put aside previous notions of policy documents as simply realist or static descriptions or ideological mystifications. Policy documents are not taken as reflections of reality, nor as representations of 'settlements' between competing discourses. To view policy texts in this way would be to treat language as a neutral technology and ignore aspects of the political and active work that it does. Policy discourse acts rhetorically to work up the truth of what is described – it works to persuade us that we know the world and how we should act within it. It helps exclude and undermine alternative possible descriptions and actions. Policy language acts to reinforce and reinscribe prior regularities within discourses that make its truths possible and to which we are or become habituated even though we may also contest them. Policy masks its activity to condense, control and regularize discourses through the deployment of texts. These are active mechanisms of governance within policy processes. Policy discourses are thus imbricated with desire and power and work to exclude alternative discourses of other truths of the world that might emerge to challenge them.

Initial explorations

A poststructuralist and discursive approach drawing upon the work of Michel Foucault is productive for such a venture as it makes possible questions of the power and politics of discourses of flexibility and lifelong learning. It offers theoretical resources through which one can explore their constitution and operation. Policy studies have begun to take up such approaches in particular drawing upon Foucault's later genealogical work. This has resulted in explorations of discourses as expressions of power-knowledge that are actively constitutive of subjects, social forms and ways of thinking. However, this book draws upon Foucault's earlier work for specific explorations of flexibility and lifelong learning and on his later work for its positioning within relations of power. Crudely, some of Foucault's earlier archaeological work tends towards a more 'textual' and his later work towards a more 'critical' poststructuralism. The former is more akin to say, literary criticism, whilst the latter locates textual practices and their criticism within a broader framework of the production of knowledge and the exercise of power.

It is the more literary poststructuralism that links my interest and the relevance of this book to rhetoric. Rhetoric is part of the work of all policy discourse, just as it is of all language and communications. Policy analysts such as Stephen Ball (1990a) and Sandra Taylor *et al.* (1997) have highlighted the rhetorical work of policy and its power in public persuasion. However, even though acknowledged to be a significant aspect of policy activity, the work of rhetoric has not yet been examined in detail or to any great extent within the policy studies literature. In part, this is perhaps a consequence of rhetoric being quite generally understood to be a persuasive embellishment of language, often used to hide the truth and deceive. Analysts of policy have tended to search for the truth beneath or behind and hence adopt a realist stance. Here they either focus on the ways in which policy descriptions of the world match up with empirical evidence or ideologically mystify the 'real world'. This kind of focus has been 'natural' in the sense that it draws upon particular common sense views of the world and language, based on certain epistemological and ontological assumptions. However, in the process attention has been taken away from considerations of how policy language acts to build up representations of reality through rhetorical strategy.

The growth of modern science with its emphasis on the search for truth through a process of induction from empirical observation and experiment has resulted in little emphasis being given to the art of rhetoric. Rhetoric and truth have been held to be mutually exclusive and science has been concerned with the truth devoid of rhetoric. The persuasiveness of science has been held to rest in its truth claims not in its rhetorical practices, despite various incursions pointing to the significance of rhetoric to knowledge production in the sciences (Latour and Wolgar 1979; Nelson *et al.* 1987). Rhetorical analysis has been considered as part of the arts and humanities, while science is concerned with truth untainted by rhetoric. This can be seen within policy science but has continued to be the case within much policy sociology – 'its [rhetoric's] historical attitude towards knowledge production is much more at home with literary criticism than with sociology' (Leach 2000: 211). It is not therefore surprising that, in continuing traditions from both the empirical and social sciences, policy studies and the analysis of policy has not focused significantly on rhetoric. In this, policy studies have been bound within a certain politics of truth when questioning the truth of politics.

It is the particular discursive and rhetorical strategies that support, surround and help produce flexibility and lifelong learning as truths within policy discourses that are explored here. Policy communications are produced rhetorically and do rhetorical work (Axford and Huggins 2001; Chilton 2004). This depends in part upon prior regularities within and between discourses, which permit what can be said 'truthfully' at any one time and location. The approach in this text therefore undermines any certainty in a distinction between truth and rhetoric by examining the work of the latter in the production of the former. The position taken is that, by so doing, a dominant politics of truth can be elaborated.

The specific focus on flexibility and lifelong learning within this text is undoubtedly timely and important. They are promulgated as truths, as required responses to an increasing pace of change, the economic and social pressures of globalization and uncertainty over the future. If economies are to remain competitive within global markets and societies continue to cohere, it is argued that flexibility and lifelong learning, as the capacities and practices of individuals, institutions and educational systems, must be brought forth in the construction of learning societies. Flexibility and lifelong learning emerge within the policies of many post-industrial nations and intergovernmental agencies. For example, lifelong learning and the learning society are promoted within the United Kingdom (Kennedy 1997; NAGCELL 1997, 1999; NCIHE 1997; DfEE 1998, 1999; DfES 2003b), in Australia (DEETYA 1998), in Germany and from the Dutch, Norwegian, Finnish and Irish governments (Field 2000a). Lifelong learning and flexibility have been taken up strongly within the United Nations Education Scientific and Cultural Organization (UNESCO) (1996) and by the European Commission (1996, 2000a,b). Explorations of the means by which flexibility and lifelong learning are brought forth within policy discourses, of how they migrate across and within discourses much more widely, and their rhetorical strategies, will help the development of a notion of politics and policy as a form of communication rather than simply a struggle over truth. It will bring out how certain policy discourses come to be persuasive and powerful.

The regularity of the emergence of flexibility and lifelong learning over a period of time, across policy discourses and within differing locations points to the significance of a focus on the discursive conditions that produce, surround, and maintain them. However, this does not mean that themes or conditions will necessarily be the same within differing policy locations and times. Discourses are never uniform or unitary. They have emerged at differing times and locations over the last years and with differing emphases. John Field (2000a) traces how policies of lifelong education, rather than learning, for example, emerged within European policies during the 1960s and 1970s and were taken up by intergovernmental agencies such as UNESCO and the Organization for Economic Co-operation and Development (OECD). Lifelong education appeared again in 1993, within the European Commission in Jacques Delors' White Paper on competitiveness and economic growth (European Commission 1993). However, it re-emerged as lifelong learning in 1996 within European and national policy vocabularies after the European Commission declared that year as the European Year of Lifelong Learning.

Similarly, policy ideas of flexibility have been part of a discourse of the marketization of the economy, labour market and education within most OECD countries since the end of the 1980s. Flexibility was advocated in 1996 within a UNESCO report, also produced under the direction of the then former President of the European Commission, Jacques Delors, and at the same time within the European Union (European Commission 1996), although this was in relation to policies promoting open and distance learning. This points to both the regularity in the emergence of lifelong learning and flexibility as policy themes, as well as some of their differing meanings.

The focus on discourse and rhetoric within this book has not emerged out of a void. Not enough consideration has been given within education policy studies to the means by which flexibility and lifelong learning are constituted as policy themes. Policy studies have focused on the truth or otherwise of these notions, and their empirical effects, rather than how they are made up, forged, constructed, as truths within policy, and how they become mobilized. Policy study has largely located itself as in search of a better truth. To write this is not to assert or argue a truth but to try to find a different starting point – a different beginning – within power relations, from which to explore the significance of this omission. The focus on discourse and rhetoric is thus a discursive and rhetorical strategy, rather than a means to find better truth. This is important to make explicit at the beginning if you, the reader, are to situate yourself reflexively within the analysis that is to unfold. It is this focus and positioning that I consider productive in exploring significant aspects of the work of policy and in contributing to the study of policy in general and post-compulsory education in particular.

A poststructuralist positioning within studies of policy and post-compulsory education is of course not new. With the increasing emphasis on the discursive construction of reality, resources already exist to engage with questions of discourse. Indeed a recent edition of *Journal of Education Policy* was given over specifically to poststructuralism and policy analysis (Peters and Humes 2003). This book is positioned, to some extent in relation to the work of policy analysts such as Stephen Ball (1990a, 1994a), James Joseph Scheurich (1994) and Norman Fairclough (2000). Also in some kind of relation with post-compulsory education analysts, such as Sandra Taylor *et al.* (1997) and Richard Edwards (1997), and in continuity with my own work together with this latter author (cf. Edwards *et al.* 2004). However, the focus within this book on Foucault's earlier work locates it somewhat differently. Others have tended to explore discourses within a broader framework of the exercise of power. This is significant, as the theoretical tools that are drawn upon in any analyses are productive of the meanings able to be afforded to policy. They affect what is found and what is excluded. 'For me, much rests on the meaning or possible meanings that we give to policy; it affects "how" we research and how we interpret what we find' (Ball 1994a: 15). Within the Chapters 2 and 3 of this book, therefore, it will be important to give some indication of the meanings afforded to policy through this specific focus and positioning within Foucault's work.

Thus, although this book resonates with the work of contemporary theorists, some of whom draw upon the work of Michel Foucault, it is to some extent different in its positioning and does quite different work. This, in itself, produces certain possibilities for reflexive criticism, both of the limitations of the book and of the work of others. It is sufficient to say within this introduction that Foucault (1980) points to the requirement for forms of political analysis and criticism that may prove productive within contemporary contexts of globalization. These are contexts which are characterized by the reconfiguration of economic, social and political relations of power, for my purposes, in part through policy themes of flexibility and lifelong learning. He suggests that productive strategies are those that may modify and co-ordinate the modification of power relations within the contexts of their operation. This book explores what this might mean.

This is not to suggest that other works fall back in any simple way on ready-made choices or institutions, as is suggested quite possible in the introductory quote from Foucault above. They most certainly are and have been productive of alternative discourses with regard to policy. But they do not indicate how strategies may be 'co-ordinated' or inscribed in ways that do not end up incorporated into dominant relations of power. The relation to policy within this book thus differs, as it seeks to bring forth means to modify relations of power that bind policy and post-compulsory education analysis to policy. It seeks to discursively and rhetorically disrupt policy by theorizing and exploring aspects of the constitution and maintenance of its discourses, and to consider if the resources constituted through this activity provide strategies for alternative 'schemas of politicization' (Foucault 1980: 190).

The trajectories of exploration that are produced herein follow three trails. First, through a detailed examination of one particular policy document, Chapter 4 provides a trajectory for the exploration of discursive rules and rhetorical strategies that bring forth flexibility as a policy truth within a specific site of policy discourse. By making explicit the techniques, procedures and statuses that surround and support the production of flexibility within this document, it becomes apparent that flexibility depends for its effectiveness on 'rules of exclusion', by which it becomes possible for policy to constitute flexibility as a requirement of the age. To engage with this analysis involves considering the discursive and rhetorical rules and tactics by which flexibility is sanctioned, the techniques and procedures accorded value in this and identify those who are drawn upon and afforded status by being charged with saying what counts as true. This is a discourse of the politics of policy description in which flexibility is brought forth as a theme and positioned as a rational response within a stated policy context.

This discourse emerges from an exploration focused on an Australian Commonwealth post-compulsory education policy review document of higher education financing and policy that is commonly talked about as the *West Report* (DEETYA 1998). 'Flexible learning' emerged quite broadly as a discourse related to the reconfiguration of learning in Australian higher education institutions in the mid- to late 1990s and early 2000s. At around the same time, flexible learning became a phenomenon for discussion and debate within the Australian open and distance, higher education and more general post-compulsory education literatures. Two dominant strands of discourse were detectable within these. One strand accommodated flexible learning as pedagogy and discussed how best it could be implemented. A second, and more critical, strand pointed to the reconfiguration of higher education and vocational provision towards the market that was being attempted, encouraging flexibility and flexible learning. The politics of the constitution of specific understandings of teaching and learning through policy pressure and the complicity of both academic and policy discourses in this emerged as a significant issue. However, this pressure and relationship is not the specific focus of the discourse/theorization of Chapter 4. Rather, it becomes a more indirect theme of the book as a whole in its exploration of the exercise of power through the deployment of policy discourses and the complicity of policy studies in this. These are laid out and explored in detail within Chapter 2.

In Chapter 5, a second theorization emerges from an exploration of the migrations of flexibility and lifelong learning as metaphors within policy discourses. This trajectory takes 'metaphor' itself for its meaning-making capacities within language – it allows the meaning of metaphors itself to 'slip' across the possibilities of meaning that it provides to us. Metaphors are used powerfully and systematically within the political arena to systematize responses to political activities and attempt to control discourses (Potter 1996; Torfing 1999). They work in part within systems of metaphors that they draw from and with which they resonate. Here the exploration of flexibility and lifelong learning is the means by which they are mobilized across and within discourses as part of a globalizing migration, and in this way become established widely as 'fact'. It is a theorization of the constitution of metaphor both as and for a politics of policy description.

This second theorization leads to an evaluation of policy themes as discursively mobilized and interrelated, although given different emphases within policy documents within differing contexts. Although contexts differ and the policy themes promoted within them are not exactly the same, there is resonance between them. The post-compulsory education policy studies and education literatures have begun to describe and theorize a global spread of education policy themes and the globalization of policy processes. This produced theorizations of migration within policy discourses (Edwards *et al.* 1999; Nicoll and Edwards 2000). The work of rhetoric in this, however, has not been exhausted. By focusing on metaphor, a set of theoretical resources are made available and a space found for theorizations of the migration of flexibility and lifelong learning within and across policy discourses more widely.

The third theorization in Chapter 6 is of the genres of rhetorical work of lifelong learning as a policy theme within mostly UK policy documents. This draws upon a related set of resources from rhetorical studies. Whereas the first discourse described above focuses on the discursive conditions and rhetorical strategies of truth-building, this one explores the means by which truths can become persuasive through the operation of differing genres of rhetoric (Leach 2000). It explores the rhetorical genres drawn upon within specific policy descriptions. Different genres of rhetoric support the constitution of lifelong learning within policy discourses. At the same time by deploying them as a tool for analysis, they offer a means to expose further the political working of rhetoric in the constitution of lifelong learning as a policy theme.

Each attempts to mark the truth-making practices of politics in order to develop strategies through which alternative truths are and can be made.

Nomadic theorizing

The difficulty with this type of work is that the discourses produced may get themselves taken up as a scientific truth. Foucault (1980) warns of this tendency. Knowledge that has been subjugated and is brought forth for critical work may become re-codified and re-colonized in this way taken up as truths. The danger of these explorations is that they might bring about just such a general acceptance, to be taken up and colonized as truth of this sort, or, worse, that the work within this book itself may appear to be colonizing.

A discursive and rhetorical strategy to avoid such re-codification or re-colonization is that of the refusal of theory within this book. Theory prejudges a terrain of analysis by offering categories for analysis that are constructed prior to it. Meanings that emerge are bound by and constrained through these categories. In some senses, theory polices that which can be legitimately said. Theory 'might be said to put the cartography before the horse' (Perry 1998: 161). It prejudges a terrain for analysis by offering us maps that essentialize truth and origin, and defend and disguise themselves in this way. Scientific theory 'travels' by this means (Perry 1998). Maps can be carried from place to place to anticipate the terrain that is encountered. They offer an abstract global cartography or universal template, as on the map, through which local features may be either identified and abstracted, or discounted and ignored. Variations, what is discounted or ignored, 'can both be acknowledged and rendered residual, fixed by/in/difference, since they, unlike abstraction, do not travel...Theory...presents itself as if coming from nowhere/anywhere' (Perry 1998: 161).

This book emphasizes the process of theorizing rather than theory as a thing. Theorizing is a journey whereby the traveller actively seeks to articulate his or her located activity. It emphasizes fragmentation and incompleteness in efforts to bring to the fore locatedness as a condition of practice. These are locations from which it is possible to mount critiques of theory that 'does not (care to) know its (own) place' (Perry 1998: 162). The book thus seeks to foreground the theorizing in which I am engaging, to avoid generalized theory and pre-determined abstractions, by picking up tools and resources that appear to me to be useful within the varied discursive terrain across which I travel. This signifies the endlessness of theorizing as discursive and rhetorical analysis, and an imperative to forge new beginnings, rather than any possibility of fixing the terrain for all time.

A second strategy is in an emphasis of the activity of myself, the theorizer, as 'nomad'. This is a means to emphasize the plurality of location and authorship. The nomad is a metaphor of self as decentred subjectivity (a displaced and located subjectivity). It is an important analytic and rhetorical resource which displaces in advance any suggestion of the unification of theorizations through their potential attribution to the unity of 'author' as centred subject. The metaphor of nomadism reflexively represents the activity of travelling without any map of the lay of the land in the theorizing of policy and of its analysis.

A third strategy is the refusal of origins as starting points or ends that are productive of completed work. The enterprise of doing and travelling is thus portrayed as a collection of discontinuous trails. These trails of theorization and exploration are picked up at one time and place, leading to some extent nowhere, disconnected and fragmented. In some ways, they are, as Foucault (1980: 78) said of his own work, 'tangled up into an indecipherable, disorganized muddle'. They do not begin at predetermined beginnings nor end at predetermined ends; for neither origins nor unities are signified here.

> Still, I could claim that after all these were only trails to be followed, it
> mattered little where they led; indeed, it was important that they did not

have a predetermined starting point and destination. They were merely lines laid down for you to pursue or to divert elsewhere, for me to extend upon or re-design as the case might be. They are, in the final analysis, just fragments, and it is up to you or me to see what we can make of them.

(Foucault 1980: 78–79)

My trails of theorization are taken up and followed, and, in just such a way as indicated by Foucault, they are for you and me to make what we can of them.

These 'vagaries' are purposeful and rhetorical features of this text. However, they have emerged through my physical location and relocation in research and academic discourses in both Australia and the United Kingdom over a number of years, and out of the intertextuality of my theorizing with that of others within these locations, which has helped me to produce these statements as this text. They are a product of my own embeddedness and embodiedness (Usher *et al.* 1997). They are thus a product of prior discourses – of what these have made possible for me to say 'truthfully', while avoiding truths that are scientific in any generalizable sense.

This book then represents trails of exploration and theorizing that are adequate to this particular moment and to the discursive sites in which the constitution and work of flexibility and lifelong learning have been considered. They are theorizing which I argue is productive within current contexts where 'vast new techniques of power' are taken to require new forms of 'politicization' (Foucault 1980). The themes of flexibility and lifelong learning that are explored are not from one policy or geographical location, nor year. National policy documents that are significant in different discursive locations – Australia and the United Kingdom – are explored in various ways. The theoretical resources drawn upon are differentiated according to the questions that emerged as significant and productive to me at specific times and places and as they offered means for productive engagement with them. The theorizations that emerge are constituted through and are disparately located within trails of nomadic theorizing, as my strategy to avoid their colonization or codification, recognizing that the text, when published, is now no longer mine to do with as I wish.

Within the following chapter the post-compulsory education and policy studies literature is examined to elicit some of the meanings of flexibility and lifelong learning that have emerged. Within Chapter 3 more detail is offered of some of the positioning sketched within this introduction. It identifies the possibilities and limitations of meanings of flexibility and lifelong learning that are produced by differing approaches to policy analysis. I argue that dominant approaches to flexibility and lifelong learning policy struggle over questions of truth. I suggest that poststructuralist and rhetorical approaches to policy analysis may offer fruitful additions. I also suggest a theorizing of the policy document as a distinctive site for analysis within policy discourses. Within the seventh and final chapter, the theorizing pursued within this book is examined for its 'imagining' of a schema of politicization that may be productive in countering stabilizations within relations of power. This could be read as an exploration of the persuasiveness of my own 'theme' – rhetorically constructed. It considers the extent to which this theorizing may contribute to education policy studies through the production of discourses over the means for the constitution and mobilization of flexibility and lifelong learning as truths within policy discourses. I consider whether I have been able to reveal and place specific issues at stake in struggles over flexibility and lifelong learning and the effects of such discourses. The significance and effects of the theorizing of the book are explored, together with what may be considered some of its limitations.

The Chapter 7 concludes that these trails, as fragments, do make a contribution to the study of policy. The book produces various ways to consider discursive relations and rhetoric by drawing on resources, some of which have not previously gained much attention. Of course, by pointing to these I point to my own discursive and rhetorical practices and these are practices of power. In problematizing the discursive relations within which policy and approaches to the study of policy and post-compulsory education are caught up, one has also to acknowledge that there is no escape from them. It is a reflexive tension within the text; to be wary of overstating claims while being able to make some. In contributing to emergent discourses, any analysis becomes part of the discursive network of power that formulates truths, even though not necessarily scientific ones. This work must reflexively engage in its own strategies, motives and influences. I argue, however, that in deploying discursive and rhetorical approaches as a means to counter dominant stabilizations of power, productive work has and can be done. Discursive and rhetorical analyses are dominantly positioned as work that is unscientific and hence less than truthfull. Discourse analysis is ill-disciplined, and rhetorical analysis tantamount to the 'spin' of the spin doctor. However, theorizings of discourse and rhetoric can take policy texts as their object of analysis. By remaining neutral to questions of truth, by putting such questions aside momentarily, it can open up a space for effective and reflexive political theorizing.

The book attempts to be significant in four quite distinct ways. First, in the production of trails of theorizing that can be taken up, pursued, diverted and extended by myself or others, the work is significant in its examinations of the means by which policy themes may be constituted and take effect within policy discourses. Second, it is significant in the constitution of discourses of the rhetorical work of policy in their production of flexibility and lifelong learning. Third, in theorizing the complicity of policy studies and post-compulsory education studies in a relation of power that supports the reinforcement and maintenance of the truths of governments and in work to counter this, I point to the networks of discourse that embrace the academic and the political in the study of policy. Fourth, in beginning to reveal the extent and potential effectiveness of the rhetorical work of governments, in part made possible through the policy document, I provide further insights into the symbolic work of policy. The trails herein are local discourses of flexibility and lifelong learning. But despite or maybe because of this, they undermine previous certainties that we know what policy is by understanding what it does.

2 Meanings of flexibility and lifelong learning

What I mean is this: in a society such as ours, but basically in any society, there are manifold relations of power which permeate, characterize and constitute the social body, and these relations of power cannot themselves be established, consolidated nor implemented without the production, accumulation, circulation and functioning of a discourse. There can be no possible exercise of power without a certain economy of discourses of truth which operates through and on the basis of this association. We are subjected to the production of truth through power and we cannot exercise power except through the production of truth.

(Foucault 1980: 93)

Flexibility and lifelong learning are extensively represented as necessary truths – as necessary features of post-compulsory education systems and societies within contemporary policy rationales. They are constituted within policy, in part, through their resonance within broader societal discourses. Those who might be identified as post-compulsory education policy analysts, education policy sociologists, and post-compulsory education analysts and practitioners, variously take an interest in the themes of lifelong learning and flexibility and explore and produce multiple discourses and meanings of them. Their broad focus is to produce knowledge – further or alternative truths – which can either inform policies or practices of education, or describe or critique these.

This points in the direction of an economy of discourses of truth regarding flexibility and lifelong learning which operates through an association between discourses and the relations of power that require them. The literature explored in this chapter helps reveal the dispersions, relations and concentrations of meanings of flexibility and lifelong learning, as they have emerged within discourses of policy, and scholarly and institutional sites. It is not a complete or systematic mapping, for this is an impossibility. In line with my view of nomadic theorizing, it is not, nor could it be, exhaustive. There is an orchestration or choreographing of the literature in this chapter, rather than a mining to the point of exhaustion.

Policy and wider discourses of the economy and society intersect with those of lifelong learning and flexibility in complex ways. It is through these and the practices that they imply and bring forth that society is meant to be reconfigured. Of course, discourses are neither equally powerful nor are they the same. Differing meanings of the learning society, lifelong learning and flexibility are embedded through differing rationales, approaches to their consideration and within differing sites. These are often dispersed, fragmented and overlapping. They form alliances in complex and unpredictable ways. They are embedded within policy rationales for change and are deployed in part through policies in attempts to govern. They are constructed and are deployed within institutional sites in relation to educational practices. They emerge and are deployed within and through the media, research and scholarship and in everyday places. Meanings, however, are significant in that they realize flexibility, lifelong learning and the learning society as they inscribe and reconfigure discourses and practices. 'Discourses are not about objects; they do not identify objects, they constitute them and in the practice of doing so conceal their own invention' (Foucault, quoted in Ball 1990a: 17). Thus, an exploration of various meanings of flexibility and lifelong learning looks to their dispersions as effects of power. To say this, of course, is to adopt a particular meaning of discourse and policy which will be important to make explicit, for 'more often than not analysts fail to define conceptually what they mean by policy. The meaning of policy is taken for granted and theoretical and epistemological dry rot is built into the analytical structures they construct' (Ball 1994a: 15). I shall write more on this in the next chapter.

This chapter is written in four main sections. These are organized around certain meanings of flexibility and lifelong learning, as they are described and discussed within literatures with differing foci and concerns. The first section identifies what are characterized as institutional meanings of flexibility, emerging from those who are involved in post-compulsory education and within the literatures that are oriented to these. Meanings for those in post-compulsory education institutions are primarily focused on flexible learning and the flexible provision of education, often in a technical sense and as part of its marketization. Although critical discourses of institutional flexibility do exist within these literatures, they tend not to engage with wider debates about policy, or with the social and economic consequences, or broad desirability, of such practices. The second section reviews meanings of flexibility that are identified within the education and policy studies literatures, which do consider wider meanings of flexibility and its consequences and desirability. These focus on flexibility as a theme within policy discourses and on discourses of flexibility that emerge outside the contexts of the education institution, in order to explore its discursive, social and economic meanings and effects. The third section considers the interrelations between the policy themes of flexibility and lifelong learning and the wider discourses that they promote through literatures that take this as their focus. These are discursive explorations and thus take discourses as their context and site of effect. The fourth section considers conceptual explorations of the meanings of lifelong learning, emerging from the policy studies literature and within discourses of post-compulsory education and their analysis.

This characterization of the emergence of meanings with differing foci – on the institution, context and conceptualization – is a textual device more than a suggestion of any discrete boundaries. Although they are identified here as if they can simply be differentiated, this is not a suggestion of any unities. It is an heuristic device that I have found useful in my exploration of meanings. It has helped me to examine the dispersions and relationships between meanings and potential constraints and productivities within them. Meanings thus intersect and overlap, although policy and post-compulsory literatures do tend to have differing foci and concerns. Education policy studies literature tends to focus on questions of lifelong learning policies, and their analysis in terms of education and learning. Although there are one or two significant exceptions, they tend to subsume consideration of flexibility within the economic discourses, rather than take flexibility as a particular focus of analysis. The post-compulsory education literature, by contrast, focuses rather more on institutional discourses of flexibility and more broadly on meanings of lifelong learning. There are of course also excisions and limits to the meanings that are represented here. These are in part due to my travel and concerns as a nomadic theorizer. The exploration is then not directed in any attempt to discern the truth of flexibility or lifelong learning one way or another, but rather to expose emphases in the meanings that are at play within certain discourses. This helps me locate my own work of travelling.

Flexibility – re-engineering the institution

In Australia, it is higher education that has been most severely marketized (Taylor *et al.* 1997). As within the United Kingdom, restructuring has been driven since the 1980s primarily through a policy requirement for the 'flexible worker'. The policy logic has been that in order that this worker become a possibility, mass participation in higher education must be promoted. A shift from a Keynesian to a new market approach has underpinned this rationale for the expansion of higher education (Marginson 1993; Taylor *et al.* 1997). Rather than an expansion for the benefit of equality of opportunity and the individual and society, as within Keynesian ideology, flexibility became represented as necessary for the workforce in order that it can cope with change. Micro-economic reform and the production of multi-skilled and flexible workers are intrinsic to the new policy ideas and strategies for restructuring. In Australia, the unification of the higher education system was brought about through legislation that removed control of funding from individual States to the Commonwealth in 1974. Through this, the Commonwealth had the control to reconfigure the system to be more competitive. Institutions have had to find the increased funds to support extra students from sources other than the state. Market reform has not left the technical and further education (TAFE) sector in Australia untouched. The economic crises of the late 1980s and early 1990s resulted in workplace and industrial reforms and an increasing emphasis on training and retraining as a critical factor for national competitiveness in a global market (Trood and Gale 2001). It has been the focus of 'a well trained, flexible workforce' (Australian Education Council 1991: 13) that 'has embodied the central features of a changed government and industry agenda for vocational education and training' (Trood and Gale 2001: 163). A plethora of policy texts highlighted the lack of responsiveness and flexibility in the vocational education and training sector, and its inability to satisfy the changing needs of industry (e.g. Employment Skills Formation Council 1992; Keating 1994). Trood and Gale (2001) report on the ambiguity in such reports as to just what flexibility and responsiveness entail and an increasing discourse of uncertainty for vocational education and training (VET) teachers over what was required. Policy texts encouraged 'flexible entry and exit to courses, flexible assessment processes, learner controlled course content to meet industry needs, flexibility in the sequence of course content, flexibility in time and place of study, access to learner support, and access to and use of resource-based learning technologies' (Trood and Gale 2001: 166–67). However, they did not recognize the difficulties entailed or detail how this was to be achieved in practice.

This dual shift to decentralization and marketization within the Australian TAFE sector has been taken to its furthest in the State of Victoria. The election of the Liberal National Party coalition government in October 1992 highlighted what had already been a previous policy trend, with the emergence of policy initiatives and cuts in funding by the end of that year. The strategic direction of the State Training Board (1994) articulated the new market emphasis within Victoria as a move from: TAFE to VET; supply to demand; activity to outcome; quantity to quality; control to devolution. The TAFE Institutes in Victoria were largely reformed as training enterprises (Seddon and Angus 1999). The meanings of flexibility carried into institutions resonated with those of the neo-liberal agenda of marketization.

Meanings of flexibility emerged strongly within institutional contexts, from writers in Australia in particular but also from the United Kingdom and elsewhere. The focus of discussion tended to be on the practices of the university as an educational institution. Within the scholarly journals of open and distance learning, discussion of flexibility has been particularly prevalent. The focus has been on the emergence of flexibility as a term used within higher education institutions for provisions that might previously have been described as those of open or distance learning. Within higher, adult and continuing education, flexibility has also drawn attention to the need for change. Here discussion has been more widely on the influence of policies promoting flexibility on educational institutions, provision and pedagogies. This has been accompanied by institution-wide administrative reformation, and the promotion of discourses of technologization, marketization and managerialism (Evans 1995b; Taylor 1995).

Scholarly journals oriented to open and distance learning (cf. *Open Learning, Distance Education*) and the use of information and communication technology in learning have discussed flexibility. A core of those contributing to these discourses have had a role in support of curriculum and institutional development within universities specializing in open and distance learning in Australia and the United Kingdom, often working within staff development or educational development units within universities. However, these journals have also provided a locus for discussion encompassing a wider discourse group through the contribution of authors from other areas of the world.

This strand of institutionalized discourses has tended and continues to represent flexible learning relatively unproblematically. Flexible learning is identified as an extension and a migration of practices of distance and open learning from universities who had dominantly used these to those having had little or no such previous experience. Here flexibility is often coded as linked to increasing and widening educational opportunities rather than simply to marketization. Practices of open and distance learning were seen to have been renamed within this migration. Flexible learning is thus often not clearly distinguished from distance and open learning (Kirkpatrick 1997). Notions of open learning and distance education are thus often taken as co-terminus with those of flexible learning and as an area where specialist understandings derived from practices of open and distance learning apply.

Dominantly what has been written discusses how flexibility in learning, flexibility in the provision or the delivery of learning, or flexibility in the organization of institutions, might be achieved or achieved more effectively (cf. Bottomley 2000; Hawkridge 2000; King 2000; Thorpe 2000). Meanings of flexibility are in this way restricted to those that are technical in orientation. To say this is to point to the assumption that by increasing the flexibility of learning, known ends can be reached without any real need for question. Central to the ends of flexibility within this discourse strand are – increasing focus on the learner and individual choice in learning (flexible learning); the increase or widening of choice or access to learning within program or the ability of the institution or program to reach new student markets (flexible provision or delivery); and the organization of the institution to support flexible provision and learning (organizational flexibility). Flexibility is thus dominantly taken a priori as a benefit and as a technical characteristic of organizations, and contexts of learning and teaching, which increase the efficiency and effectiveness of learning or its provision. This 'cult of learning' (Campion 1991: 71) ignores significant questions

> The result is that learning for the learning society, for the learning organization (e.g. learning universities), and for learning individuals is presented as if it is the panacea that supposedly will miraculously cure all

our problems, whilst actually it ignores them...it is as if, 'if we wait in the right places in suitably receptive ways the technologies of learning will fly in the goodies just as the aircraft were expected to return with the cargo. If we access the learning centre/service station the requisite knowledge will flow forth like fuel from the pump ready for us to consume as we continue our travels!!'

Such discourses support the work of those involved in course, programme and institutional restructuring, largely without questioning the assumptions that underpin them. With a decentralizing of flexible practices within institutions that have not traditionally been concerned with them, texts focusing on flexibility in learning and targeting mainstream post-compulsory educational practitioners as their readership have therefore emerged (cf. Jakupec and Garrick 2000). This is illustrative of a broadening and generalizing of interest in meanings and practices of flexibility across contexts of post-compulsory educational practice and workplaces within much of the post-industrialized world.

A more critical literature regarding flexibility in the provision of learning does exist within this discourse strand (cf. Jakupec and Nicoll 1994a,b; Field 1995; Taylor 1995; Atkinson 1996; Nicoll and Edwards 1997) and was exemplified above in Campion's (1991) text. During the early 1990s, flexible learning was discussed in terms of a shift from Fordist to post-Fordist principles of production within the economy and education (Campion 1991; Edwards 1991). This was seen to have overemphasized labour market theories in the framing of changes from open and distant to flexible forms of education practice, thereby masking alternative possibilities. By placing reliance on specific theoretical frameworks (Rumble 1995), debate was criticized for having focused on issues of production rather than consumption (Field 1994) or more widely. Nunan (2000: 58) indicated three discursive positions in the relation between the producer and consumer within such frameworks. Production was positioned as determining consumption within a Fordist theory of production within the first. Changes in patterns of consumption were articulated as resulting in flexibility in production in the second. Here Fordism was seen to have at least partially been replaced by post-Fordism within contemporary post-industrial nations. In the third position, an interplay between consumers with choice and flexible producers was seen to create a production dynamic regulated by markets.

The terms Fordism, post-Fordism and neo-Fordism were commonly used as descriptors of patterns of modern production processes, and also as distinctive phases of capitalist production. Fordism described an assembly line labour process, exemplified by the Henry Ford car manufacturer at the beginning of the last century, which revolutionized understanding of modern production processes. Neo-Fordism described a new process of 'flexible production' within the automotive industry in the 1960s and 1970s, and a concomitant more general shift in capitalist accumulation. Post-Fordism denoted a turn towards leaner production and a disaggregation of the supply chain – a kind of outsourcing and 'just in time' approach to production that directly responds to consumer demand. Post-Fordism is also known as 'flexible specialization' and identifies a further phase of production. Each term describes an organization of institutional systems of production, the organizational structure that is required to sustain it and a phase of production oriented towards a market. Whatever the limitations, this strand of writing indicates an engagement with issues beyond the technical implementation of flexible learning, even though it is focused primarily on the educational institution and its provision, which is how it produces and services its markets. Empirical analysis of institutional discourses seems to support the argument that meanings of flexibility have been associated with local changes to practices rather than any concern with broader critiques and implications of such approaches. Denise Kirkpatrick (1997) explored meanings within one metropolitan Australian university, where managers had attempted to establish 'flexible learning' as a rubric and focus for change. Four discourses of flexibility emerged within the faculties in this context. 'These were efficiency; the competitive edge; equity and access; and flexible delivery (in particular the use of information technologies)' (Kirkpatrick 1997: 166). Within the first, strategies for the promotion of flexible learning were understood by academics as economic and political expediency on the part of the university, as short-term reaction rather than proactive response, and only secondarily as anything to do with education. Within the second, increasing flexibility was seen as providing a competitive edge by attracting students through increasing marketability and choice. Within the discourse of equity and access, flexible learning practices were taken to be supportive of liberal and humanistic views of education. Within the fourth, information technologies were strongly associated with flexible delivery and individuals who worked on projects funded within the university were seen to be gaining the competitive edge. An emerging discourse among more experienced academics was focused on improving the quality of teaching-learning experiences for students. These considered the role that flexible learning could play in improving student learning. These meanings of flexibility are focused upon its technical and institutional capacities – to make learning more efficient, competitive, equal or accessible, and so forth – rather than exploring its effects more broadly or critically.

Explorations of the uptake of flexibility suggest that flexible learning may be accommodated within discourses according to the role of the individual within the institution. Peter Taylor (1997), for example, examined the changes in the nature of work resulting from a move towards practices of flexible learning and how academics, academic managers and general staff within the institution understood these. Academics tended to understand flexible learning in terms of increasing access and equity to higher education, managers in terms of an increase in market share and general staff in terms of meeting clients' needs. Taylor himself concludes that there is a potential opening through a discourse of flexible learning to explore meanings beyond traditions of both face-to-face and of distance and open provisions and their limitations. Flexibility is thus taken up in some quarters as a means to change previous discourses and practices of education and learning. The discourse becomes part of change agency. It may well be that the meanings of flexibility are in part fashioned by the ends of those individuals who take part in its practices.

Flexibility is not explored as a distinct feature of policy discourse to any great extent within the post-compulsory education policy studies literature, and there appear to have been relatively few specific analyses of meanings of flexibility in economic, social or policy terms, or their effects in relation to education apart from within those discussed above. Where it is identified this is variously, for example, as policy rhetoric (Ball 1994a; Taylor *et al.* 1997), an ideological concept (Ball 1994a) or as a master concept within contemporary policy (Coffield 2002). The emphasis on flexibility in education is considered to be part of a repositioning of education in terms of the market. This particular meaning of flexibility emerges within Stephen Ball's (1994a) work. Here flexibility is argued to do work within the discourses of the educational institution to support the emergence of a correspondence between the education system and the economy through the creation of an education market. In the UK school context, a vocational emphasis within education policy through the 1980s is understood to have supported the emergence of a discourse of 'progressive vocationalism' and 'new progressive educators' (Ball 1994a: 30). This resulted in part from the involvement of the industrial lobby within policy formation processes, with their emphasis on discourses of the market, motivation and flexibility.

Policy and institutional discourses of flexibility thus emerge as significant to the processes of the repositioning and restructuring of education that are taking place more widely. Ball's (1990a) analysis of aspects of the UK 1988 Education Reform Act, relating to secondary education, has been important in finding a way in to demonstrate this. He identifies and examines the work of a theme of flexibility within various sites of policy discourse and in terms of its effects in restructuring the school. This exploration is a 'case' used to describe and analyse changes in the processes of education policy making in England. He explores the struggle of discourses surrounding flexibility. Policy is seen to have mobilized vocational discourses and constituted closer relationships between education and the economy. He illustrates a specific poststructuralist materialist approach to the analysis of flexibility. This produces a meaning of flexibility that is of a distinctive and local form, which is not generalizable to other sites because of the form of the analysis. Ball's work also points in the direction of the operation of discourses of flexibility much more widely, in their potential to reconfigure the correspondence between education and the economy within institutions of education and training. Flexibility emerges as a means to establish a synergy between discourses of 'new progressivism' within educational institutions and those of human capital required by employers and the economy:

> We have a situation in which attempts at change arising from particular theories of learning and philosophies of knowledge (which I call new

progressivism), which were intended to enhance the learning experiences and increase the motivation of students, have coincided (for want of a better word) with technological changes in industry, affecting the labour process and modes of production, which require new kinds of attitudes and competences from employees.

(Ball 1990a: 102)

This is a forging of a relationship between progressive and modernizing discourses, which resonates with the studies of Kirkpatrick and Taylor mentioned earlier. The discourse emerging from Ball's (1990a) interviews with individuals in key positions as representatives of the vocational interest within curriculum reform bodies of that time were illustrative of this new progressivism. Representatives articulated a requirement for students/employees to have a set of social skills and transferable competencies rather than subject-based knowledge. 'Flexible competencies and a predisposition to change are set over and against basic skills. The labour market training needs and educational outcomes are again intimately related' (Ball 1990a: 106).

The concept of flexibility within a discourse of vocational progressivism, along with discourses of the market, motivation and management were seen as key in a reconfiguration of the way in which formal educational knowledge was realized. The curriculum, pedagogy, evaluation and organization, and the underlying principles that shape them were all reconfigured. This was seen to mark a shift in the principles of social control and mode of regulation that are embedded within processes of social reproduction (here within education) within contemporary capitalist societies. The new mode of regulation was one ensuring the compatibility of institutional forms, networks and norms within education with market behaviour within a regime of accumulation. This shift was realized in part through the deployment of a discourse of market flexibility: 'As we have seen, such an ensemblement is realized in the key discursive concepts which articulate the industrial lobby – the market, motivation and flexibility, and management' (Ball 1990a: 124). It is therefore in part through a discourse of market flexibility that the processes of schooling, formally those of social reproduction, have become subordinate to processes of production within the economy. 'In effect, the processes of schooling are subordinated to the principles which provide organization and social control within the economy' (Ball 1990a: 124). This argument is powerfully relevant to post-compulsory education and training quite generally.

Responsiveness and flexibility are concepts that can do work to gain support for the marketization of education and training. Within the school context, they do this by appealing to the desire of parents to have a greater choice over their children's education and of managers to have greater freedom to manage. They gain support even though choice and freedom are not what is achieved. Stephen Ball's (1994a) critical social and poststructuralist work explores the extent to which managers of schools within the

United Kingdom were afforded the freedom of autonomy and flexibility that the policy suggested would ensue from a marketization of the sector. Managers argued a need to have greater autonomy and freedom so that schools could better respond to the needs or wants of parents. Ball identified various flexibilities that did emerge. These were derived from a reduction in influence of the local education authorities over the school. They included increased budgetary autonomy and contractual flexibilities. He concluded however that these flexibilities were counter-balanced by new constraints. 'It may be that flexibility is more apparent than real, or trivial rather than substantial' (Ball 1994a: 86). Through his analysis, the 'political rhetorics' for increasing flexibility and responsiveness hides a process of the restructuring of the moral environment of the school. Previously the principle of the 'common good' had been to the fore, and this moved towards one of individualism. He concluded that responsiveness (a near synonym for flexibility) is 'a matter of empty rhetoric and of ideology' (Ball 1994a: 146) that had been misapplied in relation to the school context. The rhetoric of flexibility is inappropriate because it does not recognize how the school market works. At the same time, it masks its reconfiguration of the mechanisms for the production of social values, morals and ethics that it effects.

Ball's (1994a) study is significant in producing meanings of flexibility and responsiveness as concepts that work within broader discourses to target and appeal to specific groups within the population. This is in such a way that their acceptance brings forth a wider moral shift, which then serves to further support their acceptance. In this way, they can be taken to be features of discourses that do rhetorical work within particular sites and have considerable effects. The schooling sector within the United Kingdom has undergone considerable change as a result of national policy; '[i]t is perhaps the schooling systems of England and Wales which have been subjected to the most thoroughgoing marketization, following the Education Reform Act of 1988 and subsequent legislation' (Taylor *et al.* 1997: 92). Ball's analysis suggests that specific policy concepts that emerge within ideological discourses of the market, and promote marketization in this way, appeal to particular desires and, through this, do work within sites of education and training. Policy vocabularies work to bring about change through the reconfiguration of ideological allegiances and the desires of actors.

As previously mentioned, there has been widespread policy reform of schooling over the last two decades within many post-industrialized nations, at least in part through the promotion of discourses of flexibility. Some work concludes that market-based reforms have tended to strengthen curriculum conformity rather than the reverse. Adnett and Davies (2000) provide an economic analysis of the relationship between increased competition, curriculum innovation and diversity. They assess the economic rationale that increasing competitive pressure on schools would promote curriculum innovation and diversity (flexibility) against the empirical evidence within the United Kingdom. They conclude that market-based reforms have tended to strengthen curriculum conformity rather than the reverse. Freeing up the system so that parents are afforded choice over school and curriculum appears to result, within a context of risk and uncertainty, in a conformity of parental preferences and thus a conformity of curriculum offered. Analysing a similar situation within the United States, Brown (1992) also argued that, where parents have choice over schooling, they also tend to opt for a broad and common curriculum for their children. They do not yet know what the abilities of their children are or what they will decide they want to do with their future. A common and wide curriculum in this situation is a way of shedding the risk involved in making any more specific decision at an early age (Adnett and Davies 2000).

Explorations of the economic choice theory, as it plays out in education and training contexts, and of increasing flexibility as an aspect of this, have been so far limited. These are, however, beginning to emerge in response to policy attempts to apply a generalized market choice theory to education systems. The analysis by Adnett and Davis (2000) is illustrative of this. Choice in education is not determined in isolation but is learnt from others and is influenced by 'fads and informational cascades' (Bikhchandani *et al.* 1998). Where league table ranking differentiates between schools, for example, as it does in the United Kingdom, Adnett and Davis (2000) suggest that parent selection may depend on these differences, rather than on the kind of choice suggested by orthodox demand theory. Informal networks may also provide the basis for parental decision making, rather than the formal signals that are provided to the individual parent. As decision-making parents appear to opt for an initially broad curriculum for their children, it logically follows that middle ranking providers should (and do) imitate the behaviour of successful (high ranking) schools in the local market. Innovation does not occur in this situation, even though the curriculum in high ranking schools may be obsolete. The value of what they do is coded into their ranking without questioning whether that coding is appropriate. Within very low ranking schools, curriculum innovation is more likely over a longer time span because they cannot attract the decision-making parents. But these schools are not likely to find the resources to do this successfully, and innovative staff are likely to leave. Policy arguments for the need for increasing flexibility of courses to provide greater choice have been deployed in relation to all education and training sectors, not just in relation to schooling. This kind of study is indicative of the kinds of assumptions that are made through these arguments and a potential for much more detailed analysis of marketization in post-compulsory education.

Policy ideas and strategies, such as those of flexibility, have been argued to be structural elements in processes of marketization and part of the ideological work of policy. Taylor *et al.* (1997) suggest that such ideas and strategies are produced through policy from new right ideologies. These include ideas of smaller government, competitive individualism and self-interest as the basis for the 'good society'. They work at the level of the institution to restructure it in terms of the market. Here the focus of comment is not on what flexibility or responsiveness brings with it in terms of any shift of values, but on the rational and logical relationship of policy ideas and strategies at different 'levels' of ideology and the institution. The ideology of self-interest as a basis for the good society requires particular ideas and strategies as restructuring devices at the institutional level, of choice, responsiveness and the publication of school test results or league tables. They emphasize a point made also by Ball (1994a) that, although policy ideologies and ideas may work powerfully through their interrelationships to restructure institutions, they may not in any simple way fulfil the promises that they describe. Policy presentation of the marketization of education as the solution to the problems of cost, control and performance in the public sector, within a rationale that is constructed through what were seen as new right or neo-liberal ideologies, has steered the restructuring of the system in particular ways that does not offer what it suggests. In this analysis, flexibility is a structural element of ideology. It is a restructuring device which requires particular discourses at the institutional level and, through the production of these, takes effect.

There have been analyses of the effects of policy agendas for increased flexibility within the tertiary education sector as well as schools. Terri Seddon and Lawrence Angus (1999) trace the Australian State and Commonwealth governments' agendas that aimed to redesign and 'renorm' the TAFE institution. This agenda took its lead from Osborne and Gaebler's (1993) Reinventing Government. They argue that, in requiring responsibility for the provision of services to be devolved to the institution, the market-oriented approach has had utility for governments as they no longer need to be involved in any formulation of ethical choices about the education that is to be provided. Within a market approach, previous normative issues, such as access and equity slip off the agenda within policy but also within educational institutions. This is in part because it is the individual who is afforded the responsibility for educational choice and achievement in the market model. Government processes of policy planning or 'moral suasion' are thus avoided.

The restructuring processes studied reconfigured the social organization and professional relationships that had hitherto existed and acted to 'incorporate an ethos of contractualism' (Seddon and Angus 1999: 497). This requires the individual TAFE teacher to take himself or herself as their own 'enterprise'. The teacher is redefined from public service oriented progressive educator to a competent actor and proficient manager in business. Individuals either take up the new discourse of the market, or become marginalized or lose their job. Thus in the re-engineering of educational institutions through discourses of flexibility, there are very material effects on the workforces within those institutions.

Flexibility – all change on the economic and social fronts

Flexibility can also be explored more broadly in relation to the social and economic contexts within which education is being re-narrated, re-normed and re-engineered. This is a focus found within both the education and policy studies literatures. It is here that the consequences and desirability of flexibility within the education domain are considered. There are a number of aspects to such discourses that I shall explore here.

Central to contextual discourses are changes in the type and organization of work and the skills required for employment. This is the dominant strand, which is characterized by a concern with economic productivity and competition. It is here that educational flexibility and lifelong learning become significant as policy responses. These are identified as having been taken up within policies and the thinking of national governments during the 1980s and 1990s as a response of governments to a 'crisis of capitalism' in most western countries since the early 1970s (Ball 1990a). They are associated with a general shift towards a version of human capital theory, with economic flexibility represented as a desirable and even inevitable requirement (Edwards 1997). Flexibility is then the attempt to resolve the problems of the accumulation of economic capital in situations of crisis. Here both educational flexibility and lifelong learning become significant within policy, as education systems are understood to be intrinsic in support of the economy. The value of education and learning is gauged in its responsiveness to the labour market and capacity to develop the skills required by it. Humans are capital to be maximized for their utility. Discourses promoting flexibility and lifelong learning are thus technical and instrumental responses for the maintenance of the competitiveness of nations. Within this strand, the technological and economic dimensions of discourses tend to mask their political dimensions. The focus is over the competitiveness of the economic system as a whole. It is about how to promote systemic and organizational flexibility and lifelong learning, not only within education systems and organizations but across the whole economic domain, with little discussion over the desirability of this. Arguments are focused on the changing nature and organization of work in response to the emergence of information technology. Flexibility of labour processes, labour markets and products, and consumption, become pressures for increased labour control implemented by employers.

A requirement for flexibility emerged strongly within human capital theory in the study of economics. Within this domain, the notion is that by increasing the levels of qualifications within a population economic growth would be increased. Arguments for increasing the relationship between education or learning and the economy are premised upon certain assumptions and models of economic behaviour. Although undergoing many modifications, the underpinning assumptions of neo-classical economics are maintained from early works through to those of Friedman (1955) and the wider efforts of the Chicago School of economics at that time. A basic assumption is that all human behaviour is determined by the economic interest of the individual operating within a free market. This was coupled with a hypothesis that increased education and training result in increased economic productivity.

Marginson's (1993) narration of the uptake of ideas from human capital theory within education policy is persuasive. It points to the emergence of an economic literature that begins to drive policy narrations of the requirement for flexibility within education contexts. The rate of investment return on education was argued to be higher than on physical capital, such as machinery or buildings. While it has taken different forms, a new form of human capital theory was taken up within OECD policy during the 1980s. Marginson (1993) suggests it to have emerged from a hypothesis explored by Nelson and Phelps (1966) about decision making in an agricultural context. The previous economic model had assumed a state of perfect information, which had not held up to scrutiny. Where the environment is characterized by fast techno-logical change, the individual is not in a situation of 'perfect information'. Education was proposed to enhance farmers' capacity to adopt and imple-ment new technologies. This hypothesis quickly promulgated a new strand of economic enquiry that explored potential correlations between education, information and innovation. Bartel and Lichtenberg (1987) hypothesized that, in environments of uncertainty and technological change, the highly educated were likely to be more productive than others. Furthermore, the more uncertainty inherent within an instance of technological change within a specific situation, the faster and more effectively would highly educated individuals adopt and use them. In the early stages of the use of new tech-nologies, and in situations of high levels of innovation, industries were purported to create job opportunities for the highly educated rather than lesser-educated workers. Thus, technological change was suggested to stimu-late economic competitiveness and growth. Marginson (1993) suggests that it was in response to this strand of work that the OECD constructed its subsequent 1980s policies. These required flexibility and responsiveness as a characteristic of both individuals and organizations. In Europe, this require-ment was embedded within the education policies of the OECD from 1986.

> The development of contemporary economies depends crucially on the knowledge, skills and attitudes of their workforces – in short, on human capital. In many respects, human capital has become even more impor-tant in recent years...a basic policy goal permeating education in all countries is to increase the productivity of human resources – so as to enable more valuable output of work, and thus allow higher wages and/or profits in the economy as a whole...The labour market chal-lenges that call for long-term adjustment of the educational systems stem from the pressures of international competition, technological change and, more generally, the need for flexibility.
>
> (OECD, in Marginson 1993: 48)

Education was constructed as the source of the flexibility and responsiveness of human capital that is required in relation to technological innovation and change within the environment.

As I have mentioned, a new regime of capital accumulation is understood to have replaced Fordism from the late 1960s, associated with innovation and an emphasis on developing a more qualified workforce. The dominant policy narration has been that increasing economic change brought about through globalization and technological innovation brings forth insecurity and the threat of poverty, to which increasing flexibility is the solution. By keeping labour costs as low as possible and increasing skill levels, governments have attempted to increase the desirability of their countries to those who are interested in investment.

Economic descriptions of the requirements for flexibility thus often represent increased flexibility as the needed response to economic globalization. However, Onman (1996) an economic advisor to the OECD, narrates the emergence of perceptions of a requirement for flexibility from as early as the 1950s for some manufacturing firms. This requirement was exacerbated by a widespread slowdown in the demand for goods in the United States in the 1960s. There was thus a move from Taylorist organizational structures and Fordist production methods within some firms towards those that increased their flexibility. Flexible forms for the organization and production methods thus emerged earlier than the current wave of globalization. The manufacturing company Toyota exemplified this in the later 1950s and those of the 'Third Italy' in the 1960s and 1970s. It was as a response to these successes that discourses of flexibility in production emerged more strongly towards the end of the twentieth century.

> The late 1970s and early 1980s, however, mark the watershed when the formidable dynamism and competitive strength of flexible producers led many Taylorist firms to start talking about the 'new rules' of global competition. They were reacting, above all, to the much greater capacity of flexible producers to take profitable advantage of the flexible automation technologies that began emerging in the late 1970s ... also important was the spectacular growth of flexible Japanese automakers' share of the US auto market following the second oil shock, at a time of stagnant demand growth, in the early 1980s.
>
> (Onman 1996: 18)

A crisis in Taylorism emerged from the situation of the combined emergence of flexible production and stagflation in the United States and Europe. The crisis began in the 1960s when US productivity began to lessen and was marked by industrial redeployment to sites where capital investment was less expensive in the 1970s. Abolition of controls on capital in the United States in 1974 and in the United Kingdom in 1979 allowed capital the freedom to move across national boundaries. The emergence of neo-liberalism marked a new mode of political and economic regulation from that time (Olssen and Peters 2005). However, in addition to the distribution of capital investment around the globe, there was also the 'maturing' of flexible production in some of the older industrialized countries. 'Indeed, not all OECD-based firms seeking to overcome the rigidities of Taylorism turned to low-wage production sites "offshore". Some of those firms succeeded, over time, in developing more flexible forms of organizing production at home' (Onman 1996: 18).

Strategies for reconfiguration were further brought about by the deregulation of markets within leading economies and the globalization of corporate competition and cooperation. Economic globalization was thus promoted by production trends towards flexibility.

> Poorly understood by many international economists, the crisis of Taylorist organizations is also an important cause of the 'structural' labour-market problems in OECD countries that many people there associate with 'globalization' – and more than a few mistakenly blame on imports from developing countries.
>
> (Onman 1996: 19)

Here flexibility is not a response to globalization but rather to the limits of Taylorism. Flexibility is more a condition for globalization.

Flexibility and responsiveness were not only articulated within policies as human capital requirements, significant in bringing forth innovative and profit producing practices, but also in relation to the acquisition of transferable skills and mobility of the workforce. Education underpins the latter characteristics.

> The next century will be defined by flexibility and change; more than ever there will be a demand for mobility. Today, a passport and a ticket allow people to travel anywhere in the world. In the future, the passport to mobility will be education and lifelong learning. This passport to mobility must be offered to everyone.
>
> (Group of Eight, quoted in
> Field 2000: 87)

The flexible production that had matured in the 1980s and 1990s called for an emphasis on learning through work at all levels within firms. This had significant implications for education and learning and it is there the discursive link between flexibility and lifelong learning becomes forged in strong ways.

> Flexible organizations significantly reduce waste and increase the productivity of both labor and capital by reversing the logic of Taylorism. They do so above all by integrating 'thinking' and 'doing' at all levels of operation, and in doing so eliminate many layers of middle management, which are dysfunctional in terms of information flow. Flexible organizations also avoid excessive specialization and compartmentalization by defining multi-task job responsibilities (which calls for multi-skilled workers) and by using teamwork and job rotation. In contrast to Taylor's 'one best way', they also emphasize continuous innovation in the organization of production, as well as in products and product features.
>
> (Onman 1996: 19)

For the education system there were logical conclusions. Flexibility of the labour market required an education system that could respond flexibly to the needs of that market and produce workers as flexible learners. It is here that policies for increasing and widening participation in tertiary education, and flexibility and increasing responsiveness afforded by the marketization of education and training, and incitements to become flexible and lifelong learners become significant. This allows for expansion in the pool of labour available within the market and an increase and diversification of the skills available to it. Individuals need to reskill and upskill themselves to maintain their positions within the job market and those unable to maintain their jobs will need to retrain. Flexibility and responsiveness become synonymous with increasing flexibility in both education and training provision and in support of lifelong learning. Onman argues that the pace of transition from Taylorism to post-Fordism slowed down economic growth within the OECD in the early 1990s and will continue to do so until it is complete. As he points out, resistance to change to post-Fordist flexible forms of production is perhaps not surprising.

> This resistance to change in the face of corporate downsizing, growing wage disparities, high unemployment and widespread perceptions of growing economic insecurity often leads to a search for scapegoats – notably 'globalization', immigration, and imports from developing countries.
>
> (Onman 1996: 24)

A discourse of the need for governments and international organizations themselves to become more flexible and to reorganize themselves emerges from this. Governments and international organizations, may themselves be Taylorist in form and, as such, as prone to resistance as others. They may slow up transitions in the economy through regulatory policies and behaviours that are not conducive to them. Thus the logic of flexibility also percolates into the organization of government and practices of the state, something we see represented in the need to 'modernize' government. Special-interest groups and voters may resist such transitions when they see them as a threat (Onman 1996). Policy makers (within the United States and Europe in particular) are recommended to ensure that they avoid using rationales for actions which encourage scapegoating and to support policies that ensure that the 'fruits' of the transition are shared equitably for all members of society. Policy rationales for transitions towards flexibility should avoid economic insecurity, globalization, immigration and imports, as reasons for increasing flexibilization. However, in many of the policy texts of governments and other organizations, such scapegoats are precisely to be found.

Of course, human capital theory has been critiqued, not only in terms of its effects, but also in its substantive assumptions and capacity to appear as if it reflects the way things really are. Here the propensity for 'scientific' theories of the human world to become taken up as, popularly viewed as, conflated with, scientific theories of the natural world (physics, chemistry), through their law-like characteristics, is put under scrutiny. Authors such as

Simon Marginson (1993, 1997) and Pusey (1991) have been significant in these endeavours. Human capital theory is highlighted through their work as a socially constructed discourse of the world that emerged at a particular historical moment within policy discourse, as a contingent event, which thus might have been other and is therefore changeable.

Human capital theory was certainly not taken as more than a hypothesis within some policy discourses. Marginson (1993: 43) cites a UNESCO foreword to a collection of papers putting forward the human capital argument as evidence of this:

> this is no more, and no less, than the surge of a new faith, the wishful hope that schooling could unlock the gates to let loose a stream of growth . . . there has been much hard thinking on this subject too.

Field (2000b) highlights a tension within debates that have emerged within both the European Commission (EC) and academic discourses of lifelong learning. This is over whether the notion of education for skills and mobility implies more emphasis on credentials or on more learning. Increased requirements for qualifications (especially within a funding environment emphasizing performance measurement – output – rather than curriculum) within a workforce may lead to an increased standardization and stabilization of skills rather than the reverse. Field (2000b) follows the work of the EC in 1985 to map the content of vocational qualifications within the then European member states and then legislate in 1988 to require the equivalence of all university degrees and vocational qualifications subsequent to the first two years of post-secondary training. He notes that neither the mobility of capital nor demand for mobility has appeared to have increased as a result of this qualifications framework. Furthermore, he suggests that multinational employers may consider knowledge of the company (tacit knowledge) and social capital to be more important attributes for their mobile workers than the codified knowledge and skills developed through qualifications. He also notes that the EC appeared to continue its efforts to construct this framework even after it had become clear that mobility would not result. He suggests that the political will for continuation may have been afforded by external questions over the competence or role of the EU through that period rather than the explicit rationales put forward.

A critical aspect in the discussion of contextual flexibility explores the effects of economic and labour market reform to encourage flexibility. This can be characterized as a discourse of insecurity (Edwards 1997). It suggests that increasing labour market flexibility results in increasing differentiation between a group of relatively securely employed, well-paid workers and a peripheral group of insecurely employed, part time, low paid, employed or unemployed people. Where the market environment is unpredictable, employers ensure that only core workers have job security. The consequence of increasing flexibility is therefore an increasing differentiation of the labour force between a core and periphery. In this situation, those at the periphery become a constant source of threat to those at the core, as they are at least potentially available to take jobs as they become available. Of course, it is more complex than this, as labour shortages in certain areas demonstrate. However, overall flexibility in the economy and labour market may inscribe specific populations with increasing insecurity as its social effect, just as, ironically, they are incited within policy rationale to respond to insecurity by becoming flexible.

There has been little explicit discussion or exploration of the relationship between policy or institutional discourses of flexibility and lifelong learning. Edwards (1997), however, does explore discourses of flexibility and their significance in the current promotion by a policy of lifelong learning. For him,

> it is the requirement to increase flexibility and competitiveness which has resulted in the current focus of interest on lifelong learning and its concentration in the realms of economic policy. This is a position that is shared across the political spectrum, including by business and trade union organizations, as well as major political parties and international organizations, such as the European Commission, the Organization of Economic Co-operation and Development, the World Bank and International Monetary Fund.
>
> (Edwards 1997: 41)

Here it is the contemporary emphasis on flexibility and competition within policy which constitutes the basis for an interest in lifelong learning. Even though it is discourses of competitiveness and flexibility that govern such change and require lifelong learning, a discourse of flexibility as insecurity also produces a requirement for lifelong learning. Lifelong learning is both a response to insecurity as well as a support for economic competition. However, the requirement is different depending on the position of the individual within the labour market: 'for those at the core as a means to sustain their employability; for those at the periphery to survive the interruptions to employment' (Edwards 1997: 41). Thus, rather than 'lifelong education as the master concept for educational policies in the years to come' (Faure *et al.* 1972: 182),

> instead, flexibility has become the master concept in Western societies and Faure's enlightened and democratic vision of lifelong learning has been largely and unfairly forgotten. What is being developed in the UK is best described as a flexible society, fit for the global market ... And the most appropriate slogan for the National Campaign for Learning should, in my opinion, be 'Lifelong learning: your flexible friend and your flexible future.
>
> (Coffield 2002: 188)

There appears potential for further exploration of the interrelation between discourses of flexibility and lifelong learning in relation to the contextual discourses of change within which they sit. The combined social consequences of education policies of flexibility and lifelong learning may differ in differing locations, but they appear to be powerful in the production of discourses of insecurity and indeed social exclusion. This is contradictory, as insecurity and exclusion are argued within many policy rationales to be the problems for which flexibility and lifelong learning are the appropriate solutions. Yet they may well be as much a condition for insecurity and exclusion as a response to it.

Lifelong learning as education policy/strategy

The education policy studies literature focuses primarily on policy themes of lifelong learning, rather than flexibility. Lifelong learning has been identified as a policy concept (Lawson 1982; Journal of Education Policy 1997), a policy (Lawson 1982), a myth (Hughes and Tight 1995; Strain and Field 1997), an object and strategy (Griffin 1999a), as rhetoric (Griffin 1999b), social control (Coffield 2002), and as a 'soft' policy objective (Field 2000a). This multiplicity of meanings is in part indicative of the breadth of approaches used within these analyses but also points to the difficulty of answering the question that Ball posed about policy studies needing to clarify what they are about as a condition for engaging in research. There are descriptive, evaluative and prescriptive aspects to the existing research, much of which does not work with an explicit view of the complexities of policy processes. This is further complicated by the different ways in which lifelong learning is deployed around the globe and the differing meanings it can have.

In Japan, for instance, the term lifelong education became central to education policies during the 1990s (Fuwa 2001) and has become widespread in its use. The economic crisis of the late 1990s had put pressure on commercial enterprises, which had to reconsider their in-service training practices. Increasing unemployment and the casualization of workers meant that there was an increasing emphasis on training (Wilson 2001). Fuwa (2001) outlines a situation where tertiary education participation is high. In 1997, 76 per cent of students graduating from senior high school went on to some form of tertiary education. Of these 47.3 per cent went on to university or college and the rest to vocational school. In Japan, the continuing education of the workforce is still largely conducted by companies for their own employees. This can be in conjunction with central and local authorities, but it is largely a separate system that does not interact with university provision. With high rates of extended initial education, lifelong learning is therefore focused on those already in the workforce, for whom conditions are changing. By contrast, in Thailand, lifelong learning has been equated with the possibility for adults to take up initial educational qualifications, having not had this chance earlier in their lives. It also focuses on the skilling of the unemployed to raise their standard of living in the local community (Wilson 2001). Thailand also experienced severe economic difficulties in the late 1990s. These are somewhat different from the emphases one might find in the United Kingdom, Australia, Canada or the United States.

A need to find appropriate vocabularies is emphasized by some policy analysts (Griffin 1999b; Field 2000a). For Griffin (1999b) a shift in policy emphasis over the years from lifelong education to lifelong learning signifies its move as an object of policy to a policy strategy orientation. Marketization is seen to be part of broader processes of restructuring that are taking place around the globe with implications for policy and policy analysis. Previously clear boundaries between the activities of the state and market are seen to have become blurred. The government has, in effect, become smaller as state services have been increasingly out-sourced or privatized. The relationship of people as citizens of the state has become that of consumers. The state – the practices, processes and structures of governments – is no longer that which mediates the excesses of the market. By contrast, it provides the conditions for the market's operation (Taylor *et al.* 1997). In the context of the recon-figuration of the relation between state and civil society and moves from welfare to post-welfare provision, the meaning of policy and of lifelong learning in policy terms is changed. Policy analysis within a traditional welfare policy approach considers lifelong education as an object of policy. However, in a post-welfare context, lifelong learning cannot be understood as an object that can be mandated or secured through policy. Learning requires strategies of contemporary government, rather than policy mandate. 'At the level of government strategy, people may be variously persuaded, cajoled, bribed, threatened or shamed into becoming active individual learners: their learning cannot be mandated' (Griffin 1999b: 434). Unlike Griffin, Field (2000a) argues that these processes are not the end of the welfare state but part of a transformed welfare state approach.

There are policy studies that attempt to measure the degree to which education or training takes place as a result of policy mandate. They may focus on the amount of learning, number of qualifications, or on quantities and distributions of participation and cultural capital. These are criticized as they fail to take account of new interpretative understandings of the recon-figurations of policy and its role within changing forms of governance. They inscribe a 'reductionist model in that they deal with measurement rather than interpretation' (Griffin 1999b: 435). Griffin (1999b: 437) suggests that within the latter perspective, lifelong learning might usefully be considered as a 'function of the grand narrative of social welfare reform'. Here lifelong learning brings forth reconfigurations in the traditional approach to welfare provision.

Griffin calls for analytical, critical and interpretative perspectives that can make the distinction between a learning society and one that is better educated or trained. Lifelong learning emerges from his analysis as a func-tion of individual and social life, a feature of postmodern society and as a policy strategy to incite individuals to learn. The post-welfare state is seen to have a strategic role – in managing markets, choice and autonomy – rather than one of policy formulation.

> [T]he strategy of governments is to create the conditions in which people, families, communities and organizations are most *likely* to learn for themselves, thus obviating the need for education policy in the traditional sense. This is a characteristic function of governments in post-welfare conditions.
>
> (Griffin 1999b: 440, emphasis in original)

The debate is then redirected to a question over what governments can have education policies within contemporary conditions. In situations where market conditions, social and technological change and globalization require a response of adaptation through lifelong learning, policy as mandate ceases to have much sense. 'In a logical sense, therefore policy itself is superfluous: we only have a choice between means and cannot choose the ends of policy' (Griffin 1999a: 329). This then raises a further question as to what policy and policy analysis might be, if policy itself positions us as without choice of ends. Exploring such discursive positionings becomes ever more important.

Lifelong learning thus may be typical of a new form of policy that is emerging. These are 'new policy objectives' (Field 2000a: 249) that require action by civil society rather than the implementation of policy by the state. They are 'soft' as they deal with issues that are unable to be directly achieved through agencies of the state. Policy goals aiming for the reform of education systems and institutions remain, alongside this new type of policy (Field 2000a). There is the suggestion here then that in discourses of lifelong learning we reach certain limits of the state's competence and of policy. Rather than act itself, the state incited its citizens to act, if only in particular ways. However, both Griffin and Field are reflecting shifts in only certain parts of the globe and only certain aspects of the discourses at play.

There are various discourses of lifelong learning influencing education policy development. Drawing on the work of Ball, Edwards (1997) categorizes these as cultural restorationist, modernizing and progressive. Each constructs distinctly differing discourses of change, thereby identifying both particular problems and policy solutions to be adopted. Within policy, various social and policy constructions of change as phenomena which are external to the world of education and training are 'deployed to act as rationales for changes within that world' (Edwards 1997: 22).

The cultural restorationist, progressive and modernizing discourses of lifelong learning are not to be taken to be entirely discrete or oppositional, as they 'share' policy responses in some cases and there are tensions internal to the various positions. For example, modernizers and cultural restorationists may both support a learning market. For cultural restorationists, a learning market can be accepted to the extent that it offers individual freedom. However, where this market undermines the traditional 'cannon' of knowledge and certain cultural values, acceptance becomes problematic. 'In other words the disorder of the market can work against the order of individual freedom and responsibility, where desires are incited which cannot be met within the confines of pre-existing traditions' (Edwards 1997: 181). The progressive discourse, however, is made marginal, as the emphasis on individualism within a market context contradicts the collective and emancipatory goals of many progressives.

Meanings of lifelong learning within policy therefore are characterized and dispersed in complex ways within discourses of policy studies and education. Lifelong learning is represented in multiple ways, as is the characterization of change associated with it. Within the policy studies literature, lifelong learning is commonly represented as a policy object or concept. Here it is analysed in terms of the extent and forms of its impact in widening and increasing participation in education within a discourse of welfare democracy. In the context of the reconfiguration of relations between state and civil society and moves from welfare to post-welfare provision, the meaning of lifelong learning in policy terms is changed. Lifelong learning is no longer an object or concept of policy, which is focused upon institutional provision. Rather, it is a policy strategy, or soft objective, focusing on learning across the social formation, and requiring responses by civil society.

Differences and dispersions

It has become apparent that there are differences and dispersions in meanings of flexibility and lifelong learning according to the focus of concern within the various discourses outlined above. There are two foci of discourses of flexibility. The first has a focus on the education institution and the second on change within wider social and economic contexts. The first focus emerges primarily from those involved with practices of open, distance or flexible learning within post-compulsory education institutions. Discourses of the institution and the market (efficiency, competition), liberal humanism (equity and access) or technicism (delivery through information technology) all produce different meanings of flexibility. Meanings ascribed by individuals within such sites may emerge which are consistent with their institutional roles or may sit in varying relations to them. This focus is illustrative of an instrumentalism within discourses of flexibility and lifelong learning. Meanings are limited by an assumption that organizational flexibility and flexible learning are positive (literal) characteristics of the organization and learning. There is lack of critique in this assumption and a lack of concern for the wider social or economic implications and consequences of flexibility. One specific discourse does focus more critically and widely on the emergence of flexible learning. It examines meanings of flexible learning and its provision in terms of the changing patterns and modes of production and consumption within post-industrialized societies and economies. This is, however, still primarily focused upon flexibility in relation to the organization and the production and delivery of learning. Although more critical, and less technical, it is limited through its largely unquestioning focus on labour market theories, and, within these, on patterns of production and demand. It is limited as it draws upon discourses that are descriptive of modes of production within industrialized societies, as if these were intended as descriptions of what flexible production methods should be *per se*.

The second focus within discourses of flexibility is upon its broader social and economic contexts and effects. There are two main strands of discourses identified. First, there is flexibility coded with competition, which is identified as the strand that attempts to explain and govern trends in the economy. This is the strand within which educational flexibility and lifelong learning become significant within policy. Second, there is a more critical strand of discourse. This is characterized as one of insecurity, whereby flexibility inscribes specific populations with increasing insecurity as its social effect. This discourse emerges primarily from broad critiques of policy.

Further meanings of flexibility emerge within a third strand of discourse, from the education studies and education policy studies literatures. These discourses critically examine the effects of policy discourses of flexibility within education discourses and the wider social consequences of such changes. The work of Stephen Ball (1990a, 1994a), Sandra Taylor *et al.* (1997) and Richard Edwards (1997) exemplify these, even though there are considerable differences between their approaches and foci. Ball explores empirically the emergence of a correspondence between the education system and the economy through the creation of an education market. A reconfiguration of policy formation processes within the 1980s and a mobilization of vocational discourses are seen to have supported a repositioning of school education and a restructuring of discourses within the school. Progressive and modernizing discourses of flexibility are seen to resonate with those of the market and support reconfigurations of pedagogy and systems for the evaluation and organization of education. These bring with them a closer correspondence between education and the economy. Processes of education that were previously considered to be those of social reproduction are now subordinated to the economy. This is taken to implicate a shift in the principle of social control and restructuring of the ethical order from that of the common good towards that of individualism within post-industrialized nations. This indicates a shift in the principle of control from that of a submissive and inflexible subject towards one which is conforming and flexible. Discourses of flexibility, of individualized choice and freedom and specific local policy strategies are required as ideas and vehicles for such reforms (Taylor *et al.* 1997).

Meanings of the interrelationships between discourses of flexibility and lifelong learning emerge from Edwards's (1997) analysis. Discourses of flexibility as competition produce the re-emergence of policy interest in and requirement for lifelong learning. The increased emphasis on flexibility produces and promotes discourses of lifelong learning and those of insecurity. Social and economic insecurity for certain groups is reinscribed and reinforced through discourses and practices of flexibility and lifelong learning, even though these are not the forms of insecurity identified within policy rationales. This interrelationship between policy rationales for flexibility and lifelong learning, and their combined economic and social effects in increasing the insecurity of differing sectors of the population, has received little attention. It points to an important avenue for further investigation. At the same time, the globalization of such interrelationships and effects reinforces the importance of their investigation (Taylor *et al.* 1997).

A conceptual focus on lifelong learning within the policy studies literature identifies two main strands of meanings of lifelong learning (Griffin 1999a,b). Within the first strand, lifelong learning is considered as a function of social welfare reform. This strand comprises mainly analytic and some more critical explorations of policy proposals for lifelong learning within a social democratic model, in terms of welfare reform and state action. The policy studies literatures are arguably constrained by a focus on the examination of the breadth and patterns of participation and redistribution of social and economic resources within society. A second strand emerges to consider lifelong learning as a policy strategy in the context of post-welfare policies and societies. It identifies lifelong learning in terms of shifts towards post-welfare societies and policy conditions, and considers action to be required by civil society rather than through direct state intervention and provision. This strand points to the potential for further explorations of lifelong learning policies in relation to postmodern forms of governance, social conditions and processes.

What can be said about the meanings of flexibility and lifelong learning that I have explored at this moment for 'checking bearings' in nomadic travels? Different meanings of flexibility and lifelong learning emerge from dispersed discourses and contexts of practice – of education policy, the study of education policy and the study of educational practices. These are fragmented. They intersect, overlap and alliances are forged in complex ways. They are not separated from broader meanings of flexibility and lifelong learning that are taken up within other contexts, such as the media and everyday places. All are mediated in anticipation of the media. They are, however, significant in that they intersect powerfully within institutionalized discourses of policy and education and are taken up and drawn upon in the rationales for and attempts to reconfigure activities. They provide discourses through which to narrate and guide action.

Empirical analysis of policy rationales for change demonstrates that they do not translate in any simple way into implementation. Indeed in welfare states, many studies indicate that policies actually benefit the middle classes more than other sections of the population, as they are able to make the most of possibilities provided by state action. Nevertheless policy discourses of flexibility and lifelong learning are powerful. It is through the examination of meanings of flexibility and lifelong learning that the extent of the interrelationships between policy discourses and those of their uptake and analysis, and their influence in the reconfiguration of the education institution and society more broadly are indicated. Here there are only certain possibilities as one cannot transcend existing meanings and meaning-making practices, even in the process of travelling. There might be horizons, but we do not fall of the edge of the world. This suggests the importance of critical focus upon policy discourses.

Change and uncertainty are commonly constructed within policy as naturally occurring and as that to which we must respond. Flexibility and lifelong learning are represented as solutions to these problems. It is through discourses of change that specific meanings of flexibility and lifelong learning become inscribed and act to construct the societies within which we live, including our systems of education, training and employment. They 'realize' our societies (Coffield 2002). They also help reconfigure forms of governance, individualize subjectivities and align populations to discourses of flexibility, lifelong learning and choice. Social relations are reconfigured through such discursive action.

Within the education institution, discourses of flexibility emphasize learning activities and provisions of learning. They tend to turn attention away from questions of the reconfigurations of the content of learning, or considerations of the wider contexts and implications of flexibility. They turn attention away from critiques of the representations of change that are embedded within policy discourses. Ideologies and values informing previous practices of education appear to be eroded within the institutional sites where ideas and strategies of flexibility are promoted. Institutions are restructured in such a way that there is an apparent attempt at increasing the correspondence between the economy and education under the sign of modernization. Progressive discourses of education are marginalized through discourses of lifelong learning, and through a wider shift from the polis to forms of the market.

One strand of policy studies discourse considers policies of lifelong learning in terms of shifts towards post-welfare societies and policy conditions. The question over what policies are for, within contexts where it is only the means of policies and not their ends that can be determined, becomes highly significant. Previous discourses of policy within social democracy are compromised. This suggests a space for the politicization of discourses. If the discourses of flexibility and lifelong learning that emerge are constrained within technicist discourses of practice and through prior discourses of the welfare state and social democracy, and if policies are not able to select their ends because of certainties over the effects of economic globalization and the need for nations to remain competitive in this situation, this points to a reinvigoration of explorations of the means by which policy discourses are constructed and operate, and for alternative approaches in such explorations. If we wish to consider this situation critically, we can focus on the means by which certain discourses of change are implicated in the realization of our societies. We can, for example, begin to explore dominant meanings of flexibility and their interrelationship with lifelong learning, as they are taken up and represented within policies. We can explore their interrelated work within policy discourses and theorize how their meanings may be dispersed, taken up and mobilized within civil societies, as well as within contexts of education. How they shape up what we conceive as the probable as well as that which is possible become an important focus for analysis.

One site for such analysis is the representations of flexibility and lifelong learning within policy texts. Change and uncertainty are commonly constructed within policy texts as naturally occurring and as that to which we must respond. Flexibility and lifelong learning are represented as solutions to these 'problems'. One place to start would be by asking questions over the means by which particular discourses of change and uncertainty become powerfully constructed within and through policies and over the mechanisms for their mobilization. These are questions over the power of particular representations of the 'natural' characteristics of the world and the responses that then become 'required' of populations.

3 A political, discursive and rhetorical terrain

> For me, much rests on the meaning or possible meanings that we give to policy; it affects 'how' we research and how we interpret what we find.
>
> (Ball 1994a: 15)

The previous chapter examined meanings ascribed to flexibility and lifelong learning within various contexts of education and education policy scholarship. These indicated dispersions and concentrations of meanings that are produced, taken up, reconfigured and deployed according to the activities and concerns of actors within differing sites. What can and cannot be said of flexibility and lifelong learning is both made possible and constrained by the discourses available within these locations.

From this exploration the question emerges of how to engage in policy analysis at a time when flexibility and lifelong learning have become a greater focus for policy at local, national and supranational levels. Griffin's (1999a,b) question as to what policy and policy analysis might be within the contemporary period resonates with an uncertainty that is articulated more broadly within the policy studies literature. Policy analysts have identified and discussed various approaches in terms of the meanings of policy that they produce, their productivities and limitations. Arguments for alternative and more critical approaches have arisen forcefully. This chapter turns to this literature. From an examination of discussions of various approaches, meanings afforded policy, I claim a space for poststructuralist and rhetorical approaches to policy study. I then identify and discuss the approaches that are then taken up in considering flexibility and lifelong learning within the three trails of nomadic exploration within Chapters 4, 5 and 6.

As has been indicated, the book seeks to undermine and make vulnerable dominant discourses of flexibility and lifelong learning by pointing out that these have been inhibited by attempts to think in terms of totality and truth. In this context, any certainty that the trails of theorizing and examination that are followed could offer definitive or generalizable answers, 'truths', to questions of flexibility or lifelong learning is eroded. However, poststructuralist analyses drawing upon various concepts from Foucault's work and from rhetorical analysis do allow for the production of alternative meanings. These are not by any means meant as replacements for others. They are just other kinds of meanings. They are argued, however, to be of the variety that may act to 'counter' relations of power within and between policy and more dominant approaches to policy analysis at this time. As a 'beginning' or starting point, therefore, this chapter is less concerned with the substance of policy than with exploring different approaches to policy analysis and their possible relationships with policy processes themselves.

The chapter is written in four parts. First, there is a review of discussions about available meanings of policy analysis and approaches that they make possible. Second, there is a section identifying a space for poststructuralist theorizings of policy texts. Within a third, various aspects of Foucault's work and rhetorical analysis are brought together as resources for a productive point of departure for subsequent explorations of the rhetorical work of policy descriptions of flexibility and lifelong learning. This section lays out details of rhetorical analysis as a supplement to the concepts drawn from Foucault. It delineates beginnings for three trails of exploration as the work of the nomadic theorizer. Within the final part, so as not to suggest closure or the construction of any unities of theory, the chapter 'takes stock' of the travelling that has been achieved. It reviews the trail that has been followed within this chapter, to contrast the travelling of the nomadic theorizer, kitted up with these particular tools, in relation to alternatives that could have been taken up within the kit bag. Thus, it delineates what this mode of travel offers to policy analysis and its constraints.

Approaches to policy analysis

There has been much debate in the last ten years or so as to the methods most appropriate for the study of policy and the need for more 'useful' methods than have hitherto been to the fore. Underlying this debate has been, on the one hand, concerns about the validity of existing approaches – what makes it more than opinion – and, on the other, concerns over the lack of impact on policy makers and policy making of such analyses. This discussion indicates increasing dissatisfaction within policy studies with the capacity of dominant theoretical resources to address contemporary issues and problems of policy. These concerns are found in many areas of policy studies, but this section focuses on education policy literature.

Discussion of the nature of policy analysis arises from dissatisfaction with both positivist and critical approaches. Particular methodologies or perspectives on policy produce meanings within certain discursive boundaries which limit their work in specific ways (Kenway 1990; Ball 1994b; Scheurich 1994; Peters and Marshall 1996; Seddon 1996). Much traditional policy work is taken to be positivist and unable to work outside pre-existing relations of power within the social formation (Marshall and Anderson 1994).

Taylor *et al.* (1997) provide a useful exposition of the range of approaches that have been described within the policy analysis literature. Positivist approaches to policy analysis were the first. These were known as 'policy sciences' in North America in the late 1940s and more widely in the 1960s. Their aim was to determine the best course of action to implement a policy goal or decision. In the United States, this approach is now found primarily within the field of political science, but it appears more widely through studies that directly inform policies which are similarly technicist and pluralist. They are often underpinned by functionalist views of the way in which societies work, whereby institutions have specific functions in terms of the working of the whole, contributing to social stability and operating through a consensus of values (Taylor *et al.* 1997). Such approaches have tended to produce evaluation and implementation studies and case studies in the United Kingdom and elsewhere. They construct a position that emphasizes objectivity and value neutrality, as any alternative would be to position themselves outside the remit of that which is 'scientific': '[a]nalysts . . . according to this [positivist] view . . . are not seen as qualified to assess the morality or the legitimacy of the goal itself' (Taylor *et al.* 1997: 18). They require this position to be able to avoid any view of their complicity in the promotion of value positions, which could be taken as meddling in politics.

Critiques of positivism emerge from alternative theoretical approaches. For example, where policy is taken to work to support the structuring of power relations within social formations, through a neo-Marxian framing within a social critical approach, positivist analysis reinforces these relations by informing and improving what already exists. The role of this approach to policy is 'analyzing and understanding its problems and discovering and devising the best solutions or, at least, ameliorizations' (Scheurich 1994: 299). Positivist approaches are thus criticized as they leave the fundamental inequalities and exercises of power within the social formation unaddressed, precisely because of their claims to value neutrality and objectivity. Critical policy analysis, in contrast to positivist forms and in response to such criticisms of it, is concerned with exploring the values, assumptions and power relations that underlie policies and seeks to transform or undermine them. Where positivism is concerned with value-neutrality, critical policy analysis takes the position that values cannot be avoided. Normative positions always underpin the processes involved in the development and implementation of policies. There can therefore be no clear distinction between positivist social scientific knowledge and values. The distinction between policy analysis and policy advocacy that is made within positivist approaches cannot be sustained. Within critical policy analysis, education is concerned with the promotion of social justice for individuals and within societies. Rather than a functionalist and value consensual model of social systems and policy, one of value conflict is taken up (Taylor *et al.* 1997). Policy is oriented to what is possible and expedient as effective responses to the demands of competing interests within society. Here a contrast is made with the 'earliest policies in education...[which]...had two main functions: to provide an account of those cultural norms which were considered by the state as desirable in education; and to institute a mechanism of accountability against which student and teacher performance could be measured' (Taylor *et al.* 1997: 2). In addition, a third function for social policy emerged from the 1960s. This was 'marshalling and managing public calls for change, giving them form and direction' (Taylor *et al.* 1997: 3). The purpose of critical policy analysis is therefore political, as it seeks to make visions and ideals visible, and is oriented, in part at least, to the examination of values as they are played out within and through policy processes.

The critical policy analysis described above is only one rendition of a critical approach; which may include interpretive, social critical and policy sociology approaches. These are identified and differentiated variously by analysts. Interpretive and critical approaches, respectively from the United States and from Britain and Australia also take an anti-positivist stance. Included with the latter are those literatures drawing specifically on neo-Marxist social conflict approaches. A policy sociology, emerging from the sociology of education in Europe and Australia tends to draw on the qualitative and illuminative techniques of sociology and focuses on questions of what is happening and why, rather than being concerned with changing the situation. For this reason, it is distinguished from broader critical sociological research, which focuses on social change. The productivities and constraints of critical approaches are explored in the policy literature and elsewhere. For example, ideology critique, classically Marxist and neo-Marxist approaches, aims to challenge economic relations of power by beginning from 'the primacy of the class struggle over social classes and individuals...[and]...from the material and social existence of knowledges' (Macdonell 1986: 62).

However, even though Marxism succeeds in breaking away from positivist or humanist discourses, it has been criticized as unable to ask questions of its own construction within the context of a dominant liberal discourse. This in itself is held to maintain the existing social order (Scheurich 1994) and thus it ultimately fails in its own endeavour (Ball 1994b) to change the social order. It offers a discourse that is oppositional to systems of power, which fails by operating from within dominant discourses. For Scheurich (1994), this is merely to achieve a 'symbolization' of concerns that are conceived in response to the dominant discourse of liberal democracy. By allowing such concerns a voice, they effect a restabilization or maintenance of the social order that might have been undermined if this had not been so. In other words, Marxist approaches can be argued to be accommodated within the political processes of liberal democracy.

From a postmodernist perspective, positivist and critical approaches are totalizing discourses where they seek truth and progress through knowledge. Lyotard (1984) refers to these as the grand narratives of modernity. Thus, even though attempting to challenge relations of power, Marxist discourses create 'totalizing effects' through the dominance-resistance binary which they set up, and by ignoring the constraints on meaning that this produces. All is reduced to class struggle. In effect, they succeed in replacing the grand narrative of humanistic progression and emancipation by another. Even though analysis begins from a different position and produces new meanings, Marxism is insufficient to break the hold of prevailing power-knowledge regimes and ultimately acts in their support and maintenance. The oppositional stance is part of established political practices, rather than an undermining of them. Of course, many Marxists would resist this interpretation of their efforts.

Each approach to policy analysis is thus productive in quite specific ways, but is also argued to have limitations. Policy theorists have suggested a refocusing of analysis (Power 1992), the use of additional strategies of analysis (Codd 1988; Scheurich 1994) and a range of alternative methods and perspectives in attempts to find ways around these limitations. Suggestions include the adoption of particular scientific frameworks and methodologies for the analysis of values (Evers 1988), and a greater focus on policy system improvement as an outcome of policy studies and the strengthening of linkages between fields (Chibulka 1994). The diversifying of opinion on suitable approaches to policy analysis led Hatcher and Troyner (1994: 161) to question coherence within the field: 'What meta-theory is necessary to achieve a non-reductionist, totalizing theoretical coherence?' Poststructuralist Marxisms have also been posited based on 'the pedagogical practice of reading and rereading Marx in a critical manner' (Peters 2003: 115) and in relation to 'texts', such as education in relation to knowledge capitalism and the neo-liberal political economy.

Whilst a range of suggestions and rationales have been put forward by analysts, the emphasis has often been placed on a need for better empirical descriptions of the effects of policies. Some have suggested a strengthening of the efficacy of policy analysis by positioning it more firmly and systematically in relation to policy formulation. The underlying assumption here is that lack of clarity and efficacy are the significant limitations of policy analysis. However, such suggestions, made without consideration of their limits and consequences, are problematic, as it is in part the categorizations – the meanings – that they afford to policy, society, and so forth that are limiting. What is required is a way of thinking about them that can understand what they do, not simply with the intention of finding better categorizations, because the limitations rest in the play of language rather than in the policy processes themselves. In policy and policy analysis, we come up against the limits of language and the categorizations possible at particular times and in particular locations. 'To put this another way, in each epoch there are oppositions ... in the heads of both thinkers and listeners. They function as the most absolute system of censure, since they are ... the things which structure what is thought, and therefore they are themselves extremely difficult to think' (Bourdieu 1992: 39).

By drawing upon the linguistic turn within studies of policy, as Stephen Ball (1994a) promotes and as his work exemplifies, discussions of what such categorizations do can be asked. What questions are made possible through them and what elided? What slights of discourse can we dream of, from which may emerge alternative resources and purposes for policy analysis? What may be appropriate for specific sites and contexts of exploration? Bourdieu (1992: 39) suggests this requires a 'double historicization' where the researcher must historicize the structures of thought that will be put to work, as well as the text to be studied. This is the reflexive challenge for policy studies as much as for other researchers. It affords the possibility of escape from the bind of theories that do not explore their own possibilities and limitations, or contemplation of their social consequences.

> The famous relativist circle, that the sociologist produces with a particular force, reminding us that nothing can be thought unless through instruments of thought which are socially constituted, is, in relation to these instruments of constraint, an instrument of extraordinary freedom.
>
> (Bourdieu 1992: 40)

This 'instrument of freedom' is exemplified through a focus on both policy and its analysis as interrelated social and discursive practices. This is a focus that has emerged in studies to address the problems of critiques which deny this kind of reflexivity. Thus a promotion of greater clarity and efficacy in policy analysis is problematic, as this reinforces relationships, constructed within language, between the world and language and reason and action that are made possible within positivist positions.

Scheurich (1994) takes up this concern in his proposal that policy analysis is in danger of becoming trapped within a theory/practice binary, which separates the effects of analysis from the objects and problems that it claims to objectively study. Policy analysts, he argues, need to recognize their complicity in the constitution of policy objects and problems in particular ways that powerfully shape policy. By drawing upon poststructuralist discursive approaches, it is not simply policy processes themselves but also the realm of policy analysis that becomes an object of study. In other words, policy analysis is itself part of the object of study and not separate from it. 'Politically speaking, post-structuralism aims to expose structures of domination by diagnosing "power/knowledge" relations and their manifestations in classifications, typologies and institutions' (Peters and Humes 2003: 112). The relation between policy and its modes of study is thus a significant focus of research. Tikly (2003) and Humes and Bryce (2003) explore the changing role of the human sciences in justifying the 'regimes of truth' drawn upon by policy makers and begin to exemplify the potential for poststructuralist approaches to undermine views of the academic disciplines, and thus approaches to policy analysis, as naturally occurring. Policy analysis emerges as part of practices through which policy is fabricated as an object of study. Policy analysis does not simply sit outside of policy, commenting upon it, but is related to the practices about which it speaks, not least in the categories it uses to frame and analyze practices. It is required therefore to be discursively reflexive of the work it does, rather than treating policy as simply independent of the practices through which it is studied. Through discourse analysis, analysts of policy can focus upon the way in which different practices of policy analysis are complicit in the constitution of policy and education objects and problems in particular ways which powerfully shape both policy and education.

Here Foucault's archaeology offers a discursive 'wedge' through which to explore a proposition that 'problems' are constructed through discursive regularities that operate within specific locations and at particular times. They make it possible for problems to be articulated in one way or another and taken up within policy and policy studies (Scheurich 1994). These regularities are discursively framed rather than sitting outside of language.

A space to explore

Contemporary critiques of the grand narratives of modernity have made space for understanding of the world as linguistically and socially constructed, and have made possible poststructuralist policy studies. Ball (1994b) has argued for the relinquishing of notions of any one unifying grand theory in favour of such approaches. These both draw upon and promote the linguistic turn in social theory, which brings to the fore the discursive work at play in policy and the fabrication of certain issues as 'problems' and specific responses as 'solutions' (MacLure 2003). Rather than seeking scientific truth or uncovering what lies behind ideology and the exercises of power therein, policy analysis examines the workings of power-knowledge and the meanings fabricated through and around policy discourses. Here ideas that the real world can be directly presented to us or that knowledge of the social world universal, law-like are made problematic. As indicated earlier, approaches drawing on discourse analysis focus not simply on policy itself but also the realm of policy analysis, which becomes an aspect of the object of study. This is because the 'truths' of policy are held to be inscribed in part by particular approaches to the study of policy.

Poststructuralist discourse analysis is productive as it permits such reflexivity on the part of the analyst, and the analysis of regularities and stabilizations within and between the different discourses of policy. Truth is conceived as a social and linguistic regularity, an aspect of power-knowledge within a socio-rhetorical community (Swales 1990). In this, different trajectories for analysis can be found, ones that begin from different points within discourse. This 'counters' the discursive effects of policies, positivist approaches that take problems or their solutions to be unproblematic and critical approaches that operate from within a dominant liberal discourse. In relation to the focus of this book, flexibility and lifelong learning are represented as objects within policy and analysis has tended to take these a priori as 'real' objects for study. The effects have been to help discursively constitute, reinforce and maintain flexibility and lifelong learning as objects, by seeking to identify or uncover their truth or falsity. They have become regularized and realized. Positivism achieves this through discourses of their functional necessity and implementation within the social formation. Critical approaches construct alternative and oppositional discourses, which tend to reinforce their facticity as objects of discourse, even while seeking to undermine them by examining what lies behind. By contrast, poststructuralist approaches allow a disidentification from discourses of truth in various ways. This makes it possible to examine the means whereby objects such as flexibility and lifelong learning are discursively constituted and fabricated, within discourses, and to trace their discursive effects within particular locations and times. These approaches actively seek to avoid unities that may impede a search for alternative meanings, through the very pluralization, fragmentation and dispersion of regularities of meanings of those objects which have been taken to be relatively stable. Poststructuralist approaches then do not look for a general and unifying truth about policy or its analysis. Thus my non-linear and non-totalizable trails of course.

Positivist and Marxist approaches in policy studies, have focused attention on static descriptions of the world, where language denotes, represents or reflects reality. Language either does or can transparently convey meaning. The former is based on empiricism, the latter on the potential for language to unmask the mystifications of the powerful embedded in hegemonic discourses. This has been 'natural' in the sense that both positivism and Marxism have drawn on dominant, and hence common sense, views of the world and of language. Here there is a gap between world and word. However, in this, attention has been taken away from considerations of how policy language 'acts' to build up truth (Potter 1996). By acknowledging the social construction of language, but resisting the anchorings of ideology critique, important work in policy analysis is made possible. A discursive approach allows questions of the way in which what is said is made up within and through the regularities of discursive practices. Discourses are made problematic and available for questioning. A discourse of discourses is in effect made possible, with its own regularities, where discourses emerge as social practices. Thus truth is discursively constituted, rather than 'fixed'. This allows exploration of the way in which policy discourses build up ideas of policy that 'permit' contestation or critique through discursive regularities and binaries that are in some ways prior to them. However, there are different ways of conceptualizing such approaches. It is to an exploration of these that I now turn.

Poststructuralist approaches to policy and post-compulsory education already exist and largely draw upon the work of Michel Foucault. Here discourse is understood as actively constitutive of subjectivity, social forms and ways of thinking. However, most of this work draws upon the later genealogical texts of Foucault. The early archaeological work of Foucault, which has been marginalized, has been positioned as more 'literary' or simply 'textual' by some, with the implication that it is less relevant to policy studies. Agger (1992) suggests that it is possible to draw a distinction between a critical poststructuralism and a literary poststructuralism. The former locates discursive practices within a broader framework of the exercise of the power, while the latter does not and is more akin to literary criticism. Crudely, it is approaches informed by the early work of Foucault and that of Derrida which tend towards more literary approaches, while it is the later work of Foucault which has been influential in critical poststructuralism and where, in a decentring of discourse within genealogical investigations, discourse is constitutive of systems of power. Through genealogy, politics is taken 'as an arena of struggle over meaning...policy texts represent the outcome of political struggles over meaning' (Taylor *et al.* 1997: 27–28). Politics is no longer able to be taken to be solely the remit of the government and the state. 'The state is here the product of discourse, a point in the diagram of power. It is a necessary but not sufficient concept in the development of an "analytics of power" – "the state can only operate on the basis of other, already existing power relations"' (Ball 1994a: 22). Within genealogical work the focus for analysis is thus no longer on the workings of the government or state as such but rather upon regimes of truth and ensembles of policy. 'In Foucault's terms we would see policy ensembles that include, for example, the market, management, appraisal and performativity as "regimes of truth" through which people govern themselves and others' (Ball 1994a: 22). Such an approach to policy analysis 'has led to an increasing emphasis on matters of meaning and a related shift towards exploring the effects of policy, rather than simply focusing on policy intentions' (Taylor *et al.* 1997: 43).

However, this already points to the power of regularities within discourses to continue to constrain thinking, even as one attempts to counter its influence. There is a danger therefore of certain types of poststructuralist policy analysis becoming an orthodoxy of its own. I want to argue for the usefulness of the ideas of the early Foucault to policy analysis, to break with such regularities regarding that work.

A few key points regarding discursive approaches are worth highlighting here. First, discourse is actively constitutive in a variety of ways – 'discourse constitutes the objects of knowledge, social subjects and forms of "self", social relationships, and conceptual frameworks' (Fairclough 1992: 39). Second, there is an emphasis on the interdependency of discourse and discursive practices as 'texts always draw upon and transform other contemporary and historically prior texts' (Fairclough 1992: 39–40). In other words, discourses are 'interdiscursive' and texts are 'intertextual' – 'any given type of discourse practice is generated out of combinations of others, and is defined by its relationship to others' (Fairclough 1992: 40). Third, discursive practices are exercises of power which pervade all aspects of social life and are successful in proportion to their ability to hide their own mechanisms. 'Power does not work negatively by forcefully dominating those who are subject to it; it incorporates them, and is "productive" in the sense that it shapes and "retools" them to fit in with its needs' (Fairclough 1992: 50). A discursive approach to the study of policy involves locating discursive practices as exercises of power and pointing to the exercises of power within those practices. This is not an uncovering of 'truth', however, but is itself an exercise of power, a discursive manoeuvre.

Ball (1994a) points out how poststructuralist approaches have made it possible to explore the complexities and messiness of responses to policies but that they may ignore the discursive constraints involved. He draws on the work of Riseborough to talk of policy effects in terms of 'secondary adjustments' within institutional discourses. Here he suggests teachers are active rather than passive in response to policies. Responses may be individual or collective and may attempt to conform with or disrupt policy intentions. Responses to policy texts are thus not determined by policy but are rather 'creative'

> Given constraints, circumstances and practicalities, the translation of the crude, abstract simplicities of policy texts into interactive and sustainable practices of some sort involves productive thought, invention and adaptation. Policies do not normally tell you what to do, they create circumstances in which the range of options available in deciding what to do are narrowed or changed, or particular goals or outcomes are set. A response must still be put together, constructed in context, offset against other expectations. All of this involves creative social action, not robotic reactivity.
>
> (Ball 1994a: 19)

However, to focus on secondary adjustments of this sort – what people do – without considering the way in which discursive circumstances are already framed, may mask the constraints of response for both teachers and researchers by privileging certain possibilities over others.

> [E]xclusive focus upon 'secondary adjustments', particularly if this takes the form of 'naïve optimism', may obscure the discursive limitations acting on and through those adjustments. We may only be able to conceive of the possibilities of response in and through the language, concepts and vocabulary which the discourse makes available to us. Thus, Offe may be right in stressing that struggle, dispute, conflict and adjustment take place over a pre-established terrain.
>
> (Ball 1994a: 22–23)

The discursive uptake of policy may therefore vary. Discursive limitations are an aspect of context within which policies are worked out. As I will argue shortly, they are in some sense prior to but also worked on within and through policy texts themselves. Thus, this points to the value of the 'literary' or 'textual' approach within poststructuralism and a focus upon the policy document as a site.

Sandra Taylor's (1997) view is that the 'fine grade' analysis of policy documents made possible by discursive approaches needs to be located in a broader context. Taylor *et al.* (1997: 43) make this same point:

> Some fine-grained analyses of policy texts focus on language – exploring linguistic strategies used to position readers...as well as the key words used...it is important that such fine-grained textual analyses are placed in a broader context.

Taylor *et al.* (1997) point also to the importance of work by Rizvi and Kemmis (1987) and Bowe *et al.* (1992) in exploring the use of language within policy documents and revealing the way in which it works to persuade the audience or make multiple readings more or less possible. However, their notion of context is problematic in terms of a poststructuralist approach drawing from the early work of Foucault: 'At its broadest, context simply refers to the antecedents and pressures leading to the gestation of a specific policy. These include the many economic, social and political factors which lead to an issue being placed upon the policy agenda' (Taylor *et al.* 1997: 45). Any return to the referent – the identification of antecedents and pressures outside of discourse – is precisely what a discursive approach questions and attempts to avoid.

In archaeology, a domain of 'statements' can be described and explored as an autonomous realm of discourse from which non-discursive practices are bracketed. This is done because discursive practices take up and transform the non-discursive in particular ways – categorizing, objectifying and so on (Dreyfus and Rabinow 1982). Non-discursive practices are, therefore, not what make it possible to encounter, speak about the discursive, or give such practices serious content, but are meaningfully framed by statements, discursive formations and regularities. The analysis is not at the level of language but of statements.

> The analysis of statements...is situated at the level of the 'it is said'...[we must understand by this]...the totality of things said, the relations, the regularities, and the transformations that may be observed in them, the domain of which certain figures, certain intersections indicate the unique place of the speaking subject and may be given the name of author.
>
> (Foucault 1972: 122)

With this view of discourse, the 'context' is only that of other discursive elements. 'Thus the archaeologist can study the *network* of discursive practices and treat it as an ensemble of interconnected elements while bracketing what Foucault will later call the "thick tissue" of nondiscursive relations which forms the background of intelligibility for those actually speaking' (Dreyfus and Rabinow 1982: 58, emphasis in original). This is the result of a 'double reduction' which allows the analyst to remain neutral to the truth claim of the statement, its meaning and the more general question of the possibility of a context free truth claim. Foucault's 'double reduction, by remaining neutral with respect to the very notion of truth, opens up the possibility of a *pure* description of discursive events. "One is led ... to the project of a *pure description of discursive events* as the horizon for the search for the unities that form within it"' (Dreyfus and Rabinow 1982: 50–51, emphasis in original). Statements, what Dreyfus and Rabinow call 'serious speech acts', make sense as products within an enunciative network from which they cannot be isolated and within which they become constituted as 'serious' by the rules of that network. Dreyfus and Rabinow (1982: 66, emphasis in original) explicate the archaeological approach by taking the university as a familiar example:

> What organizes the institutional relations and the thinking is finally the system of rules which govern what sort of *talk* about education (and which talkers) can, in a given period, be taken seriously. It is these rules 'governing' what can be seriously said that, counter-intuitive as it may first seem, ultimately 'effect' or 'establish' university life as we know it.

This relinquishing of context appears rather perverse until one grasps the strategic purpose. It is precisely in order to explore the existence of a system of rules governing serious speech within discursive networks that this is necessary. I am hoping you will take me seriously in my writing of this of course. It indicates a different politics of language than that suggested by Sandra Taylor (1997) and Taylor *et al.* (1997), as the policy text and the 'literary' or 'textual' is taken seriously within policy studies without recourse to context as we generally consider this to be.

> Foucault wants to argue that the islands of density in which serious speech acts proliferate are the result of principles which operate from within or from behind discourses to constrain what can count as objects, what sorts of things can seriously be said about them, who can say them, and what concepts can be used in the saying.
>
> (Drefyus and Rabinow 1982: 71)

What then is a statement, or, as Dreyfus and Rabinow call it, a 'serious speech act'? How is it distinguishable and why is it a useful tool in the analysis of policy? Statements are not just 'utterances', because utterances may differ, but the statement may be the same (e.g. where a different language is used to say the same thing). The statement is not a grammatical entity, because, for example, a map can be a statement. Statements are, however, speech acts. It is not, however, all speech acts that are taken for consideration as statements. 'Foucault is interested in just those types of speech acts which are divorced from the local situation of assertion and from the shared everyday background so as to constitute a relatively autonomous realm' (Dreyfus and Rabinow 1982: 48). Serious speech acts are such because they operate within this realm.

> Speech acts gain their autonomy by passing some sort of institutional test, such as the rules of dialectical argument, inquisitional interrogation, or empirical confirmation . . . By passing the appropriate tests statements can be understood by an informed hearer to be true in a way that need make no reference to the everyday context in which the statement was uttered.
>
> (Dreyfus and Rabinow 1982: 48)

Foucault is not interested in commenting on such acts or in verifying them. Nor is he interested in exploring how individuals understand each other in acts of communication. Foucault is, however, interested in the types of serious speech acts: 'the regularities exhibited by their relations with other speech acts of the same and other types – which he calls discursive formations – and in the gradual and sometimes sudden but always regular transformations such discursive formations undergo' (Dreyfus and Rabinow 1982: 49). He is therefore interested in practices and 'rules' but not in the sense that we generally take them:

> The description of the events of discourse poses a quite different question: how is it that one particular statement appeared rather than another? . . . The question proper to such an analysis might be formulated in this way: what is this specific existence that emerges from what is said and nowhere else?
>
> (Foucault 1972: 27–28)

The focus of this book then is on policy statements of flexibility and lifelong learning, as they appear as events within formal policy documents. These are taken as events upon a discursive terrain and as serious speech acts governed by certain rules of possibility and impossibility, inclusion and exclusion. By formal policies are meant those related to 'government generated policies which are developed and implemented through state bureaucracies' (Taylor *et al.* 1997: 22). The text explores to some extent how it is that these statements appear and the specific form of existence that emerges. However, these are not the same questions as those posed by Foucault, for the theorizings here differ in ways that are explored further within the next section. The policy document is taken as a specific site of discursive work, which has been hitherto relatively less explored in relation to flexibility and lifelong learning. The text takes this 'space' as one through which to examine the existence of an intersection of the sort of 'principles' or 'rules' spoken of by Foucault, supplemented by the work of rhetoric in the construction of flexibility and lifelong learning as truths within policy statements. 'Foucault found that in the course of his analyses he had discovered a vast uncharted territory... Unlike most alien territories this one is so close to us that it is very difficult to find' (Dreyfus and Rabinow 1982: 44–45). This chapter has drawn upon some aspects of the techniques selected by Foucault so that I might 'discover' my own space, my own alien territory, in order that I might grope my way across it. This is not the same territory, or even similar, nor could it be. But by taking up some similar resources it offers me a specific discourse – an 'island of density in which serious speech acts proliferate' (Dreyfus and Rabinow 1982: 71) – through which to speak seriously. Having travelled within the broad terrain of poststructuralist approaches, I now lay out more specifically the theoretical resources upon which I draw from the early work of Foucault, but also the older tradition of rhetorical analysis.

A point of departure

Foucault's notion of 'systems of exclusion' is a significant point of departure. He gives an account of his own working with this notion within his 1970 lecture at the Collège de France (Foucault 1996), and it is this that the book draws directly upon in the analyses of flexibility in Chapter 4. Foucault identifies three systems of exclusion: 'the three great systems of exclusion governing discourses – prohibited words, the division of madness and will to truth' (Foucault 1996: 343). The 'will to truth' is the operation of a specific and generalized system of exclusion from discourses that takes a particular form within contemporary times. It is a will to truth of science, within which there is a system of exclusion based upon truth and falsehood. This division has functioned within modern societies by appearing to separate power and desire from 'true' discourses. For Foucault, such systems have emerged and operated in order that 'man' might control discourse, which only points to the fear of its dangerous and uncontrollable elements.

> I am supposing that in any society the production of discourse is at once controlled, selected, organized and redistributed according to a certain number of procedures, whose role is to avert its power and dangers, to cope with chance events, to evade its ponderous, awesome materiality.
>
> (Foucault 1996: 340)

Alongside, and to some extent being increasingly incorporated into that of the will to truth are the exclusions of 'prohibition', and of 'reason and folly'.

Taking prohibited words first, there are prohibitions 'covering objects, ritual with its surrounding circumstances, the privileged or exclusive right to speak of a particular subject' (Foucault 1996: 340). These are interrelated, reinforcing and complementary to one another. They form 'a complex web, continually subject to modification' (Foucault 1996: 340). Discourses dealing with politics are one of those where Foucault considers these prohibitions operate most densely.

> I will note simply the areas where this web is most tightly woven today, where the danger spots are most numerous, are those dealing with politics and sexuality...It is as though discussion, far from being a transparent, neutral element, allowing us to disarm sexuality and to pacify politics, were one of those privileged areas in which they exercised some of their more awesome powers. In appearance, speech may well be of little account, but the prohibitions surrounding it soon reveal its links with desire and power.
>
> (Foucault 1996: 340)

The other great system of exclusion – that of reason and folly – has existed in the separation out of the words of those who are mad from those who are sane since the Middle Ages. At that time, the mad person's words were excluded from common discourse:

> His words were considered null and void, without truth or significance, worthless as evidence, inadmissible in the authentication of acts or contracts, incapable of bringing about transubstantiation...at Mass. And yet, in contrast to all others, his words were credited with strange powers, of revealing some hidden truth, of predicting the future, of revealing, in all their naïveté, what the wise were unable to perceive.
>
> (Foucault 1996: 340–41)

Foucault argues that this division has not disappeared with the emergence of scientific discourse of madness. The speech of the mad person is still invested with desire. This is evident through the work of the doctor, who attends to such speech, deciphers it through systems of analysis and the institutions that are established to exclude such persons. The speech of the mad person is still credited with terrible powers.

The scientific form of the will to truth emerged in the sixteenth and seventeenth centuries in Europe and has been productive of the whole history of scientific knowledge. This has had the effect of privileging scientific approaches to investigation over others that might be considered less rigorous or 'true':

> [A] will to knowledge emerged which, anticipating its present content, sketched out a schema of possible, observable, measurable and classifiable objects; a will to knowledge which imposed upon the knowing subject – in some ways taking precedence over all experiences – a certain position, a certain viewpoint, and a certain function (look rather than

read, verify rather than comment), a will to knowledge which prescribed (and, more generally speaking, all instruments determined) the technological level at which knowledge could be employed in order to be verifiable and useful (navigation, mining, pharmacopoeia).

(Foucault 1996: 342–43)

Foucault identifies various problems associated with this turn towards science. There are, for example, certain stabilizations in the way in which we regard what truth or knowledge are and how we approach its production. These are masked from us through our understanding of knowledge production processes. They bring us to produce certain kinds of representations of the world as truthful rather than others, which might also be possible. Foucault points to several difficulties with this. First, we do not question our will to truth. As we presuppose that we understand the source of true knowledge, we cannot then question this, or individual roles, disciplinary regimes, or the will to truth that it affords us. In other words, we are unreflexive about knowledge claims. Second, it involves us in cutting out other discourses of truth, with a consequent rarefaction of a certain form of discourse. By 'rarefaction' Foucault indicates the problem of true knowledge being taken as that which reflects the world rather than that which signifies it. Third, the effect of scientific knowledge is to produce a view of the history of discourse as the continuous, unfolding progression of knowledge. This has the effect that we do not recognize the possibilities of the unexpected event, nor the discourses that have been excluded in this process. Fourth, we give the signifier sovereignty within language. In this, by imagining that the world is out there to be deciphered, we do not recognize that we write the world, and that it is this writing that gives it its regularity. Fifth, we take language as finding its meaning in the thought and creativity of 'man', rather than in the external conditions for its existence.

Foucault argues that the division governing our will to knowledge has always been arbitrary, modifiable, institutional and potentially violent,

however – asking what has been, what still is, throughout our discourse, this will to truth which has survived throughout so many centuries of our history; or if we ask what is, in its very general form, the kind of division governing our will to knowledge – then we may well discern something like a system of exclusion (historical, modifiable, institutionally constraining) in the process of development.

(Foucault 1996: 342)

Foucault calls to the reader's attention that the present division between truth and falsehood has not always been as it is today. Thus he draws a historical distinction between truth based upon who is speaking and truth based upon what is spoken. 'That day dawned when truth moved over from the ritualized act – potent and just – of enunciation to settle on what was enunciated itself: its meaning, its form, its object and its relation to what it referred to' (Foucault 1996: 342). For Foucault, this shift did not entail a discovering of the 'real' division between truth and falsehood, however, but a shift in truth-telling practices and what could be taken seriously. By offering evidence of past configuration of the division between truth and falsehood as a political act, Foucault emphasizes the present division as historically contingent, modifiable and political, even though it is often presented to us as if it were objective and set for all time. Each configuration relies on institutional supports and the dominant forms are based upon the constraint of others.

> Finally, I believe that this will to knowledge, thus reliant upon institutional support and distribution, tends to exercise a sort of pressure, a power of constraint upon other forms of discourse – I am thinking of the way Western literature has, for centuries, sought to base itself in nature, in the plausible, upon sincerity and science – in short, upon true discourses.
>
> (Foucault 1996: 343)

What I take from Foucault and utilize in my own work is that literary or textual approaches to the analysis of policy discourses have been put aside as secondary through the success of a form of will to truth that constrains our thinking. These approaches can be productively deployed in identifying boundaries of inclusion and exclusion that policy discourses maintain and in writing accounts of them. This is not a 'literary' analysis that is merely commentary. Neither is it an attempt to be 'scientific' in another way. I am attempting to fashion the exercise of power and desire within discourses – to 'counter' it by writing alternative discursive accounts which surface among other things the rules of exclusion. Foucault indicates that the will to truth is tending to grow in strength, as for example, it incorporates economic practices into codified 'precepts and recipes – as morality too … in order to give them a firm foundation' (Foucault 1996: 343). This resonates with the notion of policy precepts and recipes of lifelong learning and flexibility and the kinds of discursive work on morals and ideas that have been exposed by Ball and Taylor *et al.*, as discussed within Chapter 2. Desire and power may be masked in this process but not eliminated.

One possibility for exploring the work of power and desire, which I draw upon in this book, is to consider the rhetorical work of language that was the concern of the Greek sophists. Contemporary understandings from applied linguistics and conversation analysis indicate that rhetoric is part of all communication. Thus the analysis of the rhetorical work of policy texts can be productive in making explicit the work of desire and power within policy discourse.

A second possibility is to draw upon Foucault's own notions of archaeological investigation. Foucault (1996) calls the form of analysis emerging from his archaeological principles 'critical'. Discourses are treated as 'ensembles of discursive events' (Foucault 1996: 356). Analysis employs a principle of reversal and a specific 'point of attack'. This principle of reversal seeks out the activities of exclusion and rarefaction to make our assumption that we know the various sources and statuses of truth problematic. By reversal of the dominant notion of that truth a point of departure is found. This book works with the assumption that descriptions of truth are discursive representations that are constitutive of the truths of the world rather than simply reflections of them. They are thus imbued with power and desire. As explored in the previous section, this is not a rejection of reality but rather a suspension of realism, in order to explore the representative work of policy discourse and the power and desire involved in the attempt to realize reality. It requires specific forms of analysis. Foucault (1996: 357) attempts within this critical work,

> to distinguish the forms of exclusion, limitation and appropriation . . . [within and external to discourses, as I have already outlined] . . . ; I shall try to show how they are modified and displaced, which constraints they have effectively exercised, to what extent they have been worked on.

He identifies various 'functions of exclusion' within specific periods of time around madness and sexuality. He is careful to point out that these examples offer only provisional guidelines for this kind of analysis: 'Of course, these only amount to somewhat symbolic guidelines, but one can already be pretty sure that the tree will not fall where we expect, and that taboos are not always to be found where we imagine them to be' (Foucault 1996: 357).

Hoping to escape the dangers of trees falling unexpectedly or at least standing under one when it does fall, this text draws on a principle of reversal of particular notions of truth and language. Initially, this involves an exploration of the possibility of making visible an intersection between rules of exclusion and rhetorical practices through close textual analysis. This is attempted within Chapter 4 of this text. It will be helpful to elaborate a little here on notions of rules of exclusion.

These rules of exclusion are complimentary to each other and to the three systems of exclusion I have discussed that Foucault indicates operate to some extent externally on discourses.

> I believe that we can isolate another group: internal rules, where discourse exercises its own control; rules concerned with the principles of classification, ordering and distribution. It is as though we were now involved in the mastery of another dimension of discourse: that of events and chance.
> (Foucault 1996: 344)

There are several such rules that Foucault suggests operate as principles of rarefaction within discourses. First, there is commentary. Discourse is graded and classified through rules that divide major narratives from lesser forms of discourse which are

> 'uttered' in the course of the day and in casual meetings, and which disappears with the very act which gave rise to it; and those forms of discourse that lie at the origins of a certain number of new verbal acts, which are reiterated, transformed or discussed.
>
> (Foucault 1996: 344)

This division is 'neither stable, nor constant, nor absolute' (Foucault 1996: 344) but functions to control the chance that we might say something other than the text itself. Second, there is the principle of rarefaction of the author, 'as the unifying principle in a particular group of writings or statements, lying at the origins of their significance, as the seat of their coherence' (Foucault 1996: 346). This principle limits the chance element within discourse through 'the action of an *identity*' (Foucault 1996: 347, emphasis in original). Third, is the principle of 'the organization of the disciplines' (Foucault 1996: 347). This functions to permit new propositions, but offers control of that which is considered to be true. A further group of rules are those 'imposing a certain number of rules upon those individuals who employ it...[discourse]' (Foucault 1996: 349). These he identifies as 'ritual' – 'Religious discourses, juridical and therapeutic as well as, in some ways, political discourses are all barely dissociable from the functioning of a ritual that determines the individual properties and agreed roles of the speakers' (Foucault 1996: 350). Key here are 'fellowships of discourse', 'doctrine', and the 'social appropriation of discourse', for example, those wrought through education systems. These rules identify those who are able to employ certain forms of discourse and deny access to others. These principles of rarefaction internal to discourses are always in flux.

There are a range of discourses that are critical of Foucault's proposition of systems and rules of exclusion. In discussing the work of Barthes and Foucault, and touching on the work of Derrida, Jonathan Potter (1996: 102), for instance, argues that '[i]n contrast to linguistic and post-structural stories of construction, conversation analysts treat reality construction as something that has to be achieved using some devices or techniques... Conversation analysis provides the final story of how fact construction gets done'. Potter (1996: 102) makes explicit within his text how rhetoric works to build up the truth of what is said:

> the use of a particular descriptive term, or even a familiar discourse, may not be enough to construct a version of events which will be treated as real or factual. Realism and factuality are worked up using a set of rhetorical devices and techniques which may be specific to particular settings.

This does not mean, however, that to explore the work of rhetoric in statements one needs only to know whether it is effective.

> Often rhetoric is treated as virtually synonymous with persuasion... However, this can easily turn the study of rhetoric into an exercise in cognitive psychology. It will treat the answer to the question of whether rhetoric is effective as dependent on an assessment of whether there has been a change in mental state in the audience... [rather]... rhetoric will be treated as a feature of the antagonistic relationship between versions: how a description counters an alternative description, and how it is organized, in turn, to resist being countered.
>
> (Potter 1996: 108)

It is the struggle to realize meaning rather than consciousness or cognition that is central here. Rhetorical analysis then offers productive capacities for the analysis of policy. The *Oxford English Dictionary* (1989) defines rhetoric as 'the art of using language so as to persuade or influence others', but for Potter (1996: 106) 'rhetoric should be seen as a pervasive feature of the way people interact and arrive at understanding'. As Foucault has pointed out, with the growth of modern science from the beginning of the Enlightenment and its emphasis on induction from empirical observation and experiment, the rhetorical and the truth were held to be mutually exclusive and science was concerned with the truth devoid of rhetoric. In the same way that truth entailed the exclusion of desire, it also acted to produce the exclusion of rhetoric, where the latter was held to often pander to the desire of the masses. The persuasiveness of science then was held to rest in its truth claims, not in its rhetorical practices. Rhetorical analysis continued as part of the arts and humanities, while science concerned itself with the truth. This continued to be the case with the emergence of the social in addition to the natural sciences.

However, in recent years, this situation has shifted somewhat. Whether or not one classifies it as part of the postmodern condition of knowledge (Lyotard 1984), or the 'linguistic turn' in the social sciences, there has been a questioning of the firm boundary between rhetoric and truth (Nelson *et al.* 1984) alongside those other systems of exclusion identified by Foucault. Perhaps nowhere is this more pronounced than in the policy arena and thus it is important for policy studies. Attempts to persuade and influence are pervasive. Lyotard (1984) suggests that this is part of the language wars of the postmodern condition. Potter (1996: 107, emphasis in original) argues that these 'wars' have a longer history, one intrinsic within communication, as offensive and defensive rhetoric: 'a description will work as *offensive rhetoric* insofar as it undermines alternative descriptions... a description may provide *defensive rhetoric* depending on its capacity to resist discounting or undermining'. It is important to bear in mind that this distinction is not between the more and less powerful, as both dimensions will be found in any discourse or text. While Potter represents rhetorical war as more than a contemporary phenomenon, Lyotard points to a radicalization of these processes through the proliferation of texts, discourses and signs. There is an incitement to rhetorical practices, which itself is reflected in the growth of discourse analysis as a way of investigating their significance.

As has been identified within the earlier analysis of the literature on life-long learning and flexibility, it is suggested that the policy rhetoric of lifelong learning is not reflected in the reality of policy strategies to pursue it or in its implementation. Reality is contrasted with rhetoric, and both are found wanting. However, this may be to devalue and misunderstand rhetoric. Implicit in forms of ideology critique is the notion that representations in texts may be mystifications of the material world by those who exercise power. Here the notion of rhetoric is often collapsed into ideological struggle. However, alternative readings are available:

> While it is true that policies are responses to particular social changes, it is also the case that these changes may themselves be represented in a variety of different ways, and accorded contrasting significance. Recent educational policy initiatives may thus be viewed as responses to the struggle over particular constructions of social, political, economic and cultural changes. The state itself puts forward its policy initiatives in the rhetorical language of reform, often presented as the only plausible response to the social and economic changes described.
>
> (Taylor *et al.* 1997: 4–5)

The study of lifelong learning and flexibility precisely as rhetoric, in addition to the resources drawn from Foucault, can point to the very real and powerful practices that are in play. Forms of discourse analysis can illuminate certain aspects of what is being attempted within and by policy texts and the mobilization of actors in and around those texts. Here the question is not about whether reality matches the rhetoric, but how descriptions become taken up as truthful and which description is more persuasive and why.

Within the rest of this book – within all three ensuing explorations – I focus on theorizations and explorations of the discursive and rhetorical work of policy discourses of flexibility and lifelong learning, significantly through an examination of documents of public policy. As I demonstrate, theoretical resources may be combined in a variety of ways to produce different types of reading/analysis that focus on a particular range of issues and forms of work. They are not part of a method to be applied but resources in an interpretative journey of reading. As I have argued, this approach contrasts with forms of analysis that are more commonly used but also indicates a difference in how the policy document is conceived. Positivist policy studies take the language of policy within documents in realist terms. Within critical analysis they are often taken as the *products* of policy processes that are indicative of the 'settlements' of discourse

> In terms of the stages of policy formulation, Rein (1983: 211) has suggested that at least three steps are involved. These are problem setting, the 'mobilization of the fine structure of government action' and the 'achievement of settlements in the face of dilemmas and trade-offs among values.
>
> (Taylor *et al.* 1997: 26)

This emphasis on policy as the settlement of competing values emerges from the concern for ideology critique within Marxist forms of analysis. Poststructuralist work has tended to focus away from discursive analysis of the policy document itself to place emphasis on the conflicts, disputes and struggles that surround and are the broader discursive contexts and effects of policy documents. Commonly used forms of analysis conceive of the policy document as text in a variety of ways. However, none of these (realist, discourse settlement, value allocation or statement of intent conceptions) consider the activity – the discursive work – of language within the text.

Within the archaeological approach taken up here, discourse is a field that is made up of the totality of spoken or written statements that occur as dispersed events. 'Before approaching, with any degree of certainty, a science, or novels, or political speeches, or the *œuvre* of an author, or even a single book, the material within which one is dealing is, in its raw, neutral state, a population of events in the space of discourse in general' (Foucault 1972: 27, emphasis in original). Discourse is not that which can be expressed through a body of rules, as in the analysis of language, nor is it a consciousness that is to be discovered behind language, as in the analysis of history. It is that which exists as the finite totality of the events of writing and speech at any one moment.

I want to emphasize here some of the limits of what I explore within the ensuing trails of analysis of flexibility and lifelong learning. As I have indicated, I draw upon some key concepts from Foucault's early work and on various approaches to rhetorical analyses. In this, I take the formal policy document as the site for analysis. I have talked about the policy statement as an authoritative site of policy discourse, in part as this is a site where Foucault indicates that rules of exclusion are likely to be operating most densely. I do not explore the processes of either policy formulation or its effects. To do this would be to draw upon categories that are already inscribed within discourses of policy and, as such, they are problematic. Policy formulation and effect entail notions of traditions, intent and influence, which constrain our ability to step outside dominant discourses. The analysis would therefore be contained within existing systems and rules of exclusion, accepting, even if at a critical distance, certain of the rhetorical practices at play. These are to be held in suspense rather than rejected. They must be revealed as coming not out of themselves but as the result of rules and justifications that must be made known and scrutinized. The explorations of flexibility and lifelong learning that follow take then an archaeological and rhetorical point of attack.

Taking stock

In this chapter, I have explored dominant approaches to the study of policy and what they might offer in an exploration of flexibility and lifelong learning. Rejecting these as limiting in specific ways, a discursive and post-structuralist approach has been proposed. A discursive and rhetorical approach, drawing eclectically on the work of Foucault, Potter and others, has been argued to be appropriate, as it can offer particular tools for explorations that offer productive ways of (en)countering policy. Various research problematics associated with such an approach have been discussed and ways of dealing with them identified.

To make its case for these explorations, I have explicated a relation of power and struggle within and between discourses of policy and the study of policy and post-compulsory education. I refuse the temptation to explore what lifelong learning and flexibility 'truthfully' are or what they 'really' mean, or to construct a narrative around this from the literature. To do so would be to represent certain unities that are to be elided. My starting point – my beginning – is one of my own theorizing, as well as of the beginning of this text. I begin in taking policy themes of lifelong learning and flexibility as emerging within pre-existing discourses in order to govern based upon certain systems and rules of exclusion. The key question I am examining is the means by which these policy concepts are constituted within and through policy texts. I do not intend to focus on how they are constituted and maintained through policy studies or post-compulsory education here, as it is sufficient to identify this power relationship and to position my work as one that seeks to create a wedge to counter it. This is to be done by producing discourses – statements – of the constitution of lifelong learning and flexibility within policy texts as truths of a different sort.

The metaphors of the nomadic theorizer and the discontinuous trail have been identified as strategies to emphasize the reflexivity, locatedness and decentredness of myself as the researcher within the explorations that follow. These demonstrate the intertextuality of my work in relation to prior texts and their refashioning in the production of alternative statements. Here the beginning for a theorizing is found as an opening for research within dominant discourses made possible at a particular location by the theoretical resources that are available and the coincidence of the interests and presence of myself as researcher. The trails that are made from these beginnings are discontinuous, as they travel to some extent both somewhere and nowhere and do not attempt to progress knowledge in any straightforward way. There is no single route/root to knowledge.

4 A realization of flexibility

In the Quentin Tarantino movie, *Reservoir Dogs*, Freddy is an undercover cop who infiltrates a bunch of robbers. In the getaway from the botched robbery, he is shot and spends most of the film bleeding profusely lying on a warehouse floor. The film tells the story of how the robbers come to be in the warehouse largely through flashbacks. It is in flashback that we discover that Freddy is an undercover cop. We also see how he learnt to go undercover. In one scene, his police colleague Holdaway is teaching Freddy how to make his cover story convincing. Central to this is providing sufficient detail. He is given a script about an event in the men's room that he has to learn. This includes the detail of whether the stalls had doors and whether there were towels or a blower for drying hands. Freddy complains about how much detail he needs to learn to play the part of a crook convincingly. For Holdaway, it is only through mastering the details that Freddy will be able to sell his story to the other members of the gang. In the film, as well as seeing Freddy complain about learning the details of his cover stories, we see him tell them to the gang and they are convinced. It is only at the end of the film that Freddy tells another member of the gang that he is a cop, and he is shot.

Jonathan Potter (1996) uses this story at the beginning of his text on *Representing Reality* because it illustrates very well the point that we have to *work* to make a description convincing. Whether real or invented, descriptions of what is, what happened, or what will happen are representations of reality, which work to convince the reader or listener. This involves strategies like attending to detail. Detailing works because we expect the person who was there to remember what happened and this helps warrant the authenticity of the account.

Even when a description is not a recounting of an event that was experienced by the narrator, detail can work rhetorically in similar ways. For example, an ethnography may convince because it demonstrates that an investigation has been thorough. It provides a 'thick' rather than 'thin' description. Detail can also be selected and organized in differing ways to make different accounts of the same event. We see this vividly in the variations of witness accounts of car crashes and so forth. Detail can also be knowingly arranged to represent a specific and advantageous description of reality rather than a disadvantageous account. This is central rhetorical work for legal representatives in a courtroom. The important point here is that, rather than consider what is being said in order to construct a 'reading' of the description in a literal sense, analysis can focus on the way in which the description is constituted in order to do something. It is less a case of what is said and more of how what is said is put together to make the description convincing. Descriptions are used within communications *to do* things. They are action oriented. The story above is not only about Freddy learning to make his story convincing, but it is also a description that works to convince a movie audience of its authenticity. We can see this in the colourful use of colloquial dialogue in the film, which helps persuade us that this could be a live conversation, even though we know that it is only a script/movie.

Whether we draw consciously on rhetorical strategies to make our descriptions more convincing or not, rhetorical strategies are at work. Representations of reality are fabricated (MacLure 2003) and this activity, as we will see, to some extent depends upon, reinscribes and reinforces rules of inclusion and exclusion. This chapter is an exploration of rhetorical practices in the constitution of a description of flexibility within policy. What it demonstrates is that this combination of theorizing makes it possible to produce an exploration of flexibility as a theme of education policy which is quite different from that elucidated by more conventional approaches to policy analysis. The chapter examines one Australian Commonwealth policy document, the *West Report* (DEETYA 1998), to explore the ways in which rhetorical strategies are deployed to constitute flexibility as an aspiration and intention of policy and attempt to persuade the reader that this proposition is both reasonable and truthful. This document is taken as an event and statement of policy discourse, as introduced within Chapter 2, and, as such, it is quite different from the kind of description being worked up by Freddy. It will be worth ascertaining that this distinction is sufficiently clear. Foucault is concerned with the examination of statements that are taken 'seriously' at any one time and by this he is indicating their autonomy from the realm of everyday discourse. Now it would perhaps be possible to make the argument that Freddy's statement will be taken seriously by the gang within a specific discourse community. And its persuasiveness or otherwise could certainly have serious consequences for Freddy. Nonetheless this kind of statement is relegated to the realm of everyday discourse within our definition and could not therefore be taken as serious. To count as serious a statement needs to be able to be proposed or considered as truth without referring to the immediate (non-discursive) context in which it is uttered. The chapter is concerned with policy statements as events. The normal everyday speech of politicians, review committees, contributors and media representatives are therefore excluded from its concern. It is concerned with examining the detail of policy statements in policy texts that are published for public consumption.

The *West Report* (DEETYA 1998) emerged at a time when there were moves within many Australian universities to provide flexible learning opportunities. The Report was to the Liberal Government of the time, drawn up by an independent review committee which had been appointed by the Minister for Employment, Education, Training and Youth Affairs, Senator Amanda Vanstone, a year prior to the publication of the final report. The Committee had been charged to develop a policy and financing framework for the higher education sector capable of satisfying Australia's social and economic needs over the next two decades. Entitled *Learning for Life, Final Report: Review of Higher Education Financing and Policy*, the report was produced following substantial work; the commission of a range of papers, extensive submissions from individuals and groups, visits to Australian universities and key stakeholder groups for consultation, the production and publication of an interim Discussion Paper, an open call for further submissions on the suggestions contained within the paper, and consideration of these. The paper was reported within a media release as 'based on eight months of intensive consultation, including discussions with all universities, student and staff groups, governments, employers, other community groups, overseas higher education agencies, and consideration of almost 400 submissions' (DEETYA 1997b). This chapter examines how the Final Report, drawn up at the end of the review process, seeks to provide authoritative meanings for practices of flexibility that it promotes – to 'fix' the facts about which it speaks and, in the process, rhetorically hide its own invention. These meanings of flexibility resonate within a range of discourses that were already in operation within the social formation and support a particular vision of the future and the recommendations for policies associated with it.

The chapter is divided into four main parts. The first explores the 'event' of policy review in terms of the discursive constraints that are its context. The second focuses on the work of the *Terms of Reference* of the review committee as discursive and rhetorical mechanisms. These work to constrain and enable the production of policy discourse through control of the work of the review committee. The third focuses on the specific rhetorical strategies at work within the Final Report as policy statement. It suggests that flexibility operates rhetorically within descriptions of a terrain to be managed, defining and limiting the 'necessary' role of the government in decision making, and positioning institutions and individuals as those who are then 'required' to act to become more flexible and responsive. This begins to elucidate the rhetorical strategies of a policy doctrine. This is an extensive section of analysis. The final section takes stock of this line of theorizing to consider what it can achieve.

External constraints

It is important to consider the various orientations to activity within and surrounding an 'event' of policy, such as is indicated by the West review and its subsequent Report. First, there is the actual activity of undertaking a review. A review of the higher education policy and funding framework is the express function of the committee. A review is a 'reassessment'. It must produce recommendations to the minister over adjustments that are seen to be required. The event itself then focuses on the work of the committee and orients the description within the document that will be produced. It is to produce a narrative of reassessment and 'improvement'. Improvement assumes a description of problems, whether current or future, their solution and recommendations for action. This is the specific orientation towards 'action' that is the work of the particular 'narrative form'.

There is a second constraint and rhetorical action in the function of such a review. This is most easily made explicit by exploring the role and entitlement afforded to a minister. A government minister is afforded category entitlement to speak on policy matters. However, she or he does not have complete authority to truth. The minister is still required, to some extent, to persuade us of the truth of what he or she says. He or she must be seen to be speaking 'within the true' for this to appear free of the influence of desire and power. Here, right at the beginning, it is apparent that there operates a system of inclusion and prohibition that identifies a minister's entitlement to speak seriously on government policy matters. As Foucault (1996: 399) indicates, it would be possible to speak the truth in a void, but 'one would only be in the true if one obeyed the rules of some discursive "policy" which would have to be reactivated every time one spoke'. 'Policy' in this context, suggests the broader discourse of the government, through which what the minister can say is constrained, and also the constraints of a wider web of systems of inclusion and exclusion. Implicit within policy is a policy of discourse with its own inclusions and exclusions. Furthermore, whether what is enunciated is persuasive as truth is determined in part by the rhetorical strategies whereby it is represented. This is a further distinction, for it would always be possible to speak 'within the true' but for this not to be accepted.

The rhetorical function of the review process and document is to persuade us that the decisions of the minister, which are likely to ensue subsequent to a review process, lay 'within the true.' Rhetoric works in two main ways. First, to some extent as a warrant for the decisions that will subsequently be made. Second, by helping to avoid any potential reading that the minister or government might have a stake in what is decided. Government ministers commonly set up independent policy reviews at times when policy decisions are to be forthcoming. These need to be received well when they are released. Policy reviews and reports operate in advance of policy decisions in the attempt to build up support for legislative decisions. This is part of their function. They do this by inviting and listening to the views of various groups and individuals. From this, certain actions can be worked up as recommended and as 'within the true'.

Whether or not the decisions that ensue will ultimately be seen as warranted is not the point here. We are concerned with the review process as a strategy that is used to help make this more likely. Warranting works by persuading us that descriptions are factual. It does this by drawing the emphasis away from the subjectivity and identity of those who produce the description. 'These are procedures designed to provide a quality of what might be called *out-there-ness*. In other words, they construct the description as independent of the agent doing the production' (Potter 1996: 150, emphasis in original). The review process and the document produced works to distance the minister as the agent in the policy process. In other words, the very fact of the consultation process and production of a review report helps persuade us that the minister's subsequent description is warranted, rational and justifiable.

Warranting and stake management strategies are groupings of rhetorical activities that are common within descriptions. Warranting work is done in all communications, but some forms are more common within specific discourse categories. For example, descriptions are written in a third person form that masks the presence of the author. Detail and narrative structure are other aspects that can help the reader to be persuaded that descriptions are 'true'. This might involve offering detailed empirical evidence or structuring a description to conform to prior narrative expectations. Warranting can also be done by representing authoritative individuals and groups as in agreement with some parts or details of a description. Or they may be positioned as supporting a description in general terms. Within empirical and disciplinary discourses, this is commonly done through citations and references, but other forms of discourse do so less formally. A policy review report is no different from any other kind of communication in drawing on these sorts of strategies.

Stake or interest management tries to avoid readings that the minister or government has a stake or interest in the decisions that are ultimately made. However, in making this point, it is important to clarify that the intention is not to suggest that ministers or governments simply have a stake or interest to hide. Readers commonly interpret policies and policy texts in terms of stake and interest.

> They treat reports and descriptions *as if* they come from groups and individuals with interests, desires, ambitions and stake in some versions of what the world is like. Interests are a participant's concern, and that is how they can enter analysis... Management of stake is one of the central features in the production of factual discourse.
>
> (Potter 1996: 110–11, emphasis original)

A policy review process helps to displace this kind of treatment and the review text draws upon rhetorical strategies that help further manage issues of interest or stake.

The situation for a minister is tricky. In setting up a review process, the signal to the public is one of ensuing decision making and action. This may be unsettling for those who might be affected. At the same time, an independent review constructs a dangerous potential for discourse to get out of control. A review committee could potentially come up with suggestions that sit quite outside what is politically acceptable or even suggest no change at all. There is then a possibility that a review process in not just a situation for discourse to be reiterated but also one for the formation of a new verbal act or 'primary text' (Foucault 1996). Through opening discourse up to discussion there is the possibility it might get out of control. However, governments are increasingly required, by media and populations alike, to be seen to be doing things that are productive. For the minister alone to say what this is to be may not be sufficiently persuasive. We, as populations, need to be persuaded that what is planned as action lies 'within the true' and that our interests are protected in this. We want to be sure that the government is acting on our behalf, rather than in its own or anyone else's interest. The event then is one that works to help excise the possibility that power and desire might be seen to be operating within government policy discourse. To do this, it must build a description of the world that we can accept as sitting 'within the true'. It must be a narrative with a logos of reassessment and for improvement, with recommendations for action that flow logically from this. The review event acts as a warrant for this narrative and manages any potential for us, as audience, to think or argue that the minister or government might have a stake in what is subsequently decided. These are then both constraints and possibilities on the event and its function within policy discourse.

I have identified three broad categories of rhetorical strategy that are drawn upon in any descriptive communication oriented towards action – narrative form, warranting and stake management. The detail of these strategies frame and manage a description in specific discourse settings. These categories overlap and intersect. For example, many rhetorical strategies act both to warrant a description and manage stake. We will see how these ideas help to illustrate the kind of rhetorical and discursive work that gets done *within* the *West Report* (DEETYA 1998).

Terms of reference

Rhetorical strategies tend to be specific to the setting rather than generalizable. 'Potentially, there are a huge number of ways in which the production of descriptions is involved with actions. Descriptions are closely bound up with the idiosyncratic particulars of settings' (Potter 1996: 111). A minister has a powerful tool available for the control and production of the description in the handing down terms of reference for a review committee. 'Terms of Reference' are used commonly in policy reviews. This allows the minister to manage the work of a review committee by 'framing' in advance the description that they can produce and the recommendations for action that can be forthcoming.

In relation to *The West Report*, the *Terms of Reference* identify a problem of change to be addressed. The next two decades are identified as likely to bring further changes with the emergence of a global market, where higher education becomes an 'international enterprise', and international links are 'vital' for the creation and advancement of knowledge. Developments in communications technology are identified as reinforcing such trends, together with their creation of changes in the delivery of higher education, the management of information, the nature of teaching and learning, and the teaching and research infrastructure. Concurrently, higher education is described as becoming increasingly important to the 'fabric' of advanced industrial societies. None of this description is particularly surprising. It is a version of that found within the contemporary policy documents of many nations.

In the *Terms of Reference*, change and development for higher education is normalized, externalized and naturalized. These are rhetorical tactics that achieve slightly different work to build up the facticity of change as precisely a normal, external and natural characteristic of the world in which we live. Change is represented as that which continues over long periods of time. It is described as having been going on for a while and it is through this strategy and this reading that we come to accept change as just such a normal characteristic of the world. Normalization is also commonly achieved in communications by listing (Potter 1996). Lists are often used to summarize or provide evidence for a general class of things. Where change is described as existing over time, and examples of it listed, these things are normalized as part of generalized change and development. It is through these kinds of descriptions that we come to expect certain things (objects, characters, etc.) within future descriptions; and we may thus tend to expect specific characteristics of the world as change and development to continue in the future.

Change works externally upon the sector. It is made to appear more real by being represented as if it were devoid of human activity. It is time, the decades, which bring change rather than humans. It is made into something external through this formulation. Further, change associated with time appears natural. It is naturalized. It is made to seem as natural as the leaves falling off trees or the weathering of the mountains. It is *being made* to look like a natural occurrence. Similar points have been made about the naturalization of globalization (Giddens 2000) and the normalization and nominalization of change (Fairclough 2000) more generally within policy discourses.

It is thus a normalized, externalized and naturalized change that is projected into the future within the description of the terms of reference. It is that which brings forth a higher education sector, an international enterprise, which delivers services to a global market. By associating the emergence of higher education as an international enterprise with natural change, the reader may infer this emergence as part of a natural progression in environmental terms. The rhetorical tactics used here allow a market discourse of education to emerge quite naturally on the terrain, and this helps to elide other possibilities. Thus the discursive terrain for the ensuing work of the Review is already being heavily produced and constrained within the description of the environment to be addressed.

Significantly, flexibility and creativity are constituted as attributes of university institutions within the *Terms of Reference*. They are identified as necessary responses to change that is to be made possible through an appropriate policy framework:

> The Review Committee will develop a comprehensive policy framework for higher education that will allow universities to respond creatively and

flexibly to change, and will ensure that the sector meets the needs of students, industry and society in general as these are likely to develop over the next two decades.

(DEETYA 1998: 177)

The point here is that it is through a description of changes that are identified as fundamental and problematic that creativity and flexibility are able to be constituted as the logical and rational responses – the solutions. This is achieved by constituting objects within a discursive terrain that count as a reflection of *how things really are* or *are going to be*. The description is thus positioned 'within the true'. As we have already seen, this is not the utterance of just anyone. It is made by one who has a privileged, and indeed perhaps exclusive right to speak on policy issues at this specific moment, within this context. It provides a rationale for action which lacks detail but it is asserted at the highest level of modalization and this signifies sure knowledge. The description acts to constitute facts. Insofar as any rhetorical activity becomes aligned with the description later on, it will further constitute that reality. The *Terms of Reference* thus set the discursive terrain for the work of the review committee and the description and recommendations that can follow.

The point at which a description starts is very important. We see its significance in the work of the legal profession in courtrooms. Here a nuanced description offered by a defendant can help ensure that the focus of subsequent discussion is advantageous to that party (Potter 1996). Narrative organization is important also. By ordering events and identifying what is to be included within a description and what is to be left out, very different descriptions of reality can be forthcoming. We have only to consider the variety found in witness accounts to see how this happens. People tend to notice different things, and in part construct what they have seen through the later organization of their descriptions. Narrative organization of this sort is not only isolated to these sorts of extreme cases. It is part of the working up of the facticity of any description, including those of policy. Indeed we cannot really give any kind of description without such organization, even though we may not think explicitly of what we are doing. The structuring of narratives is fundamental to the rhetorical work of policy.

We can already see that the creativity and flexibility of university response to change within a globalized competitive terrain is both the beginning and the intended outcome of this narrative. The policy framework is to be adjusted so that this outcome is supported. This is the terrain, characters and the order of events for the review. The start of the narrative has been determined and, with that, what is to count as a complete answer. In part, this narrative is rhetorically persuasive, because it resonates with descriptions of change, globalization and the need for flexibility that are accepted elsewhere. Narrative descriptions of this sort are commonly expected to meet up with standards of coherence and correspondence with prior descriptions if they are to pass as 'real'. Indeed it would be quite strange if every description of the world within policy differed from every other. We expect continuity, because plausible accounts are commonly taken to be produced by putting 'facts', which correspond to reality, within a coherent narrative structure. However, narratives are not just about selecting facts and putting them into an order that an audience may find persuasive, but there are particular configurations – narrative forms or plot structures – that are part of our 'cultural endowment' (Potter 1996). They are persuasive within those cultures that use them. Narrative structure may be conditioned by the forms of narrative that are part of a cultural endowment and by the ways in which the authors wish the text to act. This is the case in policy as elsewhere.

Realizing flexibility

The production of a doctrinal discourse is visible in the resonance between the description of the *Terms of Reference* and that constituted within the final Report itself. Through illustrative analysis of the *Executive Summary*, and aspects of the subsequent chapters of the report below, I examine the narrative of the world within which flexibility is positioned as a requirement. What rules of inclusion and exclusion are at play? What rhetorical strategies support the constitution of the requirement for flexibility? What work do these rules and rhetorical strategies do? These are identified as concerned with either working up the facticity and reasonableness of the description or working to protect the description from future potential undermining.

As I have suggested, the notion of narrative structure may be taken as a useful metaphor. It brings forward the idea that it is in part the structure of the story that helps to work up the plausibility of a description. This suggests a different form of analysis than one that explores a narrative for its correspondence to reality. Narrative structure can 'be thought of as a rather loose preliminary category that usefully collects together a range of disparate but important discursive phenomena' (Potter 1996: 173). Even though narrative structure cannot be seen simplistically, it is in part through the structuring of descriptions that meaning is made possible. Therefore, it is upon such strategies of structuring and the way in which these may act that an analysis of a policy statement can focus. Structure can be explored in terms of the construction of 'local' and 'global coherence'. Local coherence is at the level of relations within a piece of text, and in the 'meaning connections between utterances, producing...coherent interpretations of pairs and sequences' (Fairclough 1989: 143). Global coherence suggests 'working out how a whole text hangs together...This may involve matching the text with one of a repertoire of schemata, or representation of characteristic patterns of organization associated with different types of discourse' (Fairclough 1989: 144). For this analysis, notions of local and global coherence are considered primarily in terms of the rhetorical techniques and devices deployed. The list of headings for the Final Report (DEETYA 1998) constructs a powerful narrative structure. It has global coherence.

This indicates a unity through the logical and sequential development of an argument and the commonly understood work of an *Executive Summary* in the 'crystallization' of an overall narrative for the benefit of the reader. It is clear from the headings that there is to be an identification of changes, either emergent or required, which are then to be contrasted with a vision for the future, which thus constructs a need for action and is logically followed by an outline of the activity that will achieve this vision. The description signalled through these headings is one of change and action within which flexibility is 'important'. The structure works rhetorically to signal a realist narrative and logical extrapolation into the future.

In a realist fashion, the *Executive Summary*, might then be taken to indicate a shortened version of the overall narrative – a 'quick read' for those of executive status who are concerned to gain a crystallization of the argument and overview of the list of recommendations from the review committee to the government. However, on close analysis, this global unity of narrative structure is made possible through some quite explicit and detailed rhetorical work that occurs at the local level. Most of this takes place within the *Executive Summary*, although detail, warranting and stake management activity continues heavily within further chapters. It is key aspects of this local rhetorical work that we go on to explore here.

One aspect of this is ontological gerrymandering, whereby a problem is constructed as real and objective. Thus, key areas of 'development' are constructed within an 'operating environment', which are stable and naturally occurring, and to which we must respond (DEETYA 1998: 17–18)

> We believe that over the next two decades the operating environment of higher education institutions will be fundamentally changed by developments in four key areas.
>
> *Community expectations*
> The community's expectations of higher education institutions will increase...
>
> *Demand*
> The number of students, from both Australia and overseas, seeking access to Australian higher education will also increase...
>
> *The digital revolution*
> Developments in information technology have the potential to revolutionise...
>
> *Competition*
> Competition will increase among Australian higher education providers and among players outside established networks...

Institutional and individual flexibility are identified as the responses that will ensure that the challenge of these developments is met (DEETYA 1998: 18):

> *The importance of flexibility*
> We do not claim to know precisely how these developments will change the world over the next 20 years. However, we do know that changing patterns of demand, the digital revolution and increased competition will change our world, and it would be very unwise for institutions, or governments, to assume that they will not be touched by such developments.
>
> These broad developments, and the ultimate uncertainty of the future, underline the importance of a policy framework which gives as much flexibility as possible to universities and students, and highlights the importance of building institutions that are responsive to change.

The description selects specific characteristic developments of the future world as solid and factual. These are constructed as natural, normal and externalized aspects of the operational environment of higher education institutions, in the same way as within the *Terms of Reference*. The description works to construct a division between what is natural, and thus real and largely uncontrollable, and institutions with socially constructed characteristics. This division is not ontologically sustainable – it is 'gerrymandered'. Woolgar and Pawluch (cited in Potter 1996: 184) identify ontological gerrymandering as 'specific manipulations where parts of an argument are protected from constructionist analysis'. Gerrymandering occurs when some objects or aspects of a discursive terrain are identified as natural or real and others are socially constructed.

Within the description of the *Executive Summary*, echoing the *Terms of Reference*, particular developments are identified as parts of the future competitive environment. The environment is the contextual and unchallengeable terrain against which the higher education system is judged and found wanting. The gerrymandering of these developments is made to work by treating them as far as possible as empirical objects through a strategy of, as we have previously seen, 'out-there-ness' or, 'externalizing', which warrants the description itself as divorced from agency. But it also builds a 'real', physical, world for the operation of institutions and policies, which is outside their ability to change. These objects are mobilized as 'facts' to which institutions then have to respond. It is because these developments are externalized in this way that they can then require institutional and individual flexibility: 'These broad developments . . . underline the importance of a policy framework which gives as much *flexibility* as possible to universities and students . . . and highlights the importance of building institutions that are *responsive* to change' (DEETYA 1998: 18, emphasis added). Here, the 'broad developments' are represented as real and prior characteristics of a future world, which will exist out there. They could have been represented as constructed through social or policy actions, or even indeed, constructed through the actions of institutions or individuals themselves.

The ontological problem within this description is obvious when we consider the positioning of the institution in relation to these developments and the kinds of flexibilities that they are able to produce as their response to them. If we look closely, these actions by institutions will *produce* the very future developments that have been described as naturally occurring. For example, the text (DEETYA 1998: 17) suggests that community expectations will increase, as 'students, their parents, and their employers will expect better outcomes from universities and, in line with developments in other service industries, they will increasingly look for products tailored to their particular interests and needs'. By responding to increased community expectations through increasing flexibility, higher education institutions will be acting to construct the characteristic of community expectation rather than merely responding to it. If we consider the three other future developments – demand, the digital revolution and competition – we can see the same sort of ontological problem at play. Increasing flexibility to satisfy demand, as a response to the use of information technology, and to respond to competition, higher education institutions will at the same time increase demand, the extent of the digital revolution and competition. By increasing flexibility institutions construct the world to which they are represented as responding.

It is important to note also that flexibility could have been presented as required in relation to any development. For example, an increasing marginalization of particular social groups could just as well have been argued as a reason for increasing institutional flexibility. The constitution of particular developments does work in making *them* the characteristics around which subsequent narrative structure, rhetorical work, discussion and even activities for flexibility become focused. This is a rhetorical strategy to manage the global narrative around the inclusion of certain objects – community expectations, demand, the digital revolution and competition – rather than others. It is through the selective constitution of the terrain upon which a debate takes place that discussion around a topic commonly occurs. In this policy description, the debate is to be focussed on community expectations, demand, the digital revolution and competition, and institutional and individual flexibility in relation to these objects.

I suggested in the introduction to this chapter that detail is commonly used within accounts to help warrant their facticity. Significantly, the *West Report* indicates that we know what developments are key to the future and that flexibility is a requirement. However, it does not indicate within the *Executive Summary* exactly how we know this. 'We do know that changing patterns of demand, the digital revolution and increased competition will change our world, and it would be very unwise for institutions, or governments, to assume that they will not be touched by such developments' (DEETYA 1998: 18). Here this very lack of detail may give the assertion more force than it may have otherwise had. Potter (1996) points out that description may, in some cases, do more convincing work through lack of detail as this makes them difficult to undermine. That the *Executive Summary* lacks detail, but promises that it will be forthcoming within the main body of the text of the report, works to persuade those who read only the *Summary* that convincing detail is available without going so far as to offer it. However, within chapter 2 of the main report there is detailed description of increases in the key areas that have been identified. This may be because the very increases identified as requiring flexibility arise from increasing flexibility. They are a response rather than a precondition.

Just in case the key areas for development have not been sufficient to persuade us that flexibility is needed, uncertainty over the future may. Indeed 'ultimate uncertainty' is a detail in the description which appears at first to sit uneasily in relation to the firmness of the claims surrounding broad developments in the future. It sits as a rhetorical detail right at the heart of the beginning of the narrative. One of its actions is to make the description of the requirement for flexibility less easy to undermine. On their own, the developments may not produce a secure enough requirement for flexibility. We could work up a solid argument against flexibility, for example, by suggesting that ontological gerrymandering is at work. We could go further than this and argue that the developments imply institutional change that is very specifically *targeted to meet* the predicted patterns of demand, requirements for ICT use and competitive market. Rather than moving towards a general flexibility, the developments might just as easily indicate the need for specific strategic goals and targets in relation to them. By introducing uncertainty into the policy description, flexibility clearly becomes a more rational response.

Uncertainty thus helps prevent any future attempts at the undermining of the argument by counter argument over the details that are provided.

'*Ultimate* uncertainty' is an example of the use of the strategy of 'extreme-case' formulation (Potter 1996). It maximizes uncertainty. It again defends against the possibility of any undermining. 'Ultimately' it is because we cannot be certain over the future developments or of their detail that a quite generalized flexibility can be a convincing solution. Ultimate uncertainty over the characteristics of the future environment produces a requirement for flexibility against which it is extremely difficult to argue. The fact that the description of the problem itself begins to dissolve with this ultimate uncertainty does not necessarily matter, as most people do not do a detailed rhetorical analysis when they read a policy text or hear a political speech.

The theme of uncertainty and certainty over the future is returned to in detail at the beginning of chapter 2 of the main report. The developments are also, once more, reinforced, as the 'challenges' which must be faced. These are represented as the background against which the existing policy and funding framework are to be assessed. A following separate section reinforces lack of certainty and yet asserts some certainties over the directions of change that will ensue

> We have not attempted to make precise predictions. As physicist Niels Bohr said, 'prediction is very difficult, especially about the future' – an observation illustrated in recent times by the sudden downturn in a number of Asian economies. A policy framework that is relevant to the needs of the next century must be able to function effectively in a highly unpredictable environment and to provide the maximum possible flexibility to students and universities so that they can do likewise .... Nevertheless, we can discern a number of broad directions of change.
> (DEETYA 1998: 55)

There is a density of rhetorical activity surrounding this description that makes it useful to unpack slowly. It is an 'unreasonable' text in describing a situation of the uncertainty of predictions. The physicist, Niels Bohr, and an empirical description are drawn upon to support the description – a case being made. This is an example of footing shift. Within the *Executive Summary*, it was 'we' who knew with certainty that the future was uncertain. Within this chapter, it is Niels Bohr who offers the authoritative footing for this description. Through this, the description of uncertainty is both 'corroborated' and 'inoculated' (Potter 1996). Niels Bohr agrees with the description and thus it is difficult to suggest that the argument is biased. He is not only an individual with category entitlement as an author, but he is a physicist. His corroboration therefore has double emphasis. First, through the entitlement that he has to speak. Second, through the status afforded to scientific knowledge. In other words, the description is corroborated by the entitlement of the individual to speak of knowledge that is unbiased and independent. This removes any possibility of a reading that the committee might have a stake in the description.

Imprecision about the future is worked up as a generalized and natural state of affairs. Although the words are represented as corroborative, there is a further rhetorical strategy at play, as the description avoids the possibility of any cross examination, because the physicist's words are quoted but no reference is given. Within a certain genre of writing, the usual requirement for referencing is obviated where the individual's work is commonly known. The implication of this strategy is subtle, as it works up the status of the physicist's corroboration and, at the same, avoids cross-examination of the description. Further, it positions the reader who is not familiar with the work of Niels Bohr as one who does *not* know something commonly known and accepted.

The policy unity of problem and solution in the *West Report*, surrounded as it is by a dense web of rhetorical strategies to secure it, is warranted within the *Executive Summary* in two main ways. First, by externalization at a high level of modalization. This reifies (Potter 1996) or rarefies (Foucault 1996) the narrative as 'knowledge'. Second, by constituting a group that 'knows' this narrative to be true. A lack of detail over the constituent members of the group works to align the reader, together with the writers, as members of the group. By implying that the audience already agrees with the narrative, it helps work up such an agreement. These two strategies intersect within three small words, 'we do know' (DEETYA 1998: 18) and variations of them. As they are so significant in work to secure the local description, and the global narrative that is then made possible, we will unpack these strategies in detail. '[W]e do know' draws upon and constitutes an allegiance that is not visible. It identifies a group of people and a collective prior knowledge. The question is not to ask whether a group of people correctly distinguish between truth and falsehood but how the description acts to convince the reader of this. They act to separate individuals into groups (we who know and others who do not) and the known from the unknown. The description thus acts doubly upon the reader. The strategies are of the constitution of certain knowledge (of the truth of uncertainty, key developments and the requirement for flexibility) and of a knowing group who warrant that knowledge. The assertion 'we do know' and the presentation of the importance of flexibility as already accepted knowledge, constructs a version of the world and the group as solid and factual – certain – even if it is based on uncertainty.

The ambiguity of the membership of the knowing group is also rhetorically significant. The 'we' positions the authors and reader potentially as belonging to the same group. It is a group then who are 'in-the-know' or, indeed, speak 'within the true' (Foucault 1996). Here the positioning of individuals together is forceful. The authors are afforded status and the reader is invited to belong. The text positions the authors and reader within a group of status and consensus, and this undermines potential opposition. For, who would want to appear unknowledgeable?

A need to construct an imperative for action is explicitly identified within this policy text. 'To be successful our report must engender a sense of *urgency* about the need to reform the funding and regulatory framework for higher education' (DEETYA 1998: 16, emphasis added). This is achieved not only through an appeal to truth and reason, as we have seen, but also to the emotions. These help distract the reader from any focus on the ontological problems of the description. Affective rhetoric is deployed to construct polarized positive and negative futures. Readers are then exhorted to choose between them – the future that we can construct will be more positive than the future that is inevitable, but we need to act. The three introductory paragraphs to the *Executive Summary* sketch out a description of a potential future that works for positive affect: a '*vibrant, open* and *inclusive*' (DEETYA 1998: 15) future for Australia, which can be achieved only if we act. 'Knowledge will be the most important currency of all...If Australia is to *prosper* in this new environment...we must...become a learning society' (DEETYA 1998: 15, emphasis added). The description constructs action as desirable and necessary by appealing to the positive connotations of a lively, democratic, wealthy and prosperous society. The future is rosy, as long as we become flexible.

Rational argument is combined with the suggestion of immanent 'danger' to reinforce the urgency of the need for change. The danger is that of loss of direction for the higher education system and a policy framework that will not be able to deal with future change. 'As we observed in the Discussion Paper, many people expressed a feeling that higher education is beginning to lose its way' (DEETYA 1998: 16). The danger is loss of the ability for the system to make its social and economic contribution. This danger is exacerbated through a description of a fast pace of change:

> The sense of urgency that we are seeking to generate may surprise some. However, the Review Committee's reasoning is straightforward: the world in which universities operate is changing – and changing fast – and Australia's current policy and financing framework will *not be able to deal with those changes.*
>
> (DEETYA 1998: 17, emphasis added)

Here a certain pathos is invoked focused on specific kinds of danger, which works up a need for action. Uncertainty over the direction of change contributes to the fear that the reader is incited to feel. Only action can make us safe.

This description of danger resonates with broader discourses of uncertainty and risk that are a feature of contemporary societies. The description draws upon and reinforces a sense of fear that may be already familiar to the reader. Any troubling of the reader's emotions through the representation of 'ultimate uncertainty' over the future is exacerbated by a higher education system that has lost its way and the lack of capacity for the policy framework to cope with the situation. Action for survival will have to be taken. The authors thus position themselves very strongly through appeal to truth, reason and affect.

When people work up the facticity of descriptions, they can use various resources to indicate its origin. This can help secure facticity, or in some cases assign blame and so forth. We often see these kinds of resources used in media reports. For example, where a description is attributed to a 'community leader', or in terms of what 'the public' may think is the case. They can help the media introduce a description into a conversation without attributing it to themselves, and thereby make the description appear more authoritative, or avoid potential blame, or appearance of any stake in the description, by appearing to be merely reporting what others say in one way or another. This is the rhetorical strategy of footing. Management of any reading that the Committee might have a stake in the claim that 'we do know' is carried out within the text following the *Executive Summary*. Whereas the description has been warranted as the knowledge of a generalized group, as we have seen, there is a 'footing shift' within the rest of the report. This works to display neutrality, but also perhaps indicates the rhetorical function of the review committee. Their job is to persuade the reader that they have canvassed a whole range of authoritative opinions on the matter at hand and have come to considered conclusions.

The footing of the review – initial review, discussion paper, submissions, responses, visits and consultations – is made visible through listings within the appendices of the final report. However, the individuals and groups itemized are drawn upon selectively within the body of the report itself for the purpose of ascribing specific descriptions to specific authoritative voices. The listings first constitute a group of those with category entitlement to speak authoritatively. The second more selective group providing footing differs from this and indicate the voices that are to be identified as heard. This rhetorical feature is significant. The first community comprises intra- and intergovernmental agencies, other nations and national groups. It offers a potentially reciprocal rhetorical function across nations, wherein a wide sense of unity of agreement can be fashioned and drawn upon to warrant national policy descriptions in particular contexts. The second community serves a more specific rhetorical function within the report, as it manages the potential for any suspicion of stake in the description and contributes to the constitution of the detail of the description itself.

The description within each subsequent chapter of the report is warranted through management of footing in the second way. Indeed there are so many instances where footing supports specific details of the description that particular textual devices are used throughout to organize these. Footnotes, figures and substantial quotes from authoritative texts are liberally scattered throughout each chapter. What is perhaps notable is the number of and extent to which governmental and intra-governmental texts are drawn upon, and the extent to which certain groups are included and others are not. Through these devices, the text works up an implicit rigour to its description. In so doing, it constitutes a virtual fellowship of discourse that is productive in the constitution of a description that may operate as a doctrine. This is the doctrine of flexibility.

It is perhaps the polyvalent meaning of flexibility that enables the development of a wide fellowship in the policy-making process. In each case of its use within the report, an object and relationship is constructed as one to be managed through an increase in flexibility. This is, namely, the university approach to the teaching/scholarship/research nexus, loan conditions to universities, the policy framework, wage tariffs, decision-making processes within universities, the population, a university in terms of meeting students' diversity of need, preference and educational outcome, etc. Increased flexibility is the generalized response to all issues. It is flexibility that emerges as the coordinating theme from which the subsequent narrative of necessary change within the policy and funding framework then appears logically. By repetition of its requirement within this narrative, flexibility is reinforced.

> Flexibility and responsiveness will be the watchwords for success over the next 20 years – for organisations (including higher education institutions) and for nations. The demands made on the higher education system will grow, diversify and rapidly change. Australians will demand flexibility over what, how, when and where they study, and it will be critical for our national wellbeing that those demands be met.
>
> (DEETYA 1998: 69)

Flexibility operates as a governing theme by providing a plausible and generalizable overarching solution for the problems arising from natural and unpredictable changes in the environment, even while, at the same time, being able to be positioned as producing these changes. By fixing flexibility as a solution to a problem within a particular description of the world, it can become the focus and a general theme around which action can be rhetorically promoted, organized and success measured. The positioning of flexibility as the solution to a problem may be enough to construct a considerable expectation of flexibility as a theme governing the changes that are then suggested. An expectation of a requirement for flexibility supports the plausibility of subsequent and more detailed description of actions that are then described as necessary.

Within the global narrative, increasing flexibility becomes the theme governing the relationship between the policy and funding framework, the system, institution and individual. Any change to the policy and funding framework that affords the institution increasing flexibility in relation to its satisfaction of needs within the key areas of change becomes a requirement. The government's role then is to deregulate the system to enable institutions to compete for students. This is to be done through two major reconfigurations of relationships. First, by giving the individual funding as a lifelong learning entitlement, the student becomes the client of the institution rather than the government. This will make the institution well attuned and 'creative in response' to the needs of various clients and quick in response to changes in client groups or their requirements. Second, the government will restructure the funding framework to allow the institution freedom for 'total resource management' – wage flexibility, pricing flexibility through flexible forms of delivery, flexibility to set student fees and expand student numbers and to develop their infrastructure as they require through flexible loan systems. Rhetorically, the individual consumer and choice are mobilized as the motors for reform and flexibility is realized as a desirable and reasonable goal of policy.

Taking stock

It is time to take stock of where we are with regard to this trail of exploration and theorizing. The chapter began by pointing out work that detail can do in constructing a persuasive narrative through an illustration from Tarantino's movie *Reservoir Dogs*. Detail is a commonly used rhetorical strategy and has been deployed within the analysis of this chapter in order to persuade you the reader. The exploration has not been concerned with whether those who construct policy descriptions draw knowingly on rhetoric and systems of inclusion and exclusion in what they do. Neither has it been concerned with identifying the truth of the matter. By contrast, it identified some detail of what is done, in order that what is done in the name of truth is revealed as the operation of power and desire within a policy statement, to expose some details of that work.

The chapter has begun to reveal detail in the working of desire and power both external to and within policy statements through: the imbrication of rules of inclusion and exclusion within and surrounding the event; in the building of truth through the operation of rules with quite specific rhetorical strategies and tactics; and in the building of such truth in the form of a doctrine, that it may function to control discourse and excise the chance event through its replication, and circulation. What does this say about the possibility of utilizing these tools for analysis as a means to politicize? What hooks have I here to convince the reader that this is both true and exciting?

Within communications people work to convince each other that their descriptions are those best for describing the true, and respondents may take this as such or seek to work to undermine them. Foucault's delineation between the statement as serious and others that are not may not hold empirically, as we know that the effect of flexibility is in the detail of its workings within other sites – largely institutional. However, this is not to say that Foucault's tactic is without utility, for it begins to reveal that the policy statement is a particular site for work where rules of inclusion and exclusion – the materiality of desire and power in Foucault's thesis – operate in quite specific ways, and densely. By combining Foucault's tactic and looking for the detail of the working of rhetoric, it has been possible to reveal quite specific aspects of the operation of desire and power in the construction of a policy narrative of flexibility. Some of these may be common within narratives of flexibility elsewhere. They may form regularities within discourse within the contemporary world of education, and convince us to act inline with that which is articulated.

Much of the detail of the analysis does not at first appear to produce much that is new in terms of what has been said of flexibility in other quarters. The capacity for flexibility to systematize discourses, for example, has been identified elsewhere. However, on closer inspection what differs is that the systematization described here emerges through an analysis of statements at a linguistic and rhetorical level. Systematization does not emerge in what is considered here as non-discursive effect – in terms of the institutional discourses that become systematized – but within statements and through rules and rhetorical strategies and tactics that lie in some sense within discourse. What then can be said of a systematization that emerges within this specific statement and in relation to rules such as these?

The policy report is an event of potential danger within policy discourses and, as this is so, is a site where the web of inclusions and exclusions is tightly woven. It is a site where truth must be built up in order that it may function as a doctrine. Here the possibility that discourse might be read as imbued with desire and power must be excised. It is also a site where the possibility of a chance event, serving to disrupt its progressive discursive unfolding, must be managed. Rules of exclusion and inclusion infuse the event as a web of functioning strategies which remain largely invisible to us. Specific rhetorical mechanisms and strategies that draw upon, reactivate and reinforce one another are at work. They demonstrate the operation of desire and power within policy discourses.

There are discursive constraints and possibilities that surround the event that function to make it possible to speak 'within the true' within public policy documents such as this. There are rhetorical features that support the constitution of both a fellowship of discourse and a doctrine of flexibility. As has been seen, this particular text constructs flexibility as a principle governing change. It has drawn upon flexibility for work in the production, control and management of the statement and proposes the reproduction and dissemination of such narratives as a description of a means to govern within contemporary times. There are various key aspects of the rhetorical activity that have been detectable, even though they are not entirely distinct or separable.

Key to the constitution of flexibility has been the rhetorical technique of ontological gerrymandering. That we can detect this indicates that our descriptions may generate a more or less stable division between what is able to be taken to be as real, empirically or naturally occurring within the world at a particular time, and what is taken to be constructed by human action. We are positioned to expect descriptions of the future where the problems of increased demand, increased competition, increased information and communication technologies, and uncertainty are represented as more or less natural characteristics of a world untainted by human activity. To the extent that this is so, they become key problems that must be faced and responded to by our action. The fact that by increasing flexibility we act in the world to help realize this description is put aside. It suggests that policy descriptions may to a certain extent be able to 'play' on instability inherent in this division, to construct advantageous descriptions, in the attempt to be persuasive. This combination of what is known about the world is rhetorically very powerful and consequently very difficult to undermine. How can one argue against certain uncertainty? These key developments are widely represented to us through various discourses. Our certainty in them is thus premised on an assumption that human activity will continue to be oriented within this particular doctrine. And so we come to construct the world in which we live in discursively and materially.

This points to a space for further investigation of the rhetorical strategies required for the constitution of themes of policy at particular times. Have they always required a gerrymandered division between what is described as natural and objective fact and that which is socially constructed? What has been able to be included as naturally occurring? And what themes as solutions have these produced? We might thus examine statements for regularities, not just for those of policy but also those upon which they explicitly and perhaps implicitly draw. Descriptions of the social and economic operate powerfully to influence our subjectivities and the descriptions of the world that can thus be persuasive.

There is also a systematization achieved through the organization and management of narrative structure. At the outset, the narrative terrain is laid out within the *Terms of Reference* to the committee. This fashions the gerry-mandering that is required within the report in order to produce details of the description for flexibility. This structure is mapped out through the overall sequencing of the chapters and subheadings within the *Executive Summary*. The local and global narrative structures are thus conditioned by the way in which the review committee is required to make the text act. It works because it conforms to narrative expectations; it seems right, coherent and well formed. By beginning with flexibility as a prior assumption, and by backgrounding its narrative work, discussion is focused away from its problematization as the means by which the narrative is managed. This helps prevent possibilities for it to be undermined. The requirement for flexibility is protected powerfully through the juxtaposition of the developments that we know to be certain. Increasing flexibility is further secured through uncertainty – for if we do not know what the future will bring then we had best be able to be flexible. *Ultimate* uncertainty protects the description and the government for the future if the key developments do not emerge as has been suggested.

It may therefore be that there are more or less regular rhetorical strategies and work to produce truth and reason within policy review reports of this kind. As the narrative structure is mapped out by *Terms of Reference*, the beginning, end, and objects to be required within the narrative become quite difficult to avoid within the Final Report. A review committee may be left with recourse only to strategies such as the amount of detail offered, the narrative start, warranting and so forth, to make their reports persuasive. What emerges strongly through this analysis is that the structuring strategies specific to this doctrinal description are already heavily fashioned and support work in the production of truth of flexibility. The extent to which such discursive strategies operate in other education policy review processes is therefore of interest.

The affective has been central to the rhetorical work of the description in attempting to persuade us that we must act. Danger works up urgency for action. The world is unpredictable, uncertain and changing fast. If we are to be safe, we must act now to secure our vision. The explicit threat is that we will not cope. The implicit one is of our failure to survive. Action is invoked by fear. Future safety, however, logically requires future certainty. Although the future that is promised appears rosy, certainty cannot emerge for the future through this discourse. Thus the desire for certainty and survival cannot be guaranteed but may result in the very fear that it is meant to address. This points to a dimension of policy discourses that attempts to mobilize populations through fear. This appears a possible fruitful avenue for further investigation. What are the affective aspects of statements that operate within policy at any one time? What work do they do and effects do they have?

In constituting Australia as a focus within the national policy statement, it becomes possible to describe it as engaged in a competitive game with other nations. This is a familiar rhetorical strategy. The danger of losing is, by inference, loss of control and the ability to achieve the rosy future that has been promised. By drawing upon and constituting a group of nations to warrant the description, and by setting them up as if they were a series of runners at a starting line, the requirement for 'the race' becomes more persuasive. This rhetorical strategy clearly produces a means by which governments can measure improvements through statistics, performance indicators and the like. And this may be necessary for governments to persuade us that they are in control, for us to know if we are 'winning', and in order that we may be incited to further productive activity. However, the reasonableness of this kind of strategy needs to be troubled. Discourses of international competition may themselves constitute dangers of quite other kinds. They serve to focus attention discursively on what other nations have or do not have as their resources. Rather than discourse focussing on internal distributions and redistributions within nations, as has been so in other times, policy discourses become reorientated to focus on the problematics of globalization and the globe. They trouble identities and allegiances within and between nations as they constitute them. There is no way to mark the end of the race within the rhetorical resources of this kind of description. At the end of the twenty years that has been projected, Australia will still be in competition and the future will still ultimately be uncertain.

The system of metaphors that is so striking here is one that constructs a system for the comparison and contrasting of the success of national activities in relation to the game. Where, for Freddy, the details for a persuasive account needed to be those of the men's room – the paper towels or the dryer, the stalls with doors or without – it may be that for a policy description, the details need to be an elegantly simple certainty about the existence of the game, its players, their positions, rules for engagement and the umpiring. What works rhetorically as doctrine, who it persuades and how seem important questions. This means taking a different starting point from descriptions that take reason or truth as their focus. Detail points to the significance of any prior acceptance of nations as global players and the work that policy descriptions do in the construction of the doctrinal allegiance of such nations.

The narrative we have examined is warranted through the work of a range of strategies of externalization and footing shifts, through modalization at a high level, and through details of consensus and corroboration. A wider authoritative virtual group who 'know' the description to be true is constituted. The reader is invited to be in allegiance with this discursive 'we'. This is work in the *constitution and reinforcement of* a virtual fellowship of discourse and doctrinal group. By representing flexibility as the knowledge of groups, the knowledge and the version of the world that it requires becomes more secure and persuasive. Fellowships serve a rhetorical function, which are common within policy descriptions, wherein unities of agreement are fashioned and drawn upon to warrant policy descriptions and proposals. Within the *West Report* it is intra- and intergovernmental agencies, other nations, national organizations and key authors from specific disciplinary groups who warrant the description, both generally and in many of its details. This helps to manage the possibility of future undermining based upon the stake of the government, minister, or committee in the discourse. Here it is the constitution of a wider doctrinal community that is the outcome of this work. Exploring the constitution of such groups in the policy process is useful.

The narrative represented within the *West Report* is not an uncommon one in policy terms, not least because much of the outcomes of the review were not taken up at the time, although the discourse that it represents has continued to resonate within Australian policy. By analysing it rhetorically it has been possible to identify specific strategies that are drawn upon within it. These are in part specific to this policy event. However, they indicate that systems of inclusion and exclusion of this kind operate, in the attempt to control power and desire within policy discourses and the chance event within them that might also be disruptive. These work together within this policy event as a tightly knit web to help constitute and reinscribe a narrative of flexibility as a policy doctrine.

Rules of inclusion and exclusion and the rhetorical techniques that support them are never stable, constant, absolute or discrete. They shift, as they are subject to modification through policy description and the work of other discourses. They operate as a complex web that helps control and produce what can be taken as 'serious' policy discourse at any one time and who can speak it. Thus, while discourses of flexibility can be found more widely than in the *West Report* and Australia, they do not necessarily stay the same, although it is useful to look for regularities of meaning and the discursive strategies through which they are represented, in order to chart their (re-) emergences and effects. Policy discourses move and migrate and attempt to be rhetorically moving. It is time for this chapter to move on.

5 Mobilizing flexibility and lifelong learning

In the Quentin Tarantino film, *Pulp Fiction*, two criminals, Vincent and Jules, are on their way to a hit. Vincent has just returned from a trip to Europe. The two converse about the differences between the United States and Europe through a discussion of fast food, in particular burgers and french fries. Vincent tells an incredulous Jules that in Paris a Quarter Pounder with cheese is called a Royale with cheese and a Big Mac is called Le Big Mac. More astonishing to Jules is the notion that in Holland people eat French fries with mayonnaise rather than ketchup. For me, this story represents certain aspects of globalization. Burgers and chips have become a ubiquitous food around the globe, part of the homogenization of eating habits associated with the spreading influence of multinational corporations. However, they are also signified differently in different spaces and places. The burger is both a Quarter Pounder and a Royale. In addition to the homogenization that takes place, however, there remains difference and heterogeneity. The Dutch use mayonnaise on their French fries rather than ketchup. This play of homogeneity and hetergeneity can also be found in the policy discourses of flexibility and lifelong learning and their global migrations.

A globalization of policy discourses has been identified as a feature of the contemporary world by many writers (Edwards 1997; Taylor *et al.* 1997; Lingard and Rizvi 1998). Explorations of this phenomenon, however, have tended to focus on material conditions encouraging it, rather than on the work of discourse in working it up. Marginson (1997: 35), for example, infers that the human capital view emerged in part as a result of a material relation between economists supportive of that particular view and the work of international bodies during the 1960s.

> There was close and continuing liaison between the human capital economists and the leading international bodies which championed the case for investment in education, particularly the OECD and the United Nations Education, Scientific and Cultural Organisation, UNESCO.

This kind of analysis is obviously important. It makes it apparent that there are social actors, engagements and interactions involved in the constitution of policy discourses. However, a discursive and linguistic view draws our attention to rhetorical work of policy statements in the construction of particular social actors, their relationships, and the 'we' that is required to act (Fairclough 2000). Various constructions of the global environment and relationships between nation-states appear significant within policy discourse and this suggests closer inspection. In relation to the United Kingdom at the turn of the century, for instance, 'the global economy is pervasively represented in the language of New Labour as an arena of competition between nations-states ... rather than multinational corporations' (Fairclough 2000: 29). Objects such as the 'global economy', 'competition' and 'nation-state' operate within systems of metaphor that work to support the uptake of these objects as factual and constitute communities that are active in relation to them.

This trail of theorizing within this chapter, therefore, considers the potential of a form of discourse analysis focusing on the work of metaphor in examining flexibility and lifelong learning within policy. How do specific policy discourses become mobilized, taken up, and recontextualized (Wodak 2000)? How have they become subject to dispersed groups and groups subject to them? I ask questions here regarding the multiple emergences of flexibility with lifelong learning within dispersed discursive sites. Chapter 4 explored a range of rhetorical strategies within one policy event. This chapter takes one rhetorical strategy, that of metaphor, and explores its potential for different forms of theorizing. The policy document is again taken as an event of discourse and statements of policy are the unity to be explored.

To read flexibility and lifelong learning as metaphors is a tactic of refusal to take them literally. At face value, this is similar to that used within the preceding chapter. Policy texts and policy analysis depend upon prior immersion in certain metaphors and metaphorical systems through which their representations of reality are worked up. Analysis of the ways in which policy descriptions and their critiques are formed and reified through such processes therefore becomes important, as any common acceptance of metaphors may circumscribe critical engagement. Reflexive consideration of these issues has been suggested to enable forms of critique that refuse or counter practices of reification.

Through an initial exploration of various ways of theorizing the work of metaphor, it became apparent that the migration of flexibility and lifelong learning is promoted in part through the constitution of communities which are subject to them and to which they are subject. There is the group represented as already persuaded of requirements for flexibility and lifelong learning. This is a group already subjected to discourses, which are implicit in knowing and a powerful actor in warranting descriptions. Its existence helps persuade the reader to read the description literally rather than metaphorically. Nations, institutions, individuals, groups and the reader are positioned, made subject and mobilized within and through such descriptions.

To take flexibility and lifelong learning as metaphors, that work in the mobilization of locally and globally dispersed subjects, is to attempt to disrupt the taken for grantedness of these concepts.

Jonathan Potter (1996) highlights the importance of metaphors that are taken from one context of discourse and used in another. This is an aspect of the intertextuality of communication, which has been considerably explored within the study of literature, linguistics and culture. In the area of policy analysis, there has been relatively little such work done. Some focus on metaphors has emerged, in particular through the work of Shapiro (1984b) in the US policy context. More recently Torfing (1999) has drawn upon the work of Laclau, Mouffe and Zizek to consider the work of metaphor within policy discourses. Within this chapter, I consider this work and others that I have found productive in my travels. The trail begins then with an exploration of the work of metaphors. The exploration is not intended to be systematic or exhaustive. It begins to scope out a theorizing, which is provisional, located and incomplete (Flyvberg 2002). Indeed, one could consider this as a process of the cobbling together or bricolage of theorizations, much as that which takes place within the domain of policy making itself.

> [N]ational policy making is inevitably a process of bricolage: a matter of borrowing and copying bits and pieces of ideas from elsewhere, drawing upon and amending locally tried and tested approaches, cannibalizing theories, research, trends and fashions and not infrequently flailing around for anything at all that looks as though it might work.
>
> (Ball 1998: 126)

This can be as true of policy analysis as it is of policy. What is suggested here is that metaphor offers potential for fresh openings in policy and in the study of policies of flexibility and lifelong learning.

The chapter charts a trail from concern with metaphorical work of flexibility to ways of understanding the work of flexibility and lifelong learning as part of a globalizing migration. It is written in four parts. In examining the potential of various tools for the theorizing of policy metaphor and in examining various policy texts, this chapter starts to tell a tale of flexibility and lifelong learning as migrating metaphors. It uses the metaphor of migration as a way of inscribing meaning into their global emergence. The text fabricates a trail that I have travelled. I have not 'applied' a method of discourse analysis to policy texts, an approach that would suggest a systematic scientific stance. This chapter, like the rest of the text, should be considered as an interpretive piece of art (Leach 2000) and might then be seen as more metaphorical than literal, as a theorizing is also a reading and in this case also a writing with its own rhetorical strategies, including the deployment of metaphor. '[M]etaphor opens potentialities of understanding rather than fixing understanding detrimentally and uniquely. A metaphor is permanently an opening for re-reading, re-interpretation' (Parker 1997: 84). The chapter is written in three parts. Within the first, theorizations of metaphor are explored. The second section explores the emergence of flexibility and lifelong learning as global metaphors. The third considers the mobilization, fixing, infections and colonizations of flexibility and lifelong learning. Centrally, the chapter is exploring the argument of Anna Yeatman (1994) that flexibility may itself be a governing metaphor for contemporary policy. Inevitably, metaphors are deployed in interpreting policy discourses metaphorically. The final section once again attempts to take stock of what has been achieved through such an analysis.

Metaphorical readings

A metaphor is commonly taken as a 'figure of speech in which a name or descriptive term is transferred to some object to which it is not properly applicable; an instance of this' (*The Shorter Oxford English Dictionary* 1992). However, categorizing metaphors in this way would be to hang on to a suggestion that there are some descriptions that are literal, that they can transparently represent the world in some way. Here metaphors are almost acting illegitimately. Rather than take this notion, this chapter seeks to make problematic the literal/metaphorical distinction and to displace, to bracket off, questions of whether or not a description is literal in order to examine the work of all policy statements as metaphor.

Metaphors are more intrinsic within language than common understandings of them might imply. Indeed, according to some, our fundamental relation to language is metaphoric (Parker 1997). Metaphors are not only intrinsic to language but constitutive of human subjects (Urry 2000). Within some approaches, they are integral to the possibility of thought and existence (Lakoff and Johnson 1980). David Howarth (2000: 189) argues that 'meaning does not exist anywhere except in the metaphorical relationships (realized in substitution effects, paraphrases, synonym formations) which happen to be more or less provisionally located historically in a given discursive formation'.

All policy statements can be taken to be metaphorical. The selection of one metaphorical system or one metaphor against another is thus highly significant. To assess what might happen as a result of the deployment of a particular metaphor within policy discourse requires engagement with details of meaning, interpretation and uptake. To some extent, these can be assessed empirically in advance, as, for example, through government focus group research and formal modelling of voter preference and behaviour (cf. Nelson *et al.* 1987), but can never be certain. An apparent rise of appreciation of the intrinsic metaphoricity of language within politics, media and the public, resonates with its increasing emphasis within the social sciences, linguistics and philosophy.

Research into the use of metaphors within a wide range of 'serious' writing demonstrates that they are deployed even though they might not be ordinarily identified as such. In some cases they may be drawn on specifically and explicitly for their persuasiveness. Leach (2000), for example, draws on the work of Evelyn Fox Keller in the biological sciences. Keller follows the migration of the metaphor 'information' from one discursive context to another. The term was appropriated within mathematics as a measure of the complexity of linear codes. Computer scientists and systems analysts within information theory then took it up. Information became described as a quantifiable object rather than qualitative. Biologists subsequently took up the term. Watson and Crick were criticized by geneticists for their incorrect use of the phrase 'genetical information' in relation to the DNA molecule. It was argued to be incorrect and inappropriate in terms of the complexity of a mathematical understanding of DNA. However, even though the phrase was contested, it is now quite commonly understood that such information is encoded within the DNA molecule. Leach (2000: 216) argues that Watson and Crick used information persuasively 'to lend a sense of complexity, newness and mathematical rigour to their work'. This example demonstrates that terms that are identified as legitimate within one discourse may migrate to others where they may be taken literally. Such migrations may be purposeful insofar as they are seen to be capable of productive work.

Metaphors are taken up and used powerfully and systematically within the political arena, although this may not always be obvious. They work in part within systems of metaphors from which they draw or with which they resonate (Shapiro 1989). For example, politicians in North America may have exploited metaphors more commonly drawn upon within sports discourses to make their arguments for war more persuasive. Shapiro found that this practice had 'figurability' in North America, as the population was familiar with both participation in sports but also in the language of speculation around outcome. Figurability is related to the extent of intertextuality between representational forms. An alternative set of meaning relations are made possible through this. In the case of sport in North American political discourse, metaphors act to systematize responses to political activities, thereby attempting to control discourses. However, figurability does not suggest in any simple way that control is guaranteed. In some contexts metaphors work because they do not look like metaphors. In either case, they can provoke strong emotive and oppositional responses. They also have metonymic properties, where meaning governing one context can become expected within others.

George Lakoff (in Potter 1996) demonstrates such work through his analysis of the different systems of metaphors used in the United States to justify their role in the Gulf War of the early 1990s. Through a series of metaphorical moves, superimpositions and elisions, a discourse of the 'business' of government as war became possible. These metaphors were drawn upon without becoming the focus of public debate at that time. Rather than discuss whether war should be looked at as politics or politics as business, talk was focused on the relative calculations of gains and losses for the United States of involvement in the Gulf War. Metaphors, then, may operate within systems to fabricate descriptions of the world. In the prior assumptions of the writers and readers of texts there can be predispositions towards accepting certain of these. Policy responses may be systematized through the judicious selection and promotion of metaphors within texts. Thus 'a failure to exercise a literary self-consciousness, then, amounts to the adoption of a depoliticizing posture' (Shapiro 1984b: 239). By ignoring the metaphoricity of language and refusing to examine our own predispositions to accept one system of metaphors over others, we refuse to examine a significant aspect of the work of governments and political action.

Prior acceptance of a metaphorical description leads to what has been termed 'vassalage' by some. It has been a term used in particular as a criticism of the researcher in the social sciences: 'In any area where factual versions of some group are taken as a start point for analysis the analyst may end up as a vassal' (Potter 1996: 98–99). It might equally be drawn upon in considering the reader who accepts the assertions or judgements within policy texts and thus the starting point for any analysis. However, the metaphor of vassalage itself has a certain rhetorical power, connoting servitude and subordination, which may underestimate the potential within activities of reading and the different meanings that arise in the recontextualizing of texts (Wodak 2000).

As we have seen, fact construction is a process of attempting to reify particular representations of the world as fixed and solid through particular rhetorical strategies. When taken literally, metaphors partially fix the play of meanings so that only certain things are likely to be said. Take the previous example of sports discourse within a context of war. Sports discourse, as Potter discusses (1996), allows a range of distinctions; winners and losers, victors and vanquished and skill and training. There are metaphors that are central, for example, competition, fair play and spectatorship. As Potter (1996: 79–80) points out, '[w]hat sports discourse provides, then, is an elaborate set of building blocks for constructing versions of how things are; these can be used to produce accounts of international relations which emphasize certain features and hide others'. It offers resources that allow for migration from one system of metaphors to another within descriptions. However, these are never complete or decidable. There always remains ambiguity and the potential for reverse or further migration in the moving of metaphors.

What then of the metaphors through which policy migration between nations is constructed, bearing in mind my own use of migration should not be taken literally? These are the ways in which globalization becomes a policy practice. Dale (1999) provides a useful typology of the mechanisms through which the migration of policy is effected – harmonization, dissemination, standardization, installing interdependence and imposition. He contrasts these with more conventional notions of policy borrowing and policy learning that work from a more national policy focus. Levin (1998) suggests that there is little systematic learning in the processes of national policy borrowing and that the latter may be largely symbolic. He suggests the notion of the 'policy epidemic' to assist in understanding such practices.

> New agents of disease tend to spread rapidly as they find the hosts that are least resistant. So it is with policy change in education – new ideas move around quite quickly, but their adoption may depend on the need any given government sees itself having. Although many people may be infected with a given disease, the severity can vary greatly.
>
> (Levin 1998: 139)

The metaphor of epidemic suggests vectors of disease transmission as a productive avenue for investigation. However, although a metaphor may look identical within differing contexts of emergence within policy discourses and enable certain systems of metaphors to be drawn upon and distinctions made, these cannot be taken to be the same within different moments and contexts of their emergence as the agent mutates. Meaning is recontextualized in its reappropriation. Foucault (1972) demonstrates that there is no principle of unity to which an object of discourse can claim stability (common style in the production of meaning, stability of concept or commonality of theme). Coherence emerges only in the regularity of dispersion. 'The discursive moments are dispersed, but the ordering effects of the relations of difference and equivalence, the workings of different kinds of overdetermination, and the nodal points are factors that give rise to a certain regularity which can be signified as a "totality"' (Torfing 1999: 99). Without ordering effects such as these, discourses and the identities fixed within signifying sequences would be totally separate and determined. The logic of difference indicates that complete closure in meaning is impossible. It is made so by the impossibility of the identification of all differences and by the 'logic of equivalence'. The latter collapses difference through expanding a signifying chain of equivalence. Equivalence emerges through the establishment of a paradigmatic relationship between words, discursive identities, within signifying chains. 'The discursive identities are inscribed both in signifying chains that stress their differential value, and in signifying chains that emphasize their equivalence' (Torfing 1999: 97). Meanings within differing discursive domains can then always be taken to be to some extent different, but also to some extent equivalent. 'The relation between difference and equivalence is, in other words, undecidable' (Torfing 1999: 97). Political discourses may operate by emphasizing one of these aspects. Here '[e]mphasis on the equivalential aspect by the expansion of chains of equivalence will tend to simplify the social and political space by delimiting the play of difference. The collapse of difference into equivalence will tend to involve a loss of meaning since meaning is intrinsically linked with the differential character of identity' (Torfing 1999: 97). A relationship between difference and equivalence and the work of metaphor emerges within this theorization. Metaphors are constituted when identities become fully equivalent.

To take stock, metaphors are used within policy to both establish facts and in troubling the status of certain notions as facts. It is important to identify how terms are positioned as literal or metaphoric and the work that they do in both of these senses. Metaphors may be taken up within discourses purposefully and positioned literally and this may be for reasons of their persuasiveness. They may act to systematize discourses by bringing to the fore particular systems of metaphors and eliding others. This is important, as systems of metaphors, where 'figurable', may lead to a form of vassalage where only certain things can be said. Explorations of the work of metaphors might be made productive through the notion of 'policy epidemic', if this can articulate the mutation of the agent, in order that the recontextualization of dispersed metaphors can be examined. It may also be achieved by examining the ordering relations of difference or equivalence that are made possible through metaphors within differing locations by their condensation or displacement of meanings and their partial fixing of signifying chains. This may be achieved by examining their ordering effects and the constitution of nodal points through master signifiers.

Such a theorizing is itself an attempt to partially fix meanings within systems of metaphors that are alternative to those already normalized within discourses of policy analysis. Through metaphors such as 'metaphor', 'migration', 'epidemic', 'figurability', 'construction', 'vassalage', 'ordering effects' and so forth, it is proposed that productive analysis may be done. What follows then is an exploration of the migration of flexibility and lifelong learning within policy discourses through these metaphors of analysis. Others will be picked up on the way in so far as they can provide useful associations. The emphasis is not upon whether or not flexibility, lifelong learning or this exploration is to be taken literally but rather to explore their propensity for their figurability and migration. The notion of metaphor is being used as a strategy of analysis, as part of a deconstructive rewriting of policy and displacement of realist assumptions that tend to dominate both policy and policy analysis. Here 'metaphor is itself a metaphor for the meaning-displacing characteristics of deconstruction' (Parker 1997: 84). In opening up the space of policy as a metaphorical object of study, this analysis attempts to avoid certain forms of vassalage.

Emergence and migration

The question posed here is one over the emergence and migration of flexibility and lifelong learning as metaphors within policy discourses. Policy analysts have noted their strong emergence at various quite specific points in time within national and intra-national policy and in differing locations around the globe. They have identified them as having migrated from discourses of capital accumulation, theories of production and of the market to economic and education policy. They have noted and theorized the pressures placed through national policies upon education to become more flexible, to be learning organizations, and to orient their pedagogical support towards the development of flexible and lifelong learners. They have identified flexibility and lifelong learning as metaphors that have the capacity to be deployed within policy and take effect in the reconfiguration of discourses within the sites in which they are taken up. Such reconfigurations may signify quite radical changes in conceptions of the social aims and purposes of education, the way in which people teach and learn, and understand what it is to be engaged in such practices. As yet, however, such emergence and migrations have not been significantly explored in metaphorical terms. Policy discourses are deployed in order that they may do metaphorical work whether this is what is intended by politicians or not.

On the one hand, the requirements for lifelong education or learning and flexibility in education are positioned to have emerged with human capital theory. Before the 1960s, neo-classical economics had suggested that increased education and training would increase economic productivity (Marginson 1993). Post-second World War Keynesian economic policies focused on economic growth and the provision of social services, such as education. During the 1960s, some economists argued that the rate of economic return for investment in human capital would be greater than for investment in physical capital. Marginson argues that this idea was taken up by the governments of many advanced industrial and developing nations and by the United Nations. Policies promoting lifelong education emerged around this time and were taken up by intergovernmental agencies such as UNESCO and the OECD (Field 2000a). Economic growth was strong, and, as Marginson (1993) suggests, it may have been that investment in education could 'figure' for a whole range of discourse groups at that time.

During the mid- to late 1960s, economists in the United States began to explore the micro-economic relationship between education, information and innovation. At the same time, investment in education did not seem to be achieving the growth that had been expected by the Keynesian model, and government support for that investment began to be undermined. Neo-liberal monetarist policies began replacing Keynesian policies in North America, Europe and many other parts of the world from the beginning of the 1970s (Hursh and Martina 2003). These focused on the deregulation of the economy, trade liberalization and reduction in welfare spending and taxation. The economic recession of the mid-1970s further undermined this support, and two decades of economic restructuring and social and political readjustment ensued (Harvey 1990). This has been characterized by some as a shift from Fordism and Keynesianism to post-Fordism or flexible specialization and a new regime of capital accumulation. On the surface, Harvey suggests, the inadequacy of Fordism and Keynesianism appeared as a lack of flexibility. The Fordist regime of capital accumulation in the United States had up to the time of economic recession overcome tendencies for capital overaccumulation primarily through strategies of temporal (the expansion of long-term investment through the formation of fictitious capital) and spatial displacement (the absorption of excess capital by moving it elsewhere). Harvey identifies three discursive positions that were adopted at that time in relation to changes towards flexibility. First, new technologies were reconfiguring labour relations and production systems. Second, flexibility was a political ideology that legitimized new forms of political practices and undermined the possibility of political action. And third, the position subscribed to by Harvey that post-Fordist flexible technologies and organizational forms were mixed with those of Fordism and that Fordism was increasingly interpenetrated by more traditional forms of organization, in particular, those from eastern Asia. For those subscribing to this third discourse there appeared at the same time an increasing propensity for acceptance within societies for ideas of privatization, entrepreneurialism and paternalism. During the mid-1980s, there was a shift towards a micro-economic version of human capital theory within the economic policies of post-industrial nations. This was taken up within OECD policy from 1986 (Marginson 1993). Education was constructed within policies as the source of the flexible and responsive human capital required in conditions of technological change.

The emergence of flexibility as a key to economic success was also a period in which there were significant growths in post-school education and lifelong learning. Over the period from the early 1970s adult participation in formal learning activities have substantially increased in many nations. Field (2000a) offers figures for the United States, Canada, Britain, Finland and the Netherlands and suggests that, although evidence is not even, overall the volume and level of participation has increased. When comparing these records, he identifies that the most pronounced increase was in North America between the mid-1980s and mid-1990s (from 20 to 38 per cent). Between 1991 and 1999, participation is estimated to have increased in the United States by a third, to a rate of 46 per cent of the adult population. In Finland, the shift is documented from between 1972 and 1995 where adult participation rose by 28 per cent. In the United Kingdom, the shift is claimed to have been 60 per cent in the decade from 1985. Of course, this is only a partial picture from published figures, and there will be other locations where adult participation in formal learning has increased in the last decades. However, there is little doubt that policy objectives to increase and widen participation in formal learning provision, to support lifelong learning through greater flexibility of provision, has had significant effects around the world.

Flexibility is argued to have found its strongest policy expression in the neo-liberal economic policies of governments of the 1980s and 1990s (Edwards 1997). Initially associated with the policies of Margaret Thatcher in the United Kingdom and Ronald Regan in the United States, flexibility has been pursued by governments of many different political persuasions and is supported by major regional and international economic organizations such as the European Union and the OECD. John Field (2000a) documents the new emphasis on lifelong learning that emerged during the 1990s. First, within the policies on competitiveness and economic growth of the European Commission in 1994 (Commission of the European Community [CEC] 1994). It was drawn upon again in 1996 through the promotion by the Commission of a European Year of Lifelong Learning, and by the OECD and UNESCO in 1996 (OECD 1996; UNESCO 1996). It was found within the New Labour government policies for education in 1998 and 1999 in the United Kingdom and for the Group of Eight in 1999 (Group of Eight 1999). It was emphasized within reports on lifelong learning in Germany, and in policy papers by governments in Holland, Norway, Finland and Ireland. Lifelong learning emerged within government policy in Japan and Thailand during the late 1990s, as response to economic crisis (Fuwa 2001; Wilson 2001). It was central to economic reform in New Zealand and Australia (Boshier 2001; Trood and Gale 2001). Lifelong learning is also reported as a policy theme within education policies in Botswana, Namibia and South Africa (Walters and Watters 2001). Its uptake might vary, but there is no denying the significance of lifelong learning within contemporary policy discourses.

The lifelong learning emphasis within education policy is suggested as the outcome of policy commitment to increased flexibility and competition (Edwards 1997). Flexibility is central to the establishment of a new discourse of capitalism and production within policy. It is represented as a necessary characteristic of economies, institutions and individuals, within a factual and generalizable discourse of how things are/should be, the collapsing of the descriptive and prescriptive distinction itself being significant. This is a description that troubles the status of any alternatives that are already in operation. It has affected a shift in emphasis within discourses of the economy (from capital to flexible accumulation) and of organizations (to the flexible firm and learning organization). It exemplifies a reconfiguration of a discursive terrain for education.

Reading migrations

Any narration of the emergence and migration of flexibility and lifelong learning above is to some extent problematic. It is easy to read as one where these themes emerge as responses to crises within the accumulation of capital or from emergent theories of the most effective and efficient ways to organize production. This would be to read these migrations through a lens of 'burgernomics' (Perry 1998). The Big Mac serves 'as an allegory on how theories of formal organization and models of the working of markets are read, when they too are launched around the globe' (Perry 1998: 152) and thus serves well as allegory here. Theories presume that organized economic activity can be taken as a series of approximations to a formal model and read as such. As Perry points out with regard to the global migrations of the Big Mac, burgernomics counts individual cases of deviation from the general model as 'residual *ad hoc*' difference or as residuals to be ironed out in the teleological 'long run'. Such an approach to theory is not equipped to consider difference, where signifiers slide promiscuously across and within the locations wherein they are taken up and read. With an approach that is able to consider variation and difference, flexibility and lifelong learning are made anew within each migration and from the locations within which they are read: 'when it comes to hamburgers, the word itself is made fresh even as the world is made flesh' (Perry 1998: 154). They migrate within and between discourses, signifying differently within differing locations. Thus my reference to burgers in the quote from the film, *Pulp Fiction*, which began this chapter. Likewise, flexibility and lifelong learning can be borrowed and cannibalized as aspects of theory and description in processes of bricolage within policy descriptions (Ball 1998).

Increasing competition, consumption, technology, insecurity, risk and globalization appear quite commonly as a complex of metaphors within such theories and descriptions. They slip within and between narratives of flexibility and lifelong learning as they are 'made up', and they 'read' differently within disparate geographical, cultural, social and discursive locations. It is not, as Perry says of the Big Mac, the product that travels, but the model and idea of it, through which it may be then realized and consumed.

The flexible organization, for example, signifies an object that has polymorphous, capacities for difference and change

> Flexible production is a dynamic and continuously changing system, due largely to its own internal emphasis on continuous innovation in the way things are done, as well as in what is produced...Such continuous change also makes it difficult empirically to delimit the universe of flexible organizations, or to measure their share of aggregate output.
>
> (Onman 1996: 20)

The signification of flexibility within a discourse of flexible production is thus as a dynamic and continuously evolving pattern of production (and consumption) that is difficult to pin down. It tends to feature self-managing expert teams, core workers and groups of suppliers as assets, and just-in-time delivery systems, but this varies considerably.

> The importance of specific features of flexible production...varies across firms (for a given level of development of flexible production) as well as across industries and countries, and over time even within a given firm. Indeed, the notion of 'one best way' is alien to flexible production.
>
> (Onman 1996: 21)

Flexibility is the master signifier within a discourse of flexible production and the flexible firm. However, by token of its polyvalence and polymorphic nature, flexibility is in some senses an empty signifier. It can be filled up differently within each context within which it is taken up. A good example of this is the way in which flexibility has come to signify a range of attributes within education discourses, which it does not signify elsewhere. Within education contexts, the flexible product is flexible at the point of consumption. This is not so elsewhere. One would not expect to be able to add extra lattice to a Big Mac after the point that one has eaten half way through it. Neither would one expect the staff to be able to serve an alternative size of chip or to give you a portion that is half Big Mac and half Chicken McNuggets. The consumer has had some choice in selecting what is consumed prior to purchase but not to change the characteristics of what is offered for purchase or the system of production that made the product. Within a theory of flexible education delivery, it is quite common to argue that the learner should have choice in mode, pace, place and content of learning. These discourses are commonly found quite outwith discourses of niche marketing or those of just-in-time production systems. This is to allow slippage from a discourse of flexible production across into to one of student centredness or self-management in learning within pedagogy. Flexibility is read differently within contexts of its occurrence not only by students but by those who use it as a descriptor within the teaching programmes.

Part of this context is that of globalization, itself a metaphor of migration, sustaining of the homogeneity and heterogeneity with which it is associated. Globalization is a key metaphor within policy narratives promoting flexibility and lifelong learning. The characteristics connoted by it are often represented as the problem to which they are the solutions. However, many have noted that globalization is not nearly as prevalent or all encompassing as such narratives imply. As Field (2000a) points out, some knowledge is more situated than others. Charles Onman (1996) argues that the shift towards flexible production is required as response to structural problems within the labour market rather than as a response to globalization. For him, globalization is used as a 'scapegoat' by those who resist moves towards more flexible forms of work organization. Thus, Onman (1996: 24–25) cautions policy makers not to use globalization as a rationale for making such shifts. For OECD policy makers, especially in the United States and Europe, this points to the importance of avoiding – and denouncing – the use of scapegoats, while pursuing policies that facilitate the transition to flexible production in ways that share the fruits of that transition with all members of society. Governments are urged to avoid policy representations of problems in ways that exacerbate fears of its consequences. Yet it may only be through mobilizing globalization as fearful that it becomes figurable for change to be promoted Such are the aporia of the policy process.

Mobilization, fixings, infections and colonizations

Theories of formal organization and models of the working of markets such as those explaining and requiring flexibility and lifelong learning are mobile in that they make generalized claims to forms of human activity. We have seen this in the way in which neo-classical economics works to hypothesize and derive generalizable rules regarding economic behaviour, which are then used to generate predictions. Theories identify invariate universal principles to which the real world is taken to approximate and against which differences can be read as anomalous. Theories thus have a propensity for reification and stabilization that is a product of their generalizability and elision of difference. They also have a propensity to slip from the descriptive to the prescriptive, to be projected into the future as the way things will or ideally ought to be. The status of flexibility and lifelong learning as rational or 'scientific' solutions to the challenges of the present is therefore important for policy, as they can be embedded and mobilized within narrative descriptions of change and progress. It is in part, therefore, through the collapsing of the descriptive and prescriptive distinction that flexibility and lifelong learning can be effectively mobilized within policy discourses.

The notion of the discursive constitution of 'myth' (Laclau, in Torfing 1999) is useful in explicating policy discourses of flexibility and lifelong learning as mobile metaphors. A myth is not only a description of a utopian vision of a promised land but represents the principle that such description is possible. They are descriptions that assume the possibility that a version of reality can be achieved, but at the same time this reality cannot be described except through metaphor. Myths 'fix' metaphors within a narrative of the world in part through their claims to generalizability and in such a way that the openness of possibilities of meaning is constrained. At the same time, any fixing requires of us a certain blindness to their metaphoric, linguistic and epistemological properties. Even though we may recognize the contingency of such narratives we may continue to act in the world as though we do not.

Over the past two decades, flexibility has migrated within policy as a rationale for the transformation of organizations, promoted in order to make them more competitive. Pedagogically this has been pursued through policies that place increasing emphasis on lifelong and flexible learning. Politically it has been pursued through deregulation and the legislative transformation of labour relations. The multi-skilled, flexible worker has been promoted as paradigmatic of the economically successful organization, moving from task to task, team-working, problem-solving and learning as they do. Alongside, and as part of this, there has been a downsizing and casualization of much employment, changes in the age and gender structure of the labour force, the development of notions of core and periphery workforce, and the growth of insecurity and absolute and relative inequality. Organizations have pursued their own flexibility through a range of strategies – numerical flexibility, functional flexibility, distancing strategies, pay flexibility. In the process, they have attempted to develop new workplace identities of the 'enterprising self' (du Gay 1996b). Educational institutions have turned towards practices for the flexible delivery of learning and flexibility in learning, and pedagogical discourses regarding these have emerged, in particular, an emphasis on student-centredness and lifelong learning, embedding an increased consumerism into the pedagogic relationship.

Flexibility has therefore migrated from discourses attempting to describe what is happening in relation to production practices and regimes of capital accumulation to those that suggest what should be done within other contexts, including education. This is an infection across domains. Flexibility and lifelong learning are not single phenomenon within these, as has already been emphasized. They are differentiated and dispersed in complex ways. As discussions of flexibility and learning have emerged and migrated between the realms of economics and other areas, such as industrial sociology, cultural studies, management, education and training, and as the influence of economic policy has been exerted increasingly on other domains, so the emphases and issues themselves have shifted. Neither flexibility nor lifelong learning therefore denotes a single thing. In many senses, the positions have become more complex precisely because of the nature and extent of their migration.

However, the increasing dominance and distribution of flexibility and life-long learning within education policy discourses has been paralleled by an increasing commodification of educational goods and services. This has been incited in part through policy strategies to open institutions up to competition pressures, and by discourses of participation, student-centredness and choice within policy and education. Commodification occurs where social domains and institutions that were not concerned with producing commodities, in the narrow economic sense of goods for sale, come to be organized and conceptualized in terms of production, distribution and consumption (Fairclough 1992). This points to flexibility and lifelong learning as intrinsic to a 'colonization of institutional orders of discourse, and more broadly of the societal order of discourse, by discourse types associated with commodity production' (Fairclough 1992: 207). Here flexibility and lifelong learning operate within systems of metaphors to

> effect a metaphorical transfer of vocabularies...into the educational order of discourse...[that]...is an attempt to restructure the practices of education on a market model, which may have...tangible effects on the design and teaching of courses, the effort and money put into marketing, and so on.
>
> (Fairclough 1992: 208)

Although flexibility emerges with different meanings within different contexts, it is through the insertion of a requirement for flexibility within one discursive domain that it becomes 'necessary' within others related to it. This affords it a peculiar propensity to migrate and to be mutually reinforcing. As flexibility is identified as an economic requirement within discourses of a crisis of capital accumulation, for example, it may become suasive within policy discourses as a necessary national response to change, economic uncertainty and increasing globalization. In this situation, flexibility also becomes a more or less totalized requirement for corporations that are bound up in the production of goods and services. At the level of the nation, flexibility appears as a characteristic to be built into the system. However, the reverse logic is also the case. As corporations are described as moving increasingly towards more flexible practices for their survival, policy descriptions in support of such moves become necessary. Onman (1996) describes discourses of flexible production as preceding those of globalization and global competition and productive of 'new rules' of global competition. In other words, it was less a response than a precursor to globalization.

Within the firm, as within education policy, discourses of external change, uncertainty and globalization may be useful to persuade workers that moves towards flexible practices are inevitable; at the same time such discourses work to support the construction of these perceptions as the 'new' reality. Workers must become flexible or lose their jobs. In order to do this, they must have access to the training and education that provides them with appropriate skilling and reskilling or knowledge. Insecurity in employment for employees and an insecurity of the wider economic environment for firms require discourses of the flexible and lifelong learner and learning organization. Education institutions must become flexible in their provision of learning and education in order to respond to this. In this way, they support learning organizations, flexible workers and flexible and lifelong learners. This is a systems logic, within which the economy, economic enterprise, worker skill, education and education supply are aligned. Central within each discourse are a complex of metaphors that appear generalizable. Flexibility, globalization, change, uncertainty, lifelong learning, competition and so on can move between differing locations, where their meanings slip and their relationships are narrated slightly differently.

The metaphors that are given emphasis through such alignments are not neutral. 'Skill', for example, might be taken to be a nodal point across discourses. It allows the matching of individual capacities with the activities that are required for increased economic efficiency and effectiveness. However, it also has meanings within a range of pedagogical discourses that are not concerned with the economy. It is not a neutral metaphor, even though it may be represented within education discourses as if it were. To say this is however to represent only one side of the picture, as education discourses were and are always already political, even though this acknowledgement may not be part of their narrative. Where 'skill', 'flexibility' or 'lifelong learning' take up positions across a range of discourses within which they appear necessary, they act to hold a certain narrative meaning in alignment, to fix the facts partially and temporarily, so they become difficult to avoid or to undermine. There appears to be a tendency, given their general level of specification, for such complexes of metaphors to migrate further, to be usefully taken up as resources and deployed always within the next part of the system that seeks to become aligned.

The operation of flexibility and lifelong learning across discourses in this way suggests the production and functioning of groups of metaphors that rhetorically affect a closer alignment of activities across and within policy. This thereby produces the very migrations and globalization about which it speaks. They systematize discourses by re-ordering relations of difference and equivalence. They do this by signifying equivalence through the attribution of a particular trait to a range of different identities (the flexible economy, flexible firm, flexible worker, flexible learner, flexible educational institution, and the lifelong learner, learning team, learning organization, learning nation and so forth). Signifying chains of equivalence are expanded through this and difference is to some extent collapsed within and by it. Meaning is lost in this process and the possibility of different identities elided. This also serves to produce what Laclau and Mouffe (1985) describe as ordering effects through the constitution of metonymic relations of contiguity, such that flexibility or lifelong learning, identified as necessary within one aspect of identity, may become expected within others. Ordering effects support the stabilization of associative or paradigmatic relationships, as different words can share a sameness while at the same time signify difference. Thus, flexible firm and flexible worker share a sameness, which they do not have as 'firm' or 'worker', and to some extent are made equivalent. 'Flexibility' and 'lifelong learning' thus help collapse the differential identities of the firm and worker by expanding signifying chains of equivalence. They may act as nodal points that unify the discursive terrain by inserting words that are to some extent devoid of content. They act as nodal points across ranges of signifying chains that fix meanings differently within different discourses. Flexibility and lifelong learning unite discourses and subjectivities aligned with them in some ways similarly to master signifiers, such as 'God' and 'Nation'. We can subscribe to them in some way and accept different meanings ascribed to them within alternative signifying chains.

The ordering effects of flexibility and lifelong learning are thus productive of effective policy work. They simplify the social and political space by delimiting the play of difference and setting up relations of contiguity between systems of objects within the discursive terrain. This helps construct a unity, which can be managed. These are discourses that through their uptake focus activities within a logic of greater effectiveness and efficiency. They are part of a group of metaphors that are dependent upon a systems logic, which is in part persuasive in relation to the discursive logic already normalized within the social formation but in part also constructs the acceptance of that logic.

A social Darwinian system, for example, may be one in which flexibility and lifelong learning resonate most forcefully, and through which they become persuasive. As we have seen, within policy texts, the common narrative has been that without flexibility and lifelong learning institutions and individuals will not be able to respond to the uncertain future environment, and that there is a danger in this. Any rejection of flexibility and learning might thus require a rejection of social Darwinism and thus an alternative metaphorical system. Within social Darwinism, the social system and its parts are likened to a biological organism, responding to changes within its environment or habitat. The environment is the natural context within which organisms live. Through this separation, the environment is uninfluenced by humankind and to a large extent uncontrollable. Here the metaphorical system makes ontological gerrymandering possible, as any change within it is thus equally uninfluencable and uncontrollable. This view constitutes an understanding of a relationship between the environment and the organism where change in the environment leads to physiological and behavioural 'misfit'. Organisms and groups that are able to react appropriately by adapting themselves in order that they again fit with the environment survive to reproduce and the species as a whole survives. Flexibility and learning thus become traits that afford the individual organism, the educational institution and the social system as a whole the ability to respond to unpredictable changes within the environment. They are required for adaptation and survival. Indeed it has been pointed out that Hayek's classical economics emphasizes selective evolution as the basis for all order. The idea of a market economy is analogous with Darwinian evolution, in that unfit systems are eliminated through market forces (Olssen and Peters 2005). The point here is not to ask whether social Darwinism represents reality truthfully, but rather to explore how a prior immersion in such a metaphorical description may predispose the reader to accept a requirement for flexibility and lifelong learning, and the need for action. In other words, resonance within a social Darwinian metaphorical system supports vassalage. It predisposes one towards a certain understanding and acceptance of the need for flexibility and lifelong learning. At a general level they are persuasive because their representation within policy discourses resonates with broader metaphorical systems that are already commonly accepted.

What does this tell us of the metaphorical work of flexibility and lifelong learning within discourses of education policy and their propensity for migration? Metaphors may be more or less productive, more or less suasive in relation to figurative ideas and analogies that already dominate within particular locations. In a review of theorists who consider the potential of metaphors of mobility, Urry (2000) argues that the work of the state is in 'policing' a territory that is increasingly transformed by a proliferation of nomadic flows. Permeability and flow are represented as the 'new' norms of social and state organization, within which we might position flexibility and lifelong learning as operational and operationalizable. Flexibility and lifelong learning invoke such permeability and open up territories to both international and intra-national flows. For Urry, such permeability and opening are material as well as constructed through language. However, it is in part through metaphorical work that a place is made for an emphasis on permeability and flow. Flexible and lifelong learning, flexible course production and the workplace learning for the learning organization incite globalization and its vocabularies.

There is a politics in this of course. To emphasize flow is to potentially reinforce metaphors of globalization, and this indicates the necessity for reflexive engagement in the politics of such selections. Flow, network and fluid require and focus our attention on those technological infrastructures and human activities that compress time-space and emphasize movement across previous boundaries (Urry 2000). Policy metaphors of structures and hierarchies of control are argued by him to become less persuasive in contexts where those of flow and network are to the fore. Discourses of flow may act therefore to reinforce those of requirements towards flexibility and lifelong learning, even as they appear merely to describe them.

The emphasis on and dispersal of flexibility and lifelong learning across and within discourses may be supported through the globalizing processes of policy networks, whereby globalization itself becomes a powerful metaphor of flows in the contemporary social imaginary. In a study interested in how an international organization, such as the OECD, constructs an agenda, given its diverse membership from differing nation-states and other international organizations, Taylor *et al.* (1997: 71) note that there has been a congruency on policy positions on educational issues, 'in particular around the recurring rhetoric of quality, diversity, flexibility, accountability and equity'. The OECD is part of the sphere of influence of UNESCO, the World Bank, the International Labour Organization, the Commonwealth Secretariat and the European Union (EU), all with an interest in education policy. The study concludes that the OECD's already strong ideological commitment to globalization and the relationship between the economy and education may be further enhanced by this congruence of agendas. In this respect, Lingard and Rizvi (1998: 271–72) suggest that the role of the OECD in higher education policy has been

> as an institionalizing mechanism for the idea of an integrated global economy underpinned by the ideology of market liberalism … the OECD has been a significant mechanism for encouraging the global flows of people, information and ideology, and, indirectly, of educational policies.

The migration of flexibility and lifelong learning can be considered as brought forth through scapes and flows, the networks of organizations, machines, technologies, texts and actors which constitute nodes that relay and circulate ideas among and between networks. Within the political arena, politicians, policy advisors and members of think tanks migrate corporeally, spreading certain messages. Those scapes constructed for the business of and deployment of policy and flows that emanate from them spread these ideas. The same is true for many academics, employers and managers. Conferences are sponsored to develop and promote certain themes and policy options. Academic journals and policy dissemination sites are constructed as electronic versions, as nodes within networks. Material means of spreading policy metaphors may be through the reports, books, the Internet, and the like, produced and circulated by individuals and organizations, and through the media, including, potentially, the text you are reading here. The global diaspora of people and ideas, through such processes of migration, enable the spread of policy themes as 'epidemics' (Levin 1998) and the forging of policies of flexibility and lifelong learning around the globe.

Taking stock

Flexibility and lifelong learning have been explored as interrelated themes promoting the reconfiguration of post-compulsory education systems around the globe. Discourses of flexibility and lifelong learning emerge in multiple forms within dispersed sites, including those of policy. They are in part fabricated in policy and, in their migration into different contexts there is the attempt to engender flexible and lifelong learning practices. The question explored here has been how they become mobilized, taken up, transported and recontextualized within and across these contexts. This trail of theorization has been a mobilization of lifelong learning and flexibility as metaphors and of metaphorical readings as a way of exploring them. I have started to tell a tale of migrating metaphors, and the metaphor of migration is a way of inscribing meaning into their emergence. This is where I take stock in my storying.

What has been said within this analysis of the emergence of and propensity for flexibility and lifelong learning to migrate? Flexibility has emerged within social scientific discourses and is promoted through policy and within pedagogy. This marks a migration from descriptive to prescriptive discourses, from those of what is to what ought to be, across domains. In this migration, flexibility has been supportive of the transformation of organizations, the pursuit of specific pedagogical aims and an increasing colonization of educational discourses through the equivalence of flexibility with more market-like practices. The insertion of flexibility within various discursive domains, its ability to migrate, arises from its embedding within a systems logic and certain metaphorical systems. This may be dependent upon a particular metaphorical description of the social that has been relatively stable. Flexibility operates metaphorically to expand chains of equivalence. Alternative chains require alternative metaphorical systems and perhaps even a break with systems logic.

The systems of metaphor within which lifelong learning and flexibility are constructed differ within differing locations. They are represented as literal rather than metaphorical. Their migrations may be purposeful, insofar as they are seen to be capable of productive work and are figurable. The work of various theorists has demonstrated that metaphors are used powerfully and systematically in the political arena, although the work drawn upon has tended to focus upon their work in politically sensitive moments – of war in particular – where changes in discourse may make them visible and where their work may be more apparent. The argument has been that policy responses may be systematized through the selection and promotion of certain metaphors within texts. This may indicate conflation between descriptive and prescriptive narratives of the world and can lead to vassalage through their normalization. Systems of metaphor offer building blocks for the construction of discourses and these emphasize certain possibilities and elide others.

Policy operates in part through the constitution of the metaphor of flexibility within chains of equivalence as a means for the management of a discursive terrain. The expansion of chains of equivalence limits the play of difference within discourses through the elision of alternative possibilities of meaning. Flexibility brings with it an elision of difference between identities, which helps constrain their meanings and create effective alignment between them. This reduces the discursive terrain by limiting the play of difference. A metonymic equivalence of the flexible and lifelong learner, the flexible firm and learning organization, the flexible economy and learning culture afford these discourses powerful resonance across chains of signification.

Previous discussion of the spread and stabilization of discourses of lifelong learning and flexibility has tended to focus upon globalization and globalization processes as the context for policy. However, I offer an alternative approach that looks to the work of policy description in the mobilization of particular metaphorical descriptions of the world. Through the deployment of particular metaphors and associated systems, certain forms of policy work and its analysis gets done. Metaphorical readings, through the construction and deployment of alternative systems of metaphors, can highlight what works and help produce spaces that counter the truths represented and normalized within and through policy texts. This helps avoids tendencies to vassalage. Particular constructions of the meaning of flexibility and lifelong learning may become fixed through policy representation and popular uptake. This is not to suggest that individuals necessarily take up the meanings presented within policy texts but that they become regularized within dominant relations of discourse. As new problems in education become the focus of attention, scientific methodologies and social science theories are drawn upon to create new metaphors within policy and education through which meanings may become fixed. These allow only certain possibilities of thought and exclude others. Policy thus acts to limit the possibilities of thought and response by seeking to make certain things happen. 'The effect of policy is primarily discursive, it changes the possibilities we have for thinking "otherwise"; thus it limits responses to change, and leads us to misunderstand what policy is by misunderstanding what it does' (Ball 1994a: 23).

Policy is 'a point in the diagram of power', as Ball (1994a: 22) suggests of the state. Even though policy can support the production of discourses of flexibility and lifelong learning, it cannot be seen simplistically as the source of power and meaning, but is decentred. Generic policies are polyvalent, as 'they are translated into particular interactive and sustainable practices in complex ways' (Ball 1998: 127). Policy texts are thus deeply enmeshed in the relations of power that they seek to influence and in some sense master. Reading the emergence and dispersal of flexibility and lifelong learning as metaphors within policy texts and examining the audiences mobilized within and by them helps us to understand the powerful work of discourse more fully.

Policy discourses of flexibility and lifelong learning reconfigure and stabilize specific views of the world within metaphorical complexes. Urry (2000) argues that while the social world is made up of activities, the meanings given to these tend to be local. We know that rhetorically these discourses do particular work within policy to elide and simplify the narratives of the world that we tell and thus our understandings of how we act in the world and what this does. We need to engage with what those activities that are promoted through flexibility and lifelong learning do at all 'levels'. We need to multiply language, in order that we may 'imagine' alternative worlds within which learning can be considered and may be promoted, so it can take up different emphases and effects. We need to be conscious of the discursive regularities that become stabilized between policy analysis and those of policy. These are productive, but of what? For example, what would a techno-mobile learning look like or a learning of flow? What would/could these do within policy discourses? Urry (2000) argues that policy is changing from that which emphasizes governance through discipline with regard to a territory, to one of governance as the control of flows and fluids over boundaries. However, governments in part constitute these very flows and fluids through deregulation and the constitution of global markets for education, within which we are then incited to operate. The notion of new forms of politicization that may counter the force of multinational corporations require that we work to construct and make possible alternative narratives. The tendency for corporations to homogenize descriptions of the world must be countered if we are to counter vassalage. And that entails a lot of compelling metaphorical work.

6   Realizing lifelong learning

> Language has always been important in politics and in government...
> Political differences have always been constituted as differences in language,
> political struggles have always been partly struggles over the dominant
> language, and both the theory and practice of political rhetoric go back to
> ancient times. Language has therefore always been a relevant consideration in
> political analysis. But language has become significantly more important over
> the past few decades because of social changes, which have transformed
> politics and government.
>
> (Fairclough 2000: 3)

We have now explored policy discourses of flexibility and their global
emergence with those of lifelong learning. The focus within this chapter is
on action for reform within and through the descriptions specifically
promoting lifelong learning within recent formal policy documents of the
United Kingdom and the European Union. Policy texts act internally to
build up the facticity of their own descriptions of the world and to undermine alternative possibilities in order that they may promote reform of
lifelong learning they seek to promote. Through the analysis of an ensemble
of policy documents and events that began in 1998 and is still unfolding, the
rhetorical strategies drawn upon and deployed will be made visible. Political
struggle is thus not only a question of who has the 'better' truth, but one of
the rhetorical strategies that are used and deployed successfully to persuade
within policy. Indeed, it is the attempt at the forging of a relationship between
the policies of EU member states at a national level, which is in part the
expressed intention of contemporary EU policies. This involves the deployment of quite specific rhetorical strategies. These attempt to align member
states' activities through a quite specific discourse of lifelong learning and its
associated strategies. The analysis of this chapter could thus be seen as a 'case'
in such an attempt, an attempt to see what this form of analysis can make of
it. It is limited, of course, as it forges a particular ensemble of events for
analysis, manifesting its own rules of inclusion and exclusion.

There was an agreement by heads of EU member states and governments
at the Lisbon meeting (EC 2000a) to make the European Union 'the most

competitive and dynamic knowledge-driven society by 2010'. This reform agenda has been heralded as representing a shift from a regulatory and legislative approach within policy towards one whereby it is the harmonization of policies on a supranational level that is to be achieved. This enables critical comparisons of national policies in the making of Europe as a single economic and social space (DTI 2002). Within a report paper on the status of economic reform four years subsequent to the Lisbon agreement, the aim of EU policy is articulated as increasing the flexibility of labour markets. This is to construct a single economic market and political unity that can act to counterbalance or challenge the power of the United States. Although the nature and extent of the flexibility necessary for this goal has been contested ever since, this is a representation of a significant policy aim, and one very well worth contemplating in rhetorical terms within this chapter.

What can be said about the rhetorical work attempted within and through policy agendas such as this? How do they operate rhetorically? To simply accept attempts at reform in realist terms as either working or not working, appropriate or inappropriate, or to dismiss their rhetorical work as spin or hyperbole, is to miss the significance of the work that is being attempted. To repeat, this is not to say that this is the only form of (en)counter with policy that is possible or legitimate. However, it is to suggest that additional and interesting things can be said/written/done about lifelong learning policy processes and discourses and policy more generally by adopting a discursive and rhetorical approach. And obviously there is a stake here for me in making such a claim.

For those who are interested in analysing rhetorical regularities, it is the details of the procedures – the strategies – that require focus. Potentially, there are a huge number of ways in which the production of descriptions is involved with actions. Descriptions are closely bound up with the idiosyncratic particulars of settings. However, 'the point, then, is that, although the details of what is talked about may be endlessly varied, the sorts of procedures for constructing and managing description may be much more regular, and, therefore, tractable in analysis' (Potter 1996: 111–12). Here the notions of 'offensive' and 'defensive' rhetoric, outlined by Potter (1996) that we discussed earlier, are taken up to assist the analysis. Rhetoric can be taken to work offensively to 'reify', and defensively to 'ironize' positions.

> *Reifying* meanings to turn something abstract into a material thing...These are accounts which are producing something as an object, be it an event, a thought or a set of circumstances. In contrast, we will refer to discourse which is undermining versions as *ironizing*.
>
> (Potter 1996: 107, emphasis in original)

Reifying is a strategy to put something beyond question, to build its facticity. It is one of the ways in which ontological gerrymandering is achieved.

Ironizing is a defensive rhetorical strategy, which attempts to undermine an alternative position. For instance, in policy debates, to position the discourse as spin is a way of undermining through ironizing. These are useful notions as they emphasize the struggle that goes on within policy discourses, the struggle to produce descriptions that can be taken as literal, and the ways in which they work defensively to counter alternative possibilities. Of course, to distinguish strategies in this way as simply, either offensive or defnesive, oversimplifies. However, irony and reification do point to different strategies at play in debates.

There are further resources for analysis taken up within this chapter (Leach 2000). These have been found useful in identifying and exploring the genres of lifelong learning policies and exploring the work that they try to do. Central to policy texts and processes is the work of *exigence*, which marks the problem to be addressed. 'Any exigence is an imperfection marked by urgency; it is a defect, an obstacle, something waiting to be done, a thing which is other than it should be' (Bitzer, in Leach 2000: 212). The policy event commonly makes a rhetorical space for exigence. It is a moment for the constitution of a requirement for action. Without an exigence, there is no need for policy. For the analysis of exigence, attention is paid to the timeliness (*kairos*) and appropriateness (*phronesis*) of the event, for this enhances its persuasiveness. An incitement to action that is not seen as timely nor appropriate is likely to gain little support, as many experience. Audience, what I referred to in Chapter 2 as fellowships, are mobilized within the event through the communities that are worked up and powerfully positioned as 'we', that is, those effected by the exigence.

The different genres of rhetoric can be categorized as forensic, deliberative and epideictic (Leach 2000). These are common to particular forms of institutionalized discourse, although not exclusive to them. The *forensic* genre is typically used in law courts, where discussion is oriented to representations of past events, to persuade the court of the 'truth' of what took place. It is incisive and based on the elaboration of detail. Thus Freddy had to have the details of his story straight before going undercover. The *deliberative* genre is commonly assumed to be strongly associated with the policy arena, where persuasion is focused on the best possible course of future action. It is thoughtful and reasonable. However, by focusing on policy rhetoric as deliberative, analysis would perhaps ignore the exigence at work in representing a 'picture' of the world that required action. Policy discourse is also forensic, as it focuses on past events and attempts to work up the persuasiveness of a future account in relation to this. The *epideictic* genre is associated with ceremonies and the attribution of praise and blame. This may also feature in policy, usually in the suggestion that certain people, organizations or events merit blame. 'Naming and shaming' has found many expressions in education policy. It was drawn upon powerfully by Margaret Thatcher's government in the 1980s in the United Kingdom, in the deployment of a 'discourse of derision' towards many established educational ideas and ideals (Ball 1990a). More widely, there is a ceremonial process in the ritual enactings of policy. Policy events thus draw upon more than one of these rhetorical genres.

Having identified the genres involved in any policy event, rhetorical theory suggests consideration of five further aspects (Leach 2000): invention, disposition, style, memory and delivery. Invention is concerned with ethos, logos and pathos. Ethos is that which draws upon and establishes the credibility of the author or speaker. It is about who has the authority to speak or write. Logos focuses on the logic or evidence for what is proposed. Pathos is about the appeal to the emotions. To be persuasive therefore entails having the authority, or what we termed entitlement, to write, to be able to present in a logical and reasoned way and to make it appealing emotionally for an audience. This can be part of any performance, but it is immediately apparent why these are relevant to the study of policy. Their bases might be in the writings of Ancient Greek philosophers, but we have already seen how such ideas are echoed in some of the more recent writings on discourse, upon which I have drawn.

Of the other aspects identified by Leach, disposition is the exploration of the organization of the event of discourse and its effects on the reader. Disposition was discussed in relation to narrative structure within Chapter 4. Style sits in a complex relationship between the form and the content of discourse and can relate to the kind of persuasion that can be accomplished. Memory is part of traditional analysis, to the extent to which the speaker delivers the speech on time and without reading a script. However, the cultural aspects of memory and the extent to which the audience shares them have been emphasized more recently. Delivery involves analysis of the form of dissemination and its relationship with content. In examining the policy ensemble of lifelong learning from the United Kingdom and the European Union, I intend to draw upon many aspects of the above, as part of the further illustration of the utility of discursive and rhetorical analysis to policy studies in education.

A new dawn – lifelong learning

I start by exploring aspects of the United Kingdom's New Labour government policy discourses for reform through lifelong learning. The year 1997 marked the beginning of a series of policy events in the United Kingdom, which can be represented as an ensemble of statements for the sake of analysis. Within the United Kingdom, lifelong learning has been a dominant theme within post-compulsory education policy discourse and this was realized in a Green and White Paper towards the end of the century (DfEE 1998, 1999). Green papers are consultative. White papers put forward proposals for legislation. More recently this discourse has focused to a greater extent on skills (DfES 2003b, 2005a,b), and I will explore this discursive shift to some extent.

Earlier work (Nicoll and Edwards 2000) pointed to the powerful use of 'renaissance' in the Green Paper on lifelong learning (DfEE 1998) as a way of inscribing it with meanings that might harness emotions, positive attitudes and values. It marked an entrance onto policy stage of a new age and a modernizing discourse that has become associated, both positively and negatively, with the New Labour government. A powerful strategy within this discourse was to position 'traditional' public services, including education and training, as no longer being able to meet the challenges of the future. In one way or another, this positioning has been replicated and reinforced and disseminated through the narratives of intergovernmental agencies of the European Union and the OECD, in addition to other national governments, as we saw in Chapter 5. Formal policy statements of lifelong learning within the United Kingdom have significantly changed in their rhetorical style and content since these earlier papers. I want to argue that this is, in part, an effect of wider policies.

The discursive context for the emergence of the Green and White Papers was the election of the New Labour government in May 1997 following a landslide victory that brought to an end 18 years of Conservative rule. The new government was committed to a project of modernization in all aspects of economic, social and political life. 'Newness' was to the fore, not least in the 'New' that has been put into 'Labour'. The government was to be unencumbered by the Labour Party's historical roots in the labour movement and previous commitments to nationalization and the welfare state in its established post-Second World War form. 'Third Way' thinking, between state and market, was to the fore to mark a new approach to governing. 'Joined up government' became an important catch phrase, reflecting the need to modernize the state as well as other institutions.

This was also the period of the run-up to the end of the century, in which there were numerous attempts to characterize the last century and last millennium and to look forward to the next. Attempts to characterize changes in society and economy have been many and varied. The knowledge society, the information age, post-industrial society, the learning society, postmodernity, among others, have all vied with each other, each attempting to create a wave upon which to surf into the new century. The government, attempting to locate itself in the radical dimension of change associated with the growth of the Internet and new technologies, adopted the notions of the information age, knowledge society and knowledge economy. These were linked into the millennium in terms of an urgent need to prepare for the twenty-first century. Central to that preparation were education and training and lifelong learning.

A whole raft of education policy and initiatives has therefore emerged in the years of the Labour government, including those to engender *The Learning Age: A Renaissance for a New Britain* (DfEE 1998). The exigence was both timely and appropriate in relation to the discursive context outlined earlier. The audience was likely to be receptive due to the *kairos* and *phronesis* of the policy, not least because post-school education was not seen to have been favoured by the previous Conservative government. The exigence was the construction of a problem that demanded a response and the response in this document was propounded as a renaissance through an age of learning. Yet what was the problem? And how were the exigence and response constructed rhetorically? What strategies were at work?

Once again, we find the use of 'we' signfiicant in this policy text. As we saw in relation to the *West Report*, there is an implied identity between authors and audience in the use of 'we' in the Green paper, despite readers not knowing who the authors of the text are. The only exception to this is the endorsing quote from the Prime Minister, Tony Blair that 'education is the best economic policy we have' (DfEE 1998: 1). The use of 'we' positioned the government as not imposing policy, as it is as much subject to the exigence it lays out and the imperatives to act as everyone else. Of course, whether the implied identity between the authors and audience is persuasive is open to question, as one can also disidentify with the 'we' within the text. The crisis narrative in this text could be positioned as saying something about the current state of government, in a context where states are positioned as no longer capable of governing in quite the same ways. Thus the need for policy makers to equip themselves to cope and make sense of change (Field 2000a). However, the articulation of the exigence attempts to elide such readings, to avoid a veiw that we may hold unequal positions in relation to the requirement to continue to change and the possibility that some may not wish to become lifelong learners.

Part of the way in which the New Labour government sought to construct support for its policies was initially through the pathos of its discourse. Modernization was not to take place arising from a 'discourse of derision'. By contrast, lifelong learning was positioned positively to harness the desires and values of those working in the terrain. In this sense, it was an attempt at a seductive discourse, still powerful, but in a different way rhetorically to that with which the audience had become familiar. *The Learning Age* therefore evoked renewal and rebirth and a new age, which echoed the Renaissance of arts and letters and growth of humanism in parts of Europe between the fourteenth and sixteenth centuries.

The notion of Renaissance can be said to perform in a number of ways within the policy text. The sense of rebirth associated with it pointed to new age practices, such as rebirthing, and the sense in which through lifelong learning one might be said to be continually being immersed and renewed. There was thus a refreshing aspect to the discourse. The location of the Renaissance in continental Europe also points to and codes the European credentials of the policy at a time when policy towards the European Union is fraught by division in the United Kingdom, when government wants to be 'good Europeans', but not to be seen to be 'too good'. I will return to this a little later. The Renaissance was also a rebirth of arts and letters, a challenge through culture to the absolutism of monarchy and the orthodoxies of the mediaeval church. It therefore pointed to the importance of culture to government, itself indicated in the desire to promote a 'culture of lifelong learning', as an explicit aim of policy. The policy statement is thus positioned in such a way to likely appeal to those who subscribe to both progressive and modernizing discourses within education and training and more widely within the public.

Field (2000a: 250) refers to this policy approach as part of the government's 'active attempts to mobilize civil society – including education and training providers'. It mirrors the rhetorical attempts to mobilize and motivate workers in the discourses of the learning organization and knowledge management, to which I have already referred. Its pathos was effective to the extent that it persuaded, or at least that people acted as if they were persuaded of its merits. And it was from this time that there was a marked burgeoning of 'lifelong learning' in the naming for centres for research, for education and training courses and departments, for professorial chairs and so forth. The discourse of lifelong learning blossomed in response to the changed rhetoric of government. One has only to search on the web to see this illustrated.

To question lifelong learning, as it was represented within *The Learning Age*, would appear to involve questioning that to which it can contribute at the economic, social and cultural and affective levels. Competitiveness, productivity, social inclusion and cohesion, and personal development were all marked as outcomes of developing a culture of lifelong learning. The exigence to which it was addressed embraced lack of competitiveness, social exclusion, lack of qualifications and an underdevelopment of the potential of the population. Like others (Coffield 2002; Keep and Rainbird 2002), one might question the logos – the logic or evidence – of the claims made for the requirement for lifelong learning and what it can achieve. The evidence for some of them does look sketchy no doubt. However, this appeal to logos is precisely based upon reason and evidence, when it may well be an appeal values or to the imaginary, which is more important in political practices. The lack of logs for lifelong learning is an appeal through the rhetoric of the academy rather than of politics, wherein pathos plays a significant role. Pathos – an appeal to the emotions – may be important for policy and perhaps for people, despite or maybe because of calls for more evidence-informed policy. Of course, for some, the signifiance of pathos in politics has been the basis for criticizing democracy, but it has been as important in non-democratic political regimes as well. Thus, it may be in understanding the invention of policy and the other aspects of rhetoric that we may be able to more fully engage in the offensive-defensive rhetorical wars in and around lifelong learning. An appeal to logos is not enough if we want to be politically engaged.

The exigence of lifelong learning policy within *The Learning Age* is represented as beyond the realms of the interpretation and choice of the audience. They are factual descriptions and the only certainty once again is the need to change. As inventions they work to persuasade. Ethos – the credibility of the speaker – and logos are built up through the use of the definite article and the imperative. The audience has already cast its vote, and there is no further choice to make. Pathos is intrinsic to this process. As inventions, they may to some extent represent the regularities of style and convention of formal policy texts. This can be seen in comparing policy texts with other forms of communication. Policy texts, for example, cannot adopt the style of a scientific document, which persuades us through a logos based on method and evidence. Nor can they adopt the style or conventions of an agony column which persuades through first-person intimacy, although, if they were to try, it might be quite intriguing to see the effects.

In reinscribing a historical fantasy into the future, the rhetoric of a Renaissance of learning appealed both to tradition and modernization in the United Kingdom. This is rhetoric drawing on cultural memories for many individuals within the audience addressed, even though these may be largely mythical. This is a memory to be drawn upon for the construction of a learning age and culture of lifelong learning within the United Kingdom which may then differ from those that are possible elsewhere. For example, there is no similar exigence for the learning age and a culture of lifelong learning within the Australian *West Report* (DEETYA 1998). Although lifelong learning does appear within a vision for the future within the text, it is not worked up elsewhere in the document, but rather, as we have seen, increased flexibility is emphasized. This marks a difference between the United Kingdom and Australia, one of those shifts I identified as taking place within and as part of globalization in the last chapter. To some extent, this may be a consequence of the focus of this text as recommending the policy and funding framework for higher education. The metaphor of lifelong learning may have appeared less rhetorically useful for a policy concerned with a specific education sector. There is, however, potential significance in the cultural aspects of memory to be drawn upon in different contexts in the persuasive work of policy discourse. Australia does not have the same cultural memory to invoke as the United Kingdom. Australia is already 'new'. The symbolic systems that work affectively may differ within differing sites of discourse therefore.

However, the appeal to the values and emotions of the audience is not all positive. A positioning of the traditional public services, including education and training, as no longer being able to meet the challenges of the twenty-first century within the UK policy papers is epideictic in shaming specific people and organizations as no longer up to the job. Indeed we may expect this kind of epideictic positioning as a precursor to a logos of change. We almost require it. For how could an argument for change be set up unless we had a problem that needed fixing? And problems, as we have seen, can either be those that are 'naturally' occurring or constructed by people. By starting with an assertion of a lack in the practices of specific groups or individuals, an expectation for improvement in their activities is constructed in the audience. If teachers, colleges, universities or workplaces are not up to the challenges of the future, then we expect the policy discourse to propose change. The discourse makes us anticipate and expect change, because of its narrative logic.

The exigence for lifelong learning engenders a sense of crisis. 'To continue to compete, *we must* equip ourselves to cope with the enormous economic and social change we face, to make sense of the rapid transformation of the world, and to encourage imagination and innovation' (DfEE 1998: 10, emphasis added). This is the type of crisis narrative so important to policy discourse, but here it is a crisis 'we' all face. The exigence is beyond the realm of choice and addresses itself to the reader as audience. It is a factual description and the certainty is for the need to change. In Potter's terms (1996: 108, emphasis in original), the Green Paper offers a description oriented to action, as 'for the most part, the concern is to produce descriptions which will be treated as *mere* descriptions, reports which *tell it how it is*'. Not only is it oriented to action, but it also seeks to result in action by building its own authority as a factual version of the way things are and thereby gaining support.

The exigence of the Green Paper is reifying, as it asserts the facticity of an information age, knowledge economy and competition as the logos for the imperative to act. If we take the description literally, an act is performed by the text and, at the same time, a requirement for our own action as readers is implicit within it. This reification is achieved through the forms of representation within a hierarchy of modalization (Latour and Wolgar 1979). For instance, 'we *must* equip' is used rather than 'the authors of this text think we must' or 'we should'. Descriptions can be located at various levels in a hierarchy depending upon whether they are treated as unproblematic or provisional in some way. Generally, the less provisional and more separated out from the speaker, the more solid and factual the description appears. The elision of the speaker and the lack of provisionality in the assertion of 'must' work to try and make the description reified and secure and to persuade the readership of the correctness of both the description and the action identified.

Reification is also achieved through the strategies of narrative organization and nominalization that we examined in Chapter 4. As we found there, the point at which a description starts is important to its rhetorical strategy in this as in all settings. Narrative organization depends upon the ordering of events and who is positioned as taking part and how. It is in part through the narrative structuring of the text that particular meanings are made possible. In the Green Paper, by beginning with the public services, and an education and training system which cannot cope within the new age of information, global competition and economic and social change, the narrative is structured to act in various ways. By asserting particular forms of competition and change as components of the starting point or footing, there is an attempt to circumscribe a whole prior debate about the adequacy of this representation. Beginning the narrative with certain props already on the stage avoids having to more obviously bring them on later, and this takes our attention away from them. At the same time, by positioning certain groups as 'failing', these groups are 'put on the back foot' at the outset. By positioning them negatively, their category status as potential speakers – respondents – is immediately reduced. Any wider audience is already positioned to be less likely to be persuaded by their counter-arguments. Both these moves are part of an ironizing strategy, as they undermine the potential for alternative descriptions. When we consider the number of times that this kind of narrative pattern emerges within policy discourse and elsewhere, we do not have to wonder at it. The sheer regularities of the rhetorical and discursive work in policy events and ensembles become familiar because they are familiar. There is a certain genre to which they belong and therefore the strategies of representation are often repeated to a greater or lesser extent.

Reifying certain concepts as objects rather than the outcome of human activity is critical to such processes. The props of policy discourse are brought on the stage as real objects – a chair and table – rather than as things that are being done by actors. They are the background against which policy works rather than the outcome of existing policies. Thus, the current 'failings' of education are articulated without reference to the policies which have in part resulted in them. Fairclough (2000: 27) points to the significance of this kind of nominalization, where words are used as nouns instead of verbs. Instead of representing economic processes as people applying means to materials to produce things, the actual processes and people and things involved are backgrounded, and we have instead 'the economy' as an entity. The phrase 'the new global economy' presupposes that there is a new global economy, that is, it takes it for granted, as something we all know exists. The economy as the work of many actors and actions with more or less power is lost. Global competition, the age of information, the knowledge economy and change are commonly represented as nominalizations within policy discourse. What this does is to set up a range of objects that appear to exist external to our action. At the same time, it allows the writer to avoid attributing the activity – competition, the information age, the knowledge economy and change – to any particular population or group. As we saw, this offers potential for an epideictic genre of rhetoric targeted at specific people and organizations, and the provision of a root cause for the requirement for action.

Reification is also effected by presenting authoritative individuals and groups as in agreement with the policy description, or positioning them as supporting a description in general terms. What forms of corroboration or warranting are used within a policy document? Within a policy consultation paper such as the Green Paper (DfEE 1998), corroboration activities occur both in the form of the consultation adopted and through various strategies deployed within the text itself. The document thus works both externally and internally to distance its own writers as agents and confirm that others are in agreement with it. However, as we will see, there is also work that it does to support the following White Paper (DfEE 1999). This illustrates a form of rhetorical work effected through formal policy documents, in providing support for each other and policy discourses more generally. There is an intertextuality at play here within the policy process.

Let us first scrutinize the work of the Green Paper as a policy consultation document and its role in relation to the subsequent White Paper. Green Papers are requested by government ministers in order that policy decisions inscribed in White Papers may be forthcoming at a later date. We saw this in Chapter 4 within a different statement and context of policy. Policy decisions need to be greeted with minimized opposition when they are announced. Green Papers and their ensuing consultation processes operate in advance to help this to be achieved. Green Papers build up footing for White Papers. As the latter are outcomes of consultation processes, this helps to undermine any potential subsequent reading that the governments might have any stake in what is decided – not necessarily very successfully! In making this point, it is important to clarify that the intention is not to suggest that ministers or governments generally have a stake or interest to hide. Rather, readers commonly interpret government decisions in terms of stake and interest. A prior paper and consultation process is a strategy to help this to be avoided. This is a strategy of stake management, which is, again, common within all forms of communication.

However, the text of the Green Paper itself draws upon further rhetorical strategies to manage issues of interest or stake. A consultation process that precedes a White Paper could potentially produce suggestions that sit quite outside what is politically acceptable or rhetorically felicitous. In Foucault's (1996) terms, such statements are not assimilatable within a doctrine to which people are subjected, and to whom the doctrine is subject. The danger is that there may be formulations of discourse that give rise to alternative possibilities; lying outside the doctrine. A consultation process is not just a situation for previous discourse to be reiterated, therefore, but has potential to be one for the formation of an alternative or potentially new verbal act or primary text. A strategy to control discourse used within the *West Report* consultation was to delineate its *Terms of Reference*. With the UK Green Paper (DfEE 1998) a strategy was to elide authorship entirely – there is no note to suggest who may have been involved in writing it – and to provide footing for the description by identifying a range of previous committees whose work was drawn upon. This is done within the Green Paper through a section of the text that explicitly states that it draws heavily upon specific advisory groups. These include the Committee on Widening Participation in Further Education; the committees on 16–19 qualifications and higher education; The National Advisory Group for Continuing education and Lifelong Learning; and the University for Industry Design and Implementation Advisory Group. This strategy provides footing but at the same time delineates what can be said by whom in explicitly giving a stake to a range of stakeholders within the policy making process. Another is to focus the content of the subsequent consultation comments on the detail of the proposal document. Again, this is a strategy controlling the narrative start and its focus and thus content of responses.

Reification of the imperative to learn is supported within the Green Paper through the presentation of evidence of national weaknesses in performance with regard to learning. However, rather than the argument being that global competition provides a logos for learning, as it was within the introductory exigence, the implication here is that, because of weakness in learning, or, more specifically, attainment as measured by the proxy variable of qualification, we need to improve to compete globally. The previous logos is implicitly reversed, even though this may not be noticed by the audience. The evidence of weakness in attainment is provided through a forensic analysis of the strengths and weaknesses when compared to other nations. 'The country's current learning "scoreboard" shows strengths, but also some serious weaknesses ... As the chart below shows, we lag behind France, Germany, the USA and Singapore in the proportion of our workforce qualified to level 3'(DfEE 1998, paragraphs 21 and 22). This is a common strategy used in policy texts, inciting change because of failures in relation to other countries and regions. It is one that has become more common with the rise of accountability, which requires nations to report a diverse range of statistical information to such bodies as the OECD and the European Union. The reliability of the statistics is put to one side, when they can be used rhetorically as levers for change in nation-states around the world.

The 'scoreboard' therefore ostensibly offers empirical evidence to support the logos for change. They are national measurements that pit the United Kingdom against other nations in a competition over specific forms of learning achievement. In so doing, the description fabricates and orders both a certain form of competition and a particular geographical and political division as significant. It turns our attention, within UK universities, further education colleges and workplaces, towards particular domains of activity, through which we may code these divisions. This constructs rather than describes a discourse of international competition, and with this a certain inscription of territory. France, Germany, the United States and Singapore are positioned as competitors. It is not a global inscription, as it ignores significant parts of the world, but positions 'us' in relation to these nations. There is an implicit spatial strategy in play in such policy discourses. By describing the world in such a way that evidence of the United Kingdom's lack in qualifications is clear, the activities of 'we', the reader, become required in amelioration of these deficits. We become mobilized in this international competition. Here national and international competitiveness are

> recoded, at least in part, in terms of the psychological, dispositional and aspirational capacities of those that make up the labour force ... Personal employment and macro-economic health is to be ensured by encouraging individuals to 'capitalize' themselves, to invest in the management,

presentation, promotion, and enhancement of their own economic
capital as a capacity of their selves and as a lifelong project.

(Rose 1999: 162)

Following consultation on the Green Paper, the White Paper (DfEE 1999)
was published the following year. It begins with the Preface by the then
Secretary of State for Education and Employment, David Blunkett.
The opening sentence refers back to the earlier paper: 'In the Green Paper
The Learning Age we set out our vision of how lifelong learning *could* enable
everyone to fulfil their potential and cope with the challenge of rapid
economic and social change' (DfEE 1999: 3, emphasis added). Here, the
policy text repeats the nominalizations that were the narrative start of the
Green Paper. In so doing, it reinforces and normalizes them. It gerrymanders
the same division between that which exists, that is, rapid economic and social
change, and learning throughout life as our response to that reality. However,
it differs as it builds up its own footing precisely upon the Green Paper and
consultation process that has preceded it. The description, through repetition, is rhetorically presented as quite literally the case, with no sense of the
agency that engenders particular forms of change and the implied possibility
of alternatives. This again acts to control and produce the discourse.

We do not know what happened in the consultation process, apart from
what we are told of the process. However, we can be sure that aspects of the
description within the Green Paper that promoted particular opposition are
likely to have been modified within this subsequent one. This points to a
rhetorical function of consultation, where strategies that have been less than
useful can be identified and modified. Here, for instance, it may be significant that the national scores of achievement through which the requirement
to compete is partially and territorially inscribed are not repeated in the
White Paper, given the contestation that surrounds such attempts at comparison. Detail is a rhetorical strategy that can be disadvantageous as well as
persuasive therefore. Statistics are easily picked apart and thus may act more
to undermine the logos of the exigence for change rather than build up its
facticity. In addition, there is more conditionality in the Preface to the White
Paper than in the Green Paper. The only definite article is that lifelong
learning 'will ensure' the economic transition to the future.

Rhetorically then, the claims are lesser, even as the White Paper positions
itself as a bold response to the audience for the Green Paper

> many of those who commented recommended a bold programme of
> change in national and local arrangements. They confirmed our view
> that current arrangements provided an insufficient focus on quality,
> failed to give men and women the support they need, and were
> too provider driven...There was, therefore, widespread support for
> fundamental change.
>
> (DfEE 1999: 3)

The authority for the policy is, therefore, built upon the footing of the consultation, in which the government's and respondents' views are represented as aligned and warranted, thereby legitimizing the bold modernization to which it aspires. In a sense, then, the spin is spun! The White Paper represents not only the views of government, but also those who have participated in the policy-making process. The consultation process has mobilized a policy audience who are enrolled, recontextualized and represented in the discourse of the White Paper.

Harmonizing Europe – the Lisbon agenda

No policy event takes place in a vacuum. Policy statements are intertextual, both in terms of discursive strategies and broadly content. In the United Kingdom, this is particularly apparent given its position as a member of the European Union. The Lisbon Agreement is significant for current and future lifelong learning policy strategy right across European member states and prospective member countries. It is an agreement with a major lifelong learning policy agenda, which marks a significant, encompassing and long-term attempt to unify a discursive terrain and policy activity. It attempts to gather and channel policy and wider discourses in support of the development of human capital, through which will be achieved a strong European economic market and society. The agreement was to make the EU 'the most competitive and dynamic knowledge-driven society by 2010' (EC 2000a). It has been suggested that this agenda heralds a shift from a regulatory and legislative approach to policy within the European Union towards one whereby there is the harmonization of policies on a supranational level that is to be achieved. Rather than seek to produce standardization across the EU, nation-states can pursue their own policies in relation to overall goals. Harmonization takes place on the basis of critical comparisons of national policies within the EU (DTI 2002). This is arguably a move towards policy as strategy that I discussed in Chapter 2, an incitement to regulated and accountable action rather the legislation of what that action should be.

The achievement of a competitive and knowledge-based society become a focus of policy narratives within the European Union and member states (EC 2000a). Once again, this involves a nominalization of objects that does specific rhetorical work, not least the knowledge-based society. It allows activity to be represented in a way that is depoliticized. The Presidency conclusions to the Lisbon meeting outlined the 'new challenge' that must be met by the European Union (EC 2000b: 1). Here the logos of the exigence for change is 'a quantum shift resulting from globalization and the challenges of a new knowledge-driven economy...affecting every aspect of people's lives' and 'the rapid and accelerating pace of change' (EC 2000b: 1). Thus the globalizing tendencies that I suggested were the outcomes of policies of flexibility and lifelong learning becomes positioned as the precursors for further policy in a 'virtuous' circle of discourse. The European economy must be radically transformed, and the Union's task is to 'shape these changes in a manner consistent with its values and concepts of society and also with a view to the forthcoming enlargement' (EC 2000b: 1). This is to position globalization and a knowledge-driven *economy* as the natural changes to which 'we', within the European Union, must respond, but also to shape in a way conducive to 'our' *society*.

Education and training systems were argued within the Memorandum on Lifelong Learning (EC 2000a) and again within the Presidency conclusions to the Lisbon meeting (EC 2000b), as a need to adapt to the demands of a knowledge *society*, rather than a knowledge economy. The knowledge-driven economy is then quite contradictorily represented within descriptions from even the same policy event. It is both represented as constructed by social action, and as an object already on (or at least entering) the stage of policy as a current or future problem to which we must respond. This is the construction of an equivalence and plays on the polyvalent attributes of the metaphors of both knowledge-based economies and societies. They are used interchangeably, and gerrymandered either side of a divide between that which is natural and already existing or socially constructed to be existing in the future. Their ontological and temporal status is confused and confusing. In part, this affords them their rhetorical utility, as they can be positioned and multiply ambiguously within descriptions as long as their detail is not spelt out.

Action promoted through exigences can be associated with the aspirations of multiple and specific discourse groups, to extend their potential persuasiveness. For the Presidency, beneficial outcomes of a move towards a knowledge economy include its potential to enhance the quality of life of individuals, as well as the environment. It promises economic growth, competitiveness and jobs. By describing the possibilities for the future through vocabularies that resonate with the aspirations of particular groups, they are targeted for alignment and mobilization as part of the fellowship. The exigence for the improvement of the quality of life of citizens may appeal across a range of discourses and groups; likewise, with improving the environment. The range of potential goods manifested as an outcome of a knowledge economy is expanded as far as possible in order to garner support. The promise of economic growth, competitiveness and jobs appeal equally to the employed and unemployed and to business. This is both inspirational and aspirational. There is the attempt to develop a sense of affinity between author and a differentiated audience through the text, part of which rests on an appeal to the emotions of the readership through pathos. Lifelong learning may become primarily focused on skills for the knowledge economy, but how many would not support lifelong learning when it is positioned as having so many beneficial and inspiring outcomes? Like its linked metaphor of flexibility, it would be a somewhat surprising position to espouse that one was against lifelong learning, as it would to say one wanted to be inflexible. This in itself is part of the power of the metaphors in play.

We saw earlier that Onman (1996), an economic advisor to the OECD, was keen that globalization should not be positioned as a part of the problem within policy descriptions, yet this is the case in the Presidency conclusions. Onman is pointing to the persuasive work of policy and how it can mislead. For me, it is the persuasiveness in the construction of exigencies that will rhetorically manage the allegiance of groups and stakes that is of interest. This is work in the constitution of a doctrine to which diverse groups, with quite different aspirations, can be productively subjected. It is the constitution of a system of exchange and communication through the construction of the boundaries of the doctrine, in order that it may assimilate a wide range of discourses and operate across them.

The Memorandum on Lifelong Learning itself (EC 2000a) begins by offering a footing based on a transition to a knowledge-based economy and society. This is done by reference to a previous Lisbon European Council confirmation of this necessity, and requirements from the Feira European Council that member states, the Council and the Commission should 'identify coherent strategies and practical measures with a view to fostering lifelong learning for all' (Feira Council conclusions, in EC 2000a: 3). The purpose of the Memorandum is to 'launch a European-wide debate on a comprehensive strategy for implementing lifelong learning at individual and institutional levels, and in all spheres of public and private life' (EC 2000a: 3). This represents a policy process marked by an event – public debate – which has a specific rhetorical function and location. It has a *kairos* and *phronesis* all of its own. Within a realist reading, it is appropriate that consultation should take place over weighty political decisions that are taken in the name of citizens and will affect the lives of all. Within open and democratic societies we expect this. The invitation offers the audience status as speaking subjects. This is seductive, whether or not we respond. However, at the same time, consultations act to prepare us for policy decisions. They provide footings for decisions that may be provided later. This helps to undermine any potential subsequent reading that the European Commission may have had a stake in what is decided within the overall process, despite the millions of Euros it puts into it to supporting such positions.

The Commission sets out its rationale for the discussion and makes proposalsl. This draws upon the different rhetorical genres and fulfils certain expectations within a discourse of social democracy. It works to position the audience to read the consultation process in certain ways.

> The implications of this fundamental change in perspectives and practices deserve and justify the debate proposed here. *The Member States*, who are responsible for their education and training systems, *should lead this debate*. It should also be conducted in the Member States, and not only at European level. Lifelong learning concerns everyone's future, in a uniquely individual way. The debate should take place as *close as possible to citizens themselves. The Commission intends to draw up a report in autumn 2001 based on its outcomes.*
>
> (EC 2000a: 3, emphasis in the original)

Six key messages are offered within the Memorandum to provide a framework for the ensuing debate. Each message is accompanied by 'a set of questions, the answers to which should help to clarify priority areas for action' (EC 2000a: 3). These key messages and questions act much as the *Terms of Reference* of the *West Report* (DEETYA 1998). They produce and constrain debate within specific predetermined parameters. The key messages are listed within the Memorandum (EC 2000a: 10–20) as follows (the detailed questions for each message have been omitted)

> New basic skills for all: Objective – Guarantee universal and continuing access to learning for gaining and renewing the skills needed for sustained participation in the knowledge society.
>
> More investment in human resources: Objective – Visibly raise levels of investment in human resources in order to place priority on Europe's most important asset – its people.
>
> Innovation in teaching and learning: Objective – Develop effective teaching and learning methods and contexts for the continuum of lifelong and lifewide learning.
>
> Valuing learning: Objective – Significantly improve the ways in which learning participation and outcomes are understood and appreciated, particularly non-formal and informal learning.
>
> Rethinking guidance and counseling: Objective – Ensure that everyone can easily access good quality information and advice about learning opportunities throughout Europe and throughout their lives.
>
> Bringing learning closer to home: Objective – Provide lifelong learning opportunities as close to learners as possible, in their own communities and supported through ICT-based facilities wherever appropriate.

Discussion is to be over the details of the priority areas for action in the implementation of an already decided lifelong learning strategy, which clearly resonates within an economic discourse of the development of human capital. Wider discussion of what that strategy might look like, or whether indeed such a strategy might be appropriate, is curtailed through this rhetorical device of narrative start. By starting the discussion at this point, by narrowing it down to key issues and the questions that follow on logically from these, what can be said by a respondent is severely constrained and produced.

This can be seen in the responses and their analysis. The debate is curtailed further in the range of bodies and organizations that participated in the consultation. These included: European social partners (European Centre of Enterprises with Public Participation and of Enterprises of General Economic Interest, European Trade Union Confederation, European Association of Craft, Small and Medium-Sized Enterprises (UEAPME), Union of Industrial and Employers' Confederations of Europe (UNICE); member states and the EEA countries; civil society organizations (Corporate Social Responsibility in Europe (CSR Europe), The European University Association (EUA), The European Association for the Education of Adults (EAEA), The European Vocational Training Association (EVTA), The European Forum of Vocational Education and Training (EFVET), Solidar Platform of European Social NGOs, the Youth Forum). This is a strategy to begin to construct a socio-rhetorical community afforded status as speaking subjects within the developing discourse of a lifelong learning strategy. In a Communication from the European Commission (EC 2001), entitled *Making a European Area of Lifelong Learning a Reality*, this socio-rhetorical community provides a warrant for the prior description. These are those who have been involved in the consultation process over the Memorandum. 'Over 12,000 citizens contributed to the consultation which was initiated by the Commission's Memorandum on Lifelong Learning' (EC 2001: 3). Warranting works implicitly by suggesting that those listed are in agreement with what has been decided, although, as we saw, the contributions were produced and constrained through the key messages and questions that were set within the original Memorandum. In addition, there was disagreement expressed within contributions to the consultation. However, in the Commission text, these disagreements are marginalized to formulate a 'consensus' as the outcome (EC 2001: 9).

Within this Communication, a revised definition of lifelong learning is described as arising from the consultation process.

> Responses to the consultation on the Memorandum called for a broad definition of lifelong learning that is not limited to a purely economic outlook or just to learning for adults... In addition to the emphases it places on learning from pre-school to post-retirement, lifelong learning should encompass the whole *spectrum of formal, non-formal and informal learning*.
>
> (EC 2001: 3)

In other words, there is a discursive reshaping of the terrain of lifelong learning over and within which a policy strategy has to be developed. This then embraces '*active citizenship, personal fulfillment* and *social inclusion*, as well as *employment-related aspects*... the centrality of the learner, the importance of *equal opportunities* and the *quality and relevance* of learning opportunities' (EC 2001: 4 emphasis in original). Rhetorically, the boundaries of the description are expanded, both reflecting the positioning of lifelong learning within different discourses, but also enabling it to be mobilized and mobilizable within a wide range of sites. The meaning of lifelong learning therefore migrates as it is taken up within different sites. Indeed this may be the rhetorical function of a consultation process within policy; to construct a discourse of lifelong learning that will support the migration and mobilization of lifelong learning across discourses and groups. It is quite possible that the responses to the Memorandum may have been carefully considered by the Commission in order that a definition could become mobilized in this way.

Indeed a further section within the body of the Communication text indicates just this kind of scrutiny and activity. Lifelong learning is positioned as contributing to a set of social as well as economic goals, to what others refer to as social as well as economic capital (Schuller 1998). It works to build the 'we' within policy and positions the European Commission as not imposing policy as much as working with others to shape it. This is then a powerful description. It forges a relationship between a community of respondents and policy actants, within which the latter are listening and responsive to comment and concern. It picks up on issues at stake that lie outside the questions of the Memorandum and works up responses to them to precisely help build consensus. It acts to maintain a coherence across policy events, through a narrative of the continuation of a policy process. By the relationship between old and new it works to construct a policy process and views on lifelong learning within this as a unity. It works in the constitution of a policy doctrine and the positioning of a group and territory to be subject to it.

The Communication rhetorically guards against its future possible undermining by ironizing. Counterarguments to the knowledge economy, based on the possible consequences of greater inequality and social exclusion made by respondents within the consultation process, are generalized as 'risks'. In other words, such consequences are only possibilities, but there is no necessity that they will occur. This indicates ironizing work as an aspect of the consultation process, so as to label counterarguments as 'risks' is to play down their possible significance. In the contemporary discourses of war, they are the collateral damage of what is occurring rather than integral to it. Exclusion and inequality are positioned within the Communication ambiguously, as both the consequence of action towards a knowledge-based society and what needs to be dealt with through the activities towards lifelong learning. Once again, we witness reversal, as lifelong learning becomes the strategy to address such risks, rather than, given its policy of contextualization within the discourse of the knowledge economy, as integral to them. There comes a further exigence for lifelong learning, requiring precisely 'a radical new approach to education and training', 'renewed emphasis and importance on lifelong learning' and new policies and institutions that will equip individuals in dealing with the consequences of change (EC 2001: 3). In other words, the expanded definition arising from the consultation process only acts to amplify the centrality of the discourse of lifelong learning with the European Union.

The harmonization of policies within the European Union is marshalled through 'Scorecard' reports from the Centre for European Reform. These record member states' success in implementing the Lisbon Agreement against five headings. The Commission conducts an annual review of scores in its spring report to the European Council. It attempts to hold member states to account through scorecard records and member state self-evaluations.

The national reports on lifelong learning strategies from member states and EFTA/EEA countries and acceding and candidate countries were made in response to a questionnaire sent out by the Commission. The conclusions are set out in a progress report (EC 2003). These confessional texts demonstrate that the evolution towards a lifelong learning strategy and its adoption as a guiding principle has been gradual. The questions asked of member states work rhetorically to require response in relation to what are positioned as the 'principles and building blocks for lifelong learning that were identified in the Commission's Communication' (EC 2003: 37). The progress reports have the following sub-headings:

1   General framework
2   Building partnerships
3   Insight into the demand for learning
4   Adequate resourcing
5   Facilitating access to learning opportunities
6   Creating a learning culture
7   Striving for excellence

Reporting to these headings require member states to represent their policy strategies in these terms rather than in any other. The rhetorical effect of successive reporting against these categories is, in the first place, to begin to construct discourses of lifelong learning within national contexts which may not previously have been deployed by them. Second, for those nations who did already deploy them, a discursive alignment takes place, which allows for measuring and comparability. Measurement by indicators and thus comparison between member states is a key logos underpinning the European Commission's reporting requirements. This requires the harmonization of the policy discourse in the construction of Europe as a policy entity. In the process, the reporting categories separate out skills and institutional dimensions, and act to support narratives of these as separate lifelong learning 'strands'. Within this it is the discourse of skills that has come to the fore in recent times.

The UK Skills strategy

While the discourse of lifelong learning was as important in the European Union as it was in the United Kingdom in the latter half of the 1990s, more recently policy statements in the United Kingdom (DfES 2003a,b, 2005a,b) and the European Union have turned to focus on skills. It is skills that are positioned as underpinning labour market flexibility. The emphasis on them is identified as emerging from the agreement made by EU heads of state and governments in Lisbon in 2000 for economic reform across the European Union (DfES 2003b). We, therefore, see how the discourse of flexibility in relation to the labour market, as part of economic reform, starts to reconfigure lifelong learning policy discourse to focus on skills, despite the attempts at a broader definition we saw in the prevision section. There is a discursive pull towards the economic and this has been coded through a shift in emphasis away from lifelong learning towards skills.

Policy texts of the United Kingdom have turned to focus on skills for labour market flexibility. Skills are represented within the White Paper, *21st Century Skills, Realising Our Potential: Individuals, Employers, Nation* (DfES 2003b) as important in any decision regarding the United Kingdom joining the European single currency. 'Skills underpin labour market flexibility...Increased flexibility is necessary to ensure that the economy could respond quickly and efficiently to changes in economic conditions inside the single currency area' (DfES 2003b: Foreword). We therefore witness the return to flexibility as a key part of policy discourse, in particular labour market flexibility, with the skills necessary to underpin this coming into focus. The previous UK policy exigence for lifelong learning has exited the stage. Flexibility is characterized in the relation between the supply of skills within the European labour market and its correspondence with those demanded by European employers, and the ability of the UK economy to respond to economic conditions within a single market. We saw above that insight into demand for learning within the European labour market was to be part of the context for reporting by EU member states. Here we find an orientation towards this constructed within the UK policy exigence for action. The 'we' has shifted within this description to include EU citizens and the geographical territory is reinscribed to embrace the United Kingdom as part of the European Union. There is thus a far more explicit Europeanness to the policy discourses of 2003 than there were in 1998.

However, much of the forensic rhetoric in 2003 is similar to that within the 1998 Green Paper. The 2003 policy ostensibly offers empirical evidence as warrant for the logos for change. It is focused again on higher education measures, and on basic and intermediate skills for the workforce. However, by 2003 the emphasis is on filling the 'skills gaps' rather than learning attainment. This metaphor of 'skill gap' is not politically neutral. It attempts to forge a quite different set of political divisions and geographical and socio-rhetorical alliances. Member states, through a competitive but collective endeavour, are constructed as a single unity, in efforts to forge a single economic market and produce a knowledge economy and society. Lifelong learning is noticeably absent within this policy statement. However, it is an absent presence, as, by implication, the skills strategy is part of an evolving policy process that began in the United Kingdom with the new age of lifelong learning, and in the European Union with lifelong learning as a guiding principle. The emphasis on skills within a lifelong learning agenda is supported by its separating out as a reporting category within the EC member state process, and by the UK support for this agenda. Thus

> Across the European Union, the importance of skills has been recognized in the economic reform agenda agreed at Lisbon in 2000.

The UK is a strong supporter of that agenda. Many of the topics addressed in this White Paper are issues of shared concern for all European countries.

(DfES 2003b: Foreword)

This entails a broad alignment of UK policy within that of the European Commission. However, the intertextuality of UK policy within that of the European Union and its powerful effects can also be witnessed at the micro-level. The first of the EC building blocks (EC 2000a,b, 2003) and reporting categories for member states is the 'General framework'. This discursively frames the ways in which states report and can be held accountable. This identified the legislative framework and the coordination between ministries as important national contributions to the implementation of lifelong learning strategies. The UK White Paper echoes this, but within the new focus on skills.

We will link up the work of the key Government departments involved with economic and skills issues... The same collaborative approach will apply at regional level... We will establish a new Skills Alliance, bringing together Government departments, agencies and representatives of employers and employees, to create a new social partnership for skills.

(DfES 2003b: 22)

This shift is well represented by contrasting the principles adopted in the earlier policy with the themes of the latter. Skills and employers' needs have become the focus of the policy discourse, which has effects in terms of audience, as the broad fellowship of lifelong learning becomes more narrowly focused. The principles of lifelong learning policy were:

Investing in learning to benefit everyone,
Lifting barriers to learning,
Putting people first,
Sharing responsibility with employers, employees and the community,
Achieving world class standards and value for money and
Working together as the key to success.

By contrast, the key themes characterizing the skills strategy are identified (DfES 2003b: 21–22) as:

Putting employers' needs center stage...
Helping employers use skills to achieve more ambitious longer term business success...
Motivating and supporting learners...
Enabling colleges and training providers to be more responsive to employers' and learners' needs...
Joint Government action in a new Skills Alliance.

The exigence is based more on the logos of competitiveness than the pathos of the earlier policy papers (DfEE 1998, 1999). Gone is the appeal to the liberal values and emotions of educational practioners through lifelong learning. It is a logos of skills that replaces it. The persuasiveness of the new logos is in part in its relationship with the pathos that preceded it. There is the construction of an implicit narrative of progression, through an unfolding of policy events that appear to follow logically on from each other, and through the reference and footing that each provides for the next. In 2003, the Labour Government was in the middle of its second term, and would be expected by its audience to be consolidating and pushing on the implementation of reform. The old pathos is no longer necessary for we should already be persuaded. Thus, within the policy ensemble, the 2003 policy can be positioned as a further elaboration of lifelong learning, but taking up a particular strand, which is important across Europe. However, an alternative reading suggests a narrowing of discourse and therefore of action.

Taking stock

The EU–Lisbon agreement in 2000 appears to have had some influence in supporting the reconfiguration of UK policy statements on lifelong learning. Forensic rhetoric, based on logos and ethos, appears more the name of the new game, as EU policy increasingly requires such narratives within the reporting mechanism from member states. This helps position the reader as spectator rather than actant in charge and to control and limit the discursive terrain. Within the European Union, it is the knowledge-driven or knowledge-based economy and society that is nominalized and naturalized, positioned at the start for the unfolding of the exigence for lifelong learning. Even though this positioning is not secure, EU citizens, 'we' are represented as actively constructing this economy as well as responding to it.

Member states are now required to report annually against five headings of a 'scorecard' in terms of their success in implementing the lifelong learning agreement. Though this is a policy for harmonization rather than regulation and legislation, progress of the integration of legislative and financial frameworks of member states are to be reported on. Rhetorical strategies and mechanisms of the European Commission steer national policy rhetorically at a distance. Here the invention of the 'scorecard' constructs as it controls the discursive terrain with resonances from the discourses of sports. This positions member states as in some ways competing as to which can be the best Europeans, while also positioning them as unified in a consensus on the logos and pathos of lifelong learning. They are unified within a single although internally competitive geographical terrain, economy and society, and in the desire to compete economically with the United States. In a working paper from the Centre for European Reform, a think-tank which assesses independently progress towards the EU target, and which contributed to the discussions of the European Council, Alasdair Murray (2004) writes that US growth in GDP has been strong by comparison to the growth of the European Union over the last years. It is projected to go on increasing at a faster pace, increasing ever further, rather than reducing the economic gap. Gaps work metaphorically to identify a space to be filled by policy. The paper places the GDP growth rate of Finland in first place, with the United States in second, followed by Sweden and Denmark. The success of both Sweden and Denmark is remarked upon as noticeable, as an Anglo-American economic model had not been entirely imported within those countries.

Comparisons between the various attributes of competitors are expected in sports commentating. They are very generally 'figurable' (Shapiro 1989). This seems to resonate with education policy discourse. Sports discourses place teams of players on a pitch. They position them as active in opposition to one another. They identify the rules of the game. They empty a discursive terrain of alternative forms of content. They position certain people as spectators. They articulate rules of 'fair play' (even though there may be none). They suggest to us that all is well in the world; for if we have time for the spectacle of sport, then we must be otherwise safe and secure. A discourse of competition between EU member states and others has just this capacity. Signifying chains are constructed through a discourse of the strategic advantage of nations. We 'imagine' nations as if they were players on the pitch or athletes on the track and we as the spectators. A game has no real consequences for our lives. It is just clean fun. This empties, simplifies, controls and produces the discursive terrain by orienting discussion and activity towards closing the skills gap and increasing GPD as a sport. It does work to delineate a space, inscribe territories and positions the United Kingdom and now other member states in alliance in building a collective strength to match external competitors such as the United States. There is an epideictic aspect to this in the shaming of those who lose the match, whose scorecard shows them to have achieved less in terms of realizing a European lifelong learning strategy.

Policy analysts in the United Kingdom have asked what education policy and policy analysis can be for in conditions were increasingly the ends of policy appear to be already set through market discourses. An EU policy discourse of the need to close the skills gap through lifelong learning affords national policy a potential to act in alliance with this discourse. The ends of education as well as perhaps policy may be increasingly aligned across member states through a discourse of harmonization and the mechanisms with which it is associated. Such discourses, however, fail to acknowledge the discursive shifts involved, and the reconfigurations of relations of power that take place. This positions us as less likely to be heard, and increasingly perhaps, less likely to be understood in any counterarguments.

Rhetorically, we might say, that a discourse of a market economy and life-long learning puts a cartography of human resource development through lifelong learning before the horse, or supports mobilization as burgernomics. Certainly it prejudges a terrain by essentializing the truth and origin of such discourses and hides their rhetorical work. Difference is made to appear residual or *ad hoc*. It has a tendency perhaps to rewrite a boundary between what was hitherto accepted 'within the true' and that which was excluded. Through its positioning of educators and trainers as those who are implicitly not working up to scratch, the media and general public are certainly less likely to afford individuals the category entitlement to speak 'within the true' with regard to such issues. This is the redrawing of a boundary that had previously permitted the discipline of education to generate new propositions with regard to its purposes and practices. The policy statements of lifelong learning explored within this chapter exclude the propositions of the discipline of education and policy analysis from the premise of their exigencies, and turn to those generated within economic discourses, combined with perhaps certain metaphors from the social sciences (for 'risk', 'uncertainty', 'globalization', 'the knowledge economy and society', etc. have all been documented there) in order that they may be realized.

Consultation processes afford the opportunity to reconfigure exigencies in order that discourse groups can identify with the policy discourse that is subsequently deployed and mobilized as doctrine. Through the location of a UK policy event within the context of the EU policy ensemble, the UK statements are afforded increased authority in their footing. They are increasingly reified by the weight of the groups represented to be in agreement with them. The longer the series of policy events drawing upon each other for their facticity, the harder it becomes to return to the question of whether the objects represented at the start of the exigence warrant the action made in their name. As we have seen, we construct the world that we are said to respond to by this action. And it may never be possible to clarify whether or not, or the extent to which, the world would have been other without our action.

Policy discourses attempt to position us all in this and both constrain and enable certain rhetorical strategies that we must deploy, if we are to speak truthfully within them. Policy analysis and analysts appear to have little power in this. Either they act in support or amelioration, or look for truer truth. A discourse of a market economy and lifelong learning in itself fails to take account of the potential effects of the policy narratives that it deploys, in order that we might be persuaded to act. Their reification, through constant repetition, may result in the 'forgetting' that different narratives were once desired and believed. Thus, while the rhetoric of policy might draw upon memory for its persuasiveness on the one hand, it also seeks to erase it, as part of its defensive strategies on the other. The discursive struggles in and around the realizations of lifelong learning and flexibility thereby require sophisticated discursive work if policy is to be engaged with rather than simply commented upon.

7   An 'odious' but slender wedge

> [T]he possibilities of framing critical policy analysis in postmodern conditions remains problematic, especially if 'totalizing perspectives' are ruled out in such conditions...What all this illustrates as far as policy models of lifelong learning are concerned, is that those who would criticize the social democratic approach, of the kind described...must themselves have some kind of alternative to put forward which does not fall into the same traps.
>
> (Griffin 1999b: 449)

It is commonly suggested that policy rhetoric in general and that of lifelong learning in particular is grandiose. The same claim is also made in relation to the realities of the flexible and learning organization, and learning society. The rhetoric is grandiose, but the reality is far more complex and messy. Suggestions such as these tend to assume that the goals of policy are achievable, something to be striven for and that it can produce intended outcomes. There is often an implicit suggestion that, if only the government and intra-national organizations got it right and put in more resources, a learning society, a flexible economy, flexibility in learning for full choice or access and equity, would be both possible and achievable. Lifelong and flexible learning could play a role in achieving all those goals of personal fulfilment, social inclusion and economic competitiveness that are to be found in different ways and different sites of policy rhetoric.

That approach has not been adopted here. Instead, this text has sought to argue and persuade that there is a need to explore the rhetorical work of policy discourses. Where policies present particular descriptions of the world as literal, analysts and wider audiences, such as ourselves, are strongly positioned to do work to support, critique, or undermine the facticity of these descriptions. We have only a limited number of approaches, some of which may be more persuasive than others. All have their particular productivities and constraints. What they have in common is, however, the question of truth. What a rhetorical analysis makes possible is a different kind of approach. It refuses to focus on whether or not descriptions of the world that are represented to us as factual and possible are or are not factual or possible. By contrast, it examines how rhetorical strategies are deployed in order to make descriptions felicitous, and the work that these do in the mobilization of audiences. Thus the focus shifts to the discursive practices of truth-telling in policy processes. As has been said, this idea is of course not new. We have known for a long time that different narratives of the world operate powerfully at particular times, and that the analytic resources that we deploy, both to contribute to and to engage with these, are finite and limited. What a rhetorical analysis appears to offer is the possibility of a fine grain analysis of some aspects of what is going on. It points to the work of policy in persuasion and the attempted management and mobilization of groups and populations. Here policies may not need to be achievable, but rather may need to convince us that they could be.

Lifelong learning and flexibility are policy discourses that are mobilized as part of governing, as intellectual technologies acting at a distance in the administration of populations (Miller and Rose 1993; Edwards 2002). This is performed in part through the constitution and stabilization of particular narratives of the world, which we can find either acceptable, against which we may argue, or which we might be apathetic towards. We might adopt different understandings of them, depending upon the recontextualizations to which they are subject (Edwards and Boreham 2003). In all cases, we end up working up certain facticities through our constant repetition of and commentary on specific discourses. Thus, even as we contribute to the analysis of lifelong learning and flexibility within policy, commenting upon it, we help to fabricate their facticity and ontological position. In this sense, as scholars, researchers and citizens, we are as much involved in the 'spin' of policy as those politicians and policy makers who are positioned as the darker forces of the art. To argue that lifelong learning policy or flexibility in learning is spin is to undermine the status of the policy makers involved in constituting and promoting it, and to reinforce the truth/falsehood binary that keeps us focus on our search for better truths. It masks our own rhetorical and discursive work While this may be productive, it takes attention from its/our rhetorical work and the productivity of forms of analysis that identify how particular truths become fabricated and act, and, of course, the possibilities for alternatives.

Peters and Marshall (1996) have called for forms of critical social policy within the postmodern condition. They have critiqued neo-Marxist approaches as reductionist. They ask for forms of critical policy analysis that rule out 'totalizing perspectives', which has resulted in challenges, such as those laid down by Griffin above. In part, the difficulty is in escaping the constraints and productivities of discourse *per se*, which permit only certain narratives to sit 'within the true' at any one time. Rhetorical strategies and the rules of inclusion and exclusion that help determine what can be said truthfully at any one time are implicit within these constraints. Through this text and its concern to engage the operation of the rhetorical in the construction of descriptions and realizations of truth, I have in some ways picked up the gauntlet cast down by Colin Griffin and others. The approaches that I have constructed are alternatives. While they are still reductionist in their own ways, they do not fall into the traps to which he refers. In taking different beginnings in our quite general and commonplace understandings of the work of language, these are not alternatives in any totalizing way, as they do not offer a complete picture, but a conditional form of engagement. They are beginnings to pursue or to divert elsewhere, to extend or redesign and for you and me to see what we might make of them. They are not definitive or finished.

Policy discourses of flexibility and lifelong learning have been taken as a focus in attempts to 'invent' forms of discursive and rhetorical analyses that are productive within education policy studies theorizing. This is not about the 'truths' of lifelong learning and flexibility that I have been so purposefully avoiding. This text has begun to conceive alternative forms of policy analysis which appear productive in their own ways, even though they may have problems of their own. What I mean is that it seems useful that we should be able to consider the rhetorical and discursive strategies that are drawn upon, and which must to some extent depend upon the existence and operation of more or less stabilized rules, in order that they might be countered at discursive and rhetorical levels. This reminds us that lifelong learning and flexibility are quite specifically fabricated and reinforced within and through utterances, and that they attempt to be persuasive in their multiplication, migrations and repetitions.

Our acceptance of flexibility and lifelong learning as objects to discuss and describe as policy truths of any sort act to reinforce and stabilize them as objects. We tend to treat them as if they were real and could be made more real. They become doctrinal with their own fellowships of discourse. The circulation of discourse reinforces and stabilizes the allocation of subjects to doctrinal groups and doctrines to those subjects. These discourses, knowledges and groups are never entirely stable nor constant. Neither can they always be easily detected. They need to be constantly performed in order to be realized. This leaves us with a heightened awareness of the imbrications and interconnections of our utterances within systems and rules of inclusion and exclusion. It raises questions about the extent to which these are normalized at any specific time. That we can identify the specifics of the rhetorical strategies and the discursive systems and rules that are drawn upon in the constitution of specific objects of policy discourse, indicates that we can begin to detect this 'apparatus' for the production and control of power, desire and the chance event. This creates a disruption in our commonplace assumptions that statements of truth can be made that are devoid of rhetoric or of desire or power, that reason can win out in policy.

The trails of theorizing and analysis that I have followed have suspended questions of reality and whether the objects and metaphors that I have constructed as the tools for analysis really exist, in order to construct a different starting point for analysis. I have produced trails of analysis as a means to describe practices of policy discourse in ways that do not assume a reality and, in this, have tried to avoid precisely those regularities common within our thought that seek to be grounded in the real and truth. This has made it possible to suggest a more or less systematic order upon which the *activity* of specific policy statements depends, in their constitution and promotion of lifelong learning and flexibility, and to begin the description of this describe. Through this, it has been possible to, in a sense, politicize policy statements concerning these themes by focusing on their discursive and rhetorical activity. I have not written all that could be written in this respect, as, while a book comes to an end, theorizing and politicizing is ongoing.

Griffin's work represents a strand of discourse within policy studies that is accepted as legitimate through peer review and publication. By mentioning it, and in arguing for the inclusion of forms of theorizing such as are offered in this text, I highlight an instability in the rules of inclusion within the discourses of policy studies, pointing to the emergence of fresh productive possibilities. Policy studies has over the last years been the activity of those with entitlement and role to speak within the institution of the university. This has been activity in the production and control of the formulation of new propositions within the disciplinary organization of policy studies. 'For a discipline to exist there must be the possibility of formulating – and of doing so ad infinitum – fresh propositions' (Foucault 1996: 347). This has certainly been the case within policy studies. This text is then the fashioning of an alternative approach for fresh, if also still limited propositions. As a statement, or in any case an ensemble of statements, this text is situated ambiguously within disciplinary boundaries. These function to initiate a group with a specific form of category entitlement and role within the discipline of policy studies. These are subjects which are authorized to speak critically within the discipline about policy matters and to generate new propositions. They also decide which propositions are to be counted within the true and which excluded. Of course, they are not entirely free in this. This text, as statement and as some kind of proposition, must fulfil certain conditions. It must constitute a range of recognizable objects and concepts, metaphors and metaphorical systems, made possible by that network of rules of inclusion and exclusion which delineates what can be said 'truthfully' within policy studies at this time and location. Its persuasiveness thus depends upon its conformity with certain rules, which although neither stable, constant nor absolute, produce and control the possibilities for truth-telling. Specific rhetorical strategies that are conventional to this type of event of discourse are purposefully deployed within this text to position it 'within the true'. To point to Griffin's proposition, and through this to the work of Peters and Marshall, is thus a rhetorical manoeuvre, which aligns my work as conforming to certain rules and objects, which are accepted as legitimate by authors recognized within the discipline. It thus works up its own authority as a policy analysis.

I said at the outset that I would argue for the usefulness of concepts from the early Foucault to policy analysis. These notions, I suggested, have been marginalized, positioned as more literary, with the implication that they are less relevant to policy studies. Through this text I have indicated ways in which they may be productive. Here I am not alone (Shapiro 1984a). What I have taken from Foucault and have utilized within this work is that certain approaches to the analysis of policy discourses have been put aside as secondary through the success of a form of will to truth that constrains our thinking. I hope to have convinced you that these approaches can be productively deployed within such trails of theorizing, without reducing the discourse analysis to ideology critique. By identifying the work of rhetoric and rules of inclusion and exclusion that policy descriptions draw upon, reactivate and maintain, and in writing accounts of them, I hope to have been persuasive. This has not been an analysis that is merely a commentary upon policy. Neither has it been an attempt to be scientific in another way. It is always already a form of encounter. I have been engaging with the exercise of power and desire within discourses to counter their force by exploring some approaches to their work within policy and, through this, formulating an alternative rhetoric and rules of inclusion.

I have drawn more explicitly on Foucault's notions of archaeological investigation within some trails than others in order to make this theorizing possible. Foucault (1996: 357) called the form of analysis emerging from his archaeological principles 'critical' and thus so too is my own. Within all of the trails of exploration that I have produced, discourses have been taken as 'ensembles of discursive events' (Foucault 1996: 356). Analysis has employed a principle and a specific 'point of attack', which has been my point of departure. This has entailed the reversal of a dominant notion within policy studies that truth exists, to be found out there in the real world and that a language of this can exclude power and desire. This has allowed me to remain neutral to the truth claims of the statement and the more general question of the possibility of a context-free truth claim (Dreyfus and Rabinow 1982). Through this principle, I have been able to take descriptions as discursive representations that are constitutive of the truths of policy rather than reflective of them and, as such, are imbued with power and desire. This has not been a rejection of reality, but rather a suspension of realism, in order to explore the representative work of policy discourses and the power and desire inscribed in them. I have adopted a form of close textual analysis and the analysis of rhetoric has offered one possibility for this. This has not offered a method to be applied, but resources in an interpretative art to be taken up by different actors in different locations at different times.

This moment, the final chapter, is, once more, one for taking stock, as to talk of conclusions would be to belie the rules of my own text. Taking stock seems an appropriate metaphor for a nomadic theorizer such as I, who, in reaching the end of her text, finds herself in a situation of needing to attend to various questions. Where have I begun and left off in my trails of theorizing? What discursive work have these trails attempted and achieved? Where did I set out to travel and, at what junctures and through what desires, did I divert to more appealing territories? How did the various resources taken up along the way stand up to the challenges and dangers that I encountered? And, would I choose alternative routes/roots and resources if I were to begin again? What can I, or you, make of these travels? Or, where can we go from here? These are questions for myself, who has travelled thus far, and for whom, behind, I would rather like to hear

(having been at it long enough already, repeating in advance what I am about to tell you) the voice of Molloy, beginning to speak thus; 'I must go on; I can't go on; I must go on: I must say words as long as there are words, I must say them until they find me, until they say me – heavy burden, heavy sin; I must go on; maybe it's been done already; maybe they've already said me; maybe they've already borne me to the threshold of my story, right to the door opening onto my story; I'd be surprised if it opened'.

(Foucault 1996: 339)

There is a comfort in commentary, in the continual repetition of what has already been to some extent said. I, as Foucault, would perhaps have preferred the words to speak to me, to proceed and disappear into the distance, to be able to stand within discourse without any of this risky business. However, if we rely on commentary, and Foucault includes in this category searches for the ontological meaning of discourse as well as attempts to make the past or present intelligible in present day terms, 'we are doomed historically to history, to the patient construction of discourses about discourses, and to the task of hearing what has already been said' (Foucault, in Dreyfus and Rabinow 1982: 14). In other words, there is only endless repetition. The point about the archaeological method and the nomadic theorizing that I have attempted here is that it performs a distanciation of truth to gain access to a description that can reveal a different kind of systematic order. This moment of taking stock requires me then not to comment but to speak the other words that I have been telling you. I need to say how these trails are other than commentary and how the discourses of flexibility and lifelong learning that I have begun, contribute to discourses of policy and policy studies, which do not merely repeat what has gone before.

The chapter is divided into four parts. The first three consider the trails of theorizing that I have to some extent blazed. The final part explores the significance and limitations of these dispersed fragments of travel for the politics and policies of flexibility and lifelong learning. The meanings of flexibility and lifelong learning have emerged and multiplied across a range of locations over the last years. They have been taken up powerfully and deployed in order to both constrain and enable discourses. Such discourses are found extensively in sites of education and education policy. They are also to be found in the discourses of, for example, economics, human resource management and development, organizational theory and within the social sciences and social studies. Some of these are assumed, either implicitly or explicitly, realist approaches to language and meaning. Others have been generated through critical approaches that are aligned with a neo-Marxian structural materialism. Yet others are generated through eclectic approaches that are more poststructuralist in their leanings. I have sought to begin to sketch these out, although not exhaustively. Of course, consistent with the approach taken here, these are all active descriptions. Descriptions within each and every discursive utterance act in some way. Although I have been focused on what I have called 'serious' statements of policy, there is much more to be done in their examination.

Flexibility and lifelong learning are represented within policy narratives as positive aspirations and neutral technologies. They emerge and are taken up within alternative discursive locations in complex ways and signify differently within them. Flexibility and lifelong learning mean quite different things within such locations. They are by no means neutral in the work that they do. They are located within policy narratives that are in themselves artful devices, framed by discourse and rhetoric. For instance, flexibility of the institution, as Stephen Ball and others suggested, may reconfigure collective and traditional values regarding the social purposes of education. It can thus act to reconfigure the forms of sociality that we construct and reproduce within sites of education. Flexibility can reconfigure pedagogies and curricula also within these sites. In this framing, flexibility is a mechanism whereby education is refashioned and subsumed within the purposes of 'the economy' through marketization. We cannot say, however, that flexibility acts in this way within all locations, as this gives it a transcendental rather than contextualized meaning. It also does not address the issue of how such discourses act to bring about that about which they speak and the subjects – knowledge and actors – through which action is realized and stabilized.

Realizing flexibility

Flexibility is a work of truth-building within policy narratives. It is rhetorically realized through its representations. Discursive rules which surround and permeate the policy event permit the successive emergence of flexibility as an object within statements of policy discourse. Such discourses are a performative practice, as they entail action. They are based upon the existence of rules of inclusion and exclusion, without which what anyone said as policy, whatever was uttered, could always be truthful, just or right, or otherwise persuasive. This is not the case, of course. We hear what is said and are persuaded or otherwise through a reactivation of the rules that give rise to the utterance. These are made visible through the forms of analysis I have been pursuing within this text. Rules are thus regularities that function to some extent externally to and within policy discourses. It is not then to an assemblage of discursive *practices*, external to formal policy utterances, that one must necessarily look to see how flexibility emerges at a particular time. One can look for the rhetorical strategies that constitute flexibility within the serious statements of policy events, and for the rules of inclusion and exclusion upon which these draw, and which they seek to reinforce and maintain. For Foucault (1996), it is these rules that provide the conditions for the emergence of discursive objects such as flexibility and lifelong learning and reveal the exercise of power and desire they represent.

A government does not have complete authority to truth. Indeed governments and politicians are often the most distrusted of actors. Less may be invested than hitherto in the authority or ethos of the speaker, especially in the moves towards evidence-informed policy and the focus on logos that entails. Governments within liberal democracies are required to try to persuade us of the truth of what they say. A system of inclusion and prohibition operates, which identifies a person's entitlement to speak seriously on government policy matters, but wherein truth itself lies in what *is* enunciated. As Foucault indicated (1996: 349), it would be possible to speak the truth in a void, but 'one would only be in the true if one obeyed the rules of some discursive "policy" which would have to be reactivated every time one spoke'. Rhetorical strategies help to position an utterance 'within the true', by positioning it positively in accordance within a complex web of rules, which helps to fashion what can be persuasive within any one time and place. The rhetorical work to establish, maintain and reinforce these inclusions and exclusions is implicit in all discourse. This web in part operates external to discourse: inclusions and prohibitions on who has the authority to speak, and distinctions between reason and folly, truth and falsehood. We have seen the positioning of utterances as within and outside the true in the analysis of the *West Report*. We have seen how the authority of individuals and groups other than the government, or its designated speakers, is inscribed and reinforced through strategies to work up the persuasiveness of policy utterances. We have seen that this is done through inclusions and exclusions that are required in order that what is uttered is not read as if the government might have a stake or interest in what is represented, and so that certain objects can be represented as external to the human world and others within it. Such strategies have been seen to be powerfully active in constituting and normalizing a narrative of the requirement for flexibility and the necessity for our action towards it. It is a narrative still in play in both Australia and beyond.

The dispersions of flexibility within policy discourses and the regularity of its representation point to stabilizations within a web of rules of inclusion and exclusion that have supported their emergence and continuation. Flexibility is produced through ritual recitation, indicating a fellowship of discourse. Ritual functions in the preservation and reproduction of flexibility within a particular representation of the world. The roles of speaking and listening are not interchangeable in this. The *Terms of Reference* to the policy review Committee within this statement identified flexibility with a representation of the world that is already to some extent fixed and it is a version of this which must be 'recited'. Foucault suggests that such ritual practices, where particular unities within discourse function to allow 'secret-appropriation' and 'non-interchangeability' of knowledge, indicate schemas of exclusivity and disclosure that work within our societies and which constitute fellowships of discourse. These schemas are institutionalized and maintained by the ways in which the utterances of the fellowship are separated out by the ritual conventions and practices surrounding and supporting them, by the necessary positions, gestures, circumstances and signs accompanying the speech of those afforded such entitlement. The policy review and report that has been analysed in Chapter 3 confirms the kind of institutionalized schema of exclusivity and disclosure of which Foucault speaks.

Flexibility is also constituted powerfully as an object within a particular doctrinal representation of the world. The proposition, 'we do know that' (DEETYA 1998: 18) key developments, change and uncertainty are certain, draws upon and reinforces specific rules dividing truth from falsehood. This underlines the requirement for flexibility and subjects a group to a particular representation of the world and that representation to the group. However, it is also the structuring of the narrative within this statement that has been revealing. It permits the unfolding that focuses on the inflexibilities of the then existing policy and funding framework, the institution and individual and identifies ways in which flexibility can be made possible. The discourse of flexibility simplifies and provides a systematic narrative, whereby the institution, individual and community are placed in an unmediated relationship with each other through changes to the policy and funding regime. There is a symmetry in the discourse, as all will benefit from the increased flexibilities sought. It is flexibility that will bind organizations, individuals and communities.

Flexibility is often accepted as a policy object that emerges through specific discourses of the management of the economy and institutions, which are then taken up and deployed within policy. The tendency then is to focus on whether or not these discourses are verifiable or right, how they may best be implemented, or how they mask social and economic structures of power. However, my rereading of flexibility suggests the significance of local explorations of the operation of power and desire *within* and through the policy descriptions – how descriptions are constituted discursively and rhetorically and with what effect. What the analysis demonstrates is some of the means by which flexibility is constituted and represented persuasively, based upon the normalization of particular rules of inclusion and exclusion.

Key to these rules and strategies appears to be a regularity in the constitution of specific objects that are placed upon the discursive terrain and the gerrymandering of the division between those that are to be taken as real and those socially constructed. In principle, this gerrymandering permits the generation of any number of policy descriptions of problems and their solutions. However, through the regularity of its inclusions and exclusions, through its reactivation and reinscription, discursive stabilization permits only certain forms of the division. It is the regularity of the division between the real and the socially constructed that enables certain divisions to be more persuasive than others. This is a rarefaction of knowledge (Foucault 1996) where the descriptions that this division enable are taken to reflect the world rather than fabricate it. It masks the power and desire implicit within such divisions and their function in the maintenance of ritual and the formation and dissemination of a doctrine. My trail of theorizing points to the fellowship of discourse that is required for the constitution of a wider doctrinal group and the functioning of doctrine through which flexibility can be the theme around which activity is organized. Both ritual and doctrine help to control the possibility for a chance event within policy discourses. That the description is unsurprising points to the regularity of its dispersion within policy statements, a regularity of the rhetorical strategies drawn upon to fabricate it and of the system of exclusion that lies to some extent immanent within it.

Certainty in the truth of flexibility is warranted by constituting the authoritative doctrinal community of actors, nations and international organizations, who are represented as those who 'know'. This community is in part drawn upon to warrant the description. It is a doctrinal community of nations that 'we' are pitted against in competition. There is a danger in inflexibility, as if we loose the competition, we will fail to achieve our rosy future. The positioning of the nation in competition with others works rhetorically to permit the assessment, monitoring and management of our activities through the comparison of national statistics.

This trail has produced a discourse of the constitution and conditions of the emergence and work of a specific discourse of flexibility. Policy discourses need to be persuasive. There is a web of regularities that control and manage what is able to be taken within the true at any one time, which includes what can be legitimately uttered in opposition. Truth is fashioned within a society at a given time in ways that are relatively stable. However, the boundaries between what can be accepted and what is not is never completely fixed. Regularities are reinforced and reinscribed by the rhetorical strategies through which a particular description is worked up. There may be a certain amount of play in this. Policy thus works through the constitution of 'true' descriptions of the world which are persuasive to the extent that they can be worked up rhetorically so as to sit 'within the true' at any one time and location. As we have seen, these discourses are constrained through doctrinal allegiances and the rules of fellowship of discourse and ritual, which overlap and intersect. Rhetoric works within utterances through the institutionalization of ritual spaces for speaking and writing and affords status to those who are permitted to speak or write. It is through the intersection of rules of exclusion and inclusion, and operation of rhetoric within events of discourse that policy operates to produce, reinscribe, control and manage its discourses. Here, rather than policy studies examining policy description as empirical utterance, discourse can be explored for the ways in which it acts to construct the world through statements, thereby opening up possibilities for developing strategies to engage with such acts rather than simply comment upon them.

Policy review processes emerge through this exploration as rhetorical spaces whereby what can be said may to some extent be explored by those who are permitted to speak. Not all statements may be constrained through the ritual mechanism of 'terms of reference'. It may be that utterances can be to some extent tested and accepted or rejected, insofar as they are assimilable within the parameters of doctrinal allegiances. However, this kind of possibility is external to the space that I have taken up within my own theorizings, as it retains the unity of the individual as agent that I have been so concerned to avoid. It is possible to suggest from my own theorizings that the descriptions that are most rhetorically persuasive are those that can be successfully externalized, warranted, taken to be without stake or interest and translatable within a whole range of discourses. The conundrum here, of course, is that in making this argument, in saying, implicitly, 'we know that...' I reactivate a rhetorical strategy that was drawn upon within the policy text analysed. Could

I be falling into the trap that I am attempting to point out? This is not the case. That it is not so depends upon a 'nice' point. Nonetheless it is a true one in terms of this text. When I say 'we know that', I point to the possibility of this proposition as acceptable within the true and attempt to both warrant this and subject a group to this discourse. We are condemned to draw upon rules of exclusion as they exist at any one time and location, if what we say is to be able to be taken 'within the true', to be in some ways intelligible. The difference between policy statements, readings of them, and the statement here in terms of the rules of exclusion at play and deployment of rhetorical strategy, is that I have reversed a dominant assumption about such descriptions and doctrines. This is the assumption that truth exists to be found 'out there' in the real world, and that language can exclude power and desire to represent this. By saying 'we know that', I am pointing to that which has been masked by power and desire and has been revealed through this reversal and this description. I am playing a language game, but with all seriousness.

The approach I have adopted avoids questions of truth in order to look for the regularities of discourse, the truth-making practices in policy statements. It offers a discourse that is warranted through disciplinary understandings of the working of rhetoric and discourses derived from literary theory, conversation analysis and philosophy. It deploys a rhetorical strategy that calls upon the reader to, in part, act as 'witness' to the truth of the description. This does not escape the work of desire and power. Reflexively, it exposes its own rhetoric and complicity within systems of inclusion and exclusion, even as it explores these in relation to specific policy texts. It has held in suspense a division between truth and falsehood that is quite commonly taken to lie between truth and rhetoric. It has positioned rhetoric as part of the making of truth, rather than that which embellishes the truth or attempts to deceive. Rhetoric may certainly play a role in embellishment and deception, but it does more than this, which can only be understood in relation to the wider play of discourse.

Flexibility and lifelong learning as migrating metaphors

Where there are policies of flexibility, they are often associated with discourses of lifelong learning. Such discourses are not confined, but flow within and as part of the wider flows of globalization. Flexibility and lifelong learning migrate. They are effective to a greater or lesser extent and in different ways across different contexts. Here both flexibility and lifelong learning can be read as metaphors, as also can the metaphors through which their emergence is articulated, such as the metaphor of migration. Here their meanings migrate, as they are taken up within different contexts and statements.

Policy texts and policy analysis depend for their persuasiveness upon our prior immersion in certain metaphors and metaphorical systems through which their representations of reality are worked up and reified. Analysis of the ways in which policy propositions and their critiques are formed and reified through such processes is therefore important, as any common acceptance of metaphors may circumscribe critical engagement. To take a metaphor literally is to focus on its denotative meanings rather than its connotations, or to assume that a definitive meaning exists independently from the work to establish a certain meaning as true. Reflexive consideration of these issues enables a further form of critique that refuses or counters practices of reification.

Metaphors may be drawn on within policy discourses for their figurability, their potential to systematize responses to political activities and to fix the play of meanings. Migrations may be purposeful insofar as metaphors are seen to be capable of productive work. Political discourses here emphasize differences and equivalences in meanings across discursive domains. This suggests that it may be through the insertion of metaphors such as flexibility and lifelong learning within policy discourses that reordering effects are achieved, identities become equivalent and alternative potential meanings are displaced.

Flexibility is figurable within a systems logic that aligns the economy, educational system and institution, individual and firm, and gives emphasis to certain metaphors within each location. It has the capacity to align activities across and within domains and this helps to enhance its mobility. It fixes relationships across signifying chains and thus delimits the play of difference. This is not to suggest that descriptions of flexibility are necessarily taken up within differing locations. However, it mobilizes a generalized discourse, which elides differences and allows these to be read as symmetrical. Flexibility operates within systems of metaphors, within which there is a regularity in the danger for human populations from a natural environment which changes and is uncontrollable. These may resonate with existing representations of the circumstances of humanity within social systems. Social Darwinism, for example, inscribes a system of metaphors within which the relation of society to the environment, parts to the whole and danger for populations are similar. It may be through the resonances between metaphorical systems within policy representations and those operating in the wider society that specific metaphors become figurable.

Lifelong learning and flexibility are commonly represented as interrelated discourses of response to change. They are constituted within systems of metaphor, reified and targeted to populations through the constitution of audiences. The systems of metaphor and rhetorical strategies deployed in such reifications and attempts to persuade are therefore important to examine. Many policy texts constitute a nation of citizens as a community under threat. However, they do this through differing metaphorical complexes and reify the description by constituting different communities to warrant them. For instance, the *West Report* builds up a metaphorical system whereby the individual's desires become aligned with those of the nation through a discourse of equity and competition. Australia is positioned as a nation in competition with others within the OECD, but also one seeking the achievement of universal access to post-secondary education. Populations and individuals must become flexible and lifelong learners, if Australia is to succeed. The 1997 *Fryer Report* in the United Kingdom, by contrast, draws upon metaphors of the 'centrifugal forces' of the 'global economy' that 'tear up' the bonds between citizens. Lifelong learning then takes on meaning in the development of networks of bonds between citizens. Both these texts thus represent a metaphorical narrative of a national community in threat from forces outside, even though the community and danger it faces are not entirely the same. However, they are overlapping, subjecting individuals and attempting to align their activities towards lifelong learning and increasing flexibility.

Policy discourses then draw upon and deploy metaphors within descriptions of action and these operate powerfully to shape reactions. Metaphorical readings are a way of countering attempts to inscribe specific meanings in such discourses. To not take the work of metaphor seriously is to suggest that policy descriptions are literal, that they *can* transparently represent the world in some way. I have made problematic this literal/metaphorical distinction by displacing, bracketing off, questions of whether or not a description is literal, in order to examine the metaphorical work of policy description. Metaphors work within these descriptions and constitute groups who are subject to them as their reality. Uncritical acceptance of a metaphorical description leads to vassalage.

This theorizing is an attempt to partially fix meanings within an alternative system of metaphors. Through theorizings of 'figurability', 'construction', 'vassalage', 'ordering effects', and so forth, I have attempted a productive rereading of flexibility and lifelong learning. Reflexively it is significant to note that the system of metaphors that I have constructed resonates to some extent with the one that I have identified within the policy texts that I have analysed. It is the danger of vassalage that I have been exhorting readers to be persuaded of and attempt to avoid. It may be that such unities of discourse lie at the very roots of our thoughts. However, despite this, the analysis charted a trail from the concern with metaphorical work in discursive migrations to ways of understanding the migration of flexibility as part of a globalizing process. It also started to tell a tale of lifelong learning as migrating metaphor and of the metaphor of migration as a way of inscribing meaning into its global emergence. This suggests the potential for other such fabrications drawing upon theorizings of metaphor and alternative metaphors and metaphorical systems in constructing fresh openings in policy and in the study of policies of lifelong learning. It suggests metaphorical readings as an interpretive art. Reflexive consideration of the metaphorical work of policy description may enable forms of critique that refuse or counter practices of reification and the attempted migrations within such descriptions.

Further explorations of the regularities and systems of metaphor that emerge within dispersed events of policy discourse and of the audiences that they require and work up are possibilities. For, if we are to escape vassalage, or keep a certain openness to the forms of vassalage we adopt, we must identify the regularities of the representations that we become subject to and recognize the communities within which we become positioned. What work do these do through our acceptance of them as literal descriptions? What orientations to danger do they require? To what mobilizations of activity, aspiration and desire are we made subject through them? What and who are discarded as anomalous in these processes? In examining what is excluded we may find alternative systems of metaphor at play, which could be drawn upon productively. Thus, in the elision of differences, who and what is elided within different locations? Anna Yeatman (1994) also indicates the productivity of metonymy in the politicization of metaphor. What metonymical relations do stabilized systems of metaphor permit and how might these be pursued? Perhaps, at the broadest, one might explore the possibilities of alternative metaphorical systems of sociality. What systems might it be possible to conceive apart from those dependant upon systems logic and upon danger, fear and uncertainty? Lyotard (1984), for example, offers a theorizing of a form of relational sociality rather than systems sociality, which might be productive. We could also explore systems of metaphor and communities subject to these that have been drawn upon in the past and outside those of the West to see how these have differed and thus how we are constrained within the present by making comparisons with alternative representations.

Lifelong learning as policy rform

In arguing for the importance of rhetorical analysis to policy studies, I position myself as against the notion that policy can be dismissed as 'spin'. This dismissal is a form of grandstanding that exonerates the commentator from engagement in the politics of policy. Rhetorical analysis helps to point to the politics of discourse that is at play in policy-making processes.

In relation to lifelong learning policy, this trail illustrated that the pathos drawn upon and utilized within policy discourses can be important to identify and explore. It suggested that the persuasiveness of exigence may be increased by deploying pathos that draws upon specific cultural memories, where this is both timely and appropriate to the event of the policy utterance. An analysis of the pathos of lifelong learning within UK policy texts indicated that lifelong learning can make a space for the reconfiguration and resinscription of the boundaries of learning through a redelineation of the terrain to be managed. Lifelong learning is positioned positively through pathos to harness the desires and values of those working in the terrain. It is an attempt at a seductive discourse, which appeals to desire. This is both inspirational and aspirational, appealing to the values and emotions of practitioners within the arena.

The rhetoric of renaissance and opportunity appeals both to tradition and modernization in such discourses. Here the emphasis on pathos is not a lack of policy. It emphasizes and deploys specific strategies of rhetoric within policy. There is thus a moral positioning of the individual and maybe even imperative to be adaptable or flexible, wherein self-improvement is aligned with renewal of educational practices and national prosperity. A historical resonance is afforded through a reference back to an earlier period of 'self-improvement' and moral rectitude, the era of industrial supremacy and empire. A revival of the role of certain institutions in education is persuasive. For who would not be persuaded of a requirement for libraries and museums to be more flexible and responsive to individual learning? Or, of the danger of a library or museum that could not support the nation in global economic competition? Education here is the motivation of those without and involves the persuasion of these 'needy' individuals of the joys of learning. The trail points to the imbrication of the conventions of writing and representation within policy texts with those of their interpretation and reception. As the latter are reconfigured through shifting practices in communicative forms, pathos may become more effective, despite or maybe because of increasing discourses of evidence-informed practice.

This trail points to the power of differing theorizings of rhetoric to illuminate differing features of policy and the work it does. It indicates the potential for explorations of policy conventions of representation, writing and speaking, and of their reading, listening and reception within differing discursive locations. It points to the potential of explorations of the dissemination of policy within and through a range of communicative practices and their intersections or otherwise with wider reconfigurations of such conventions. There are also possibilities for exploring the effectiveness of policies in their work to trouble and reconfigure the boundaries of systems and institutionalized practices and in efforts to align activities and desires more broadly. These are of course only some possibilities. However, they may be significant in their potential to explore the space that has been identified within the policy studies literature for identifying a politics of engagement in policy. For this, policy analysts may need to become spin doctors themselves, or at least, be able to consider the rhetorical in relation to their own practices. Rhetorical analysis is a strategy to analyse policy strategies, but also points to forms of engagement in the politics of policy. This cannot rely on the ethos of the analyst, nor the logos of their argument. Forms of pathos may reconfigure the terrain of education and education policy through the refashioning of desire and make it possible for different and productive policy objects to be identified. This is something with which analysts must engage rather than dismiss.

Checking bearings

By exploring within a few sample texts aspects of the work of discourse and rhetoric in – variously – the constitution, migration, and e/affective work of lifelong learning and flexibility, I have begun to formulate a politics of truth-telling in the policy process. I do not consider that this is all that can be done, nor the only thing. It is a contribution to debates about how to engage with policy. Within the first trail, by focusing on the active work of language in the constitution of flexibility, it has been possible to explore discursive regularities that are conditions of existence for its emergence. The significance of this discourse is the space it makes for the reassessment of narratives of the meanings of flexibility within policy discourses. Flexibility is often taken to be a policy object that reflects discourses of the economy and institution. In my trails, flexibility is an object that is actively and rhetorically fabricated within each instance of its utterance *within policy*. It makes it possible to examine flexibility as intrinsic to power and desire within policy discourses and the attempted elimination of chance events. Rather than critique being focused on the truth and power of discourses, a space is made for explorations of the operation of power and desire within and through policy descriptions – how statements are constituted discursively and rhetorically and what effect they have. By focusing on the migrations of flexibility and lifelong learning as metaphor within the second trail, a discourse has emerged that makes the persuasiveness of these terms problematic in a different way. Their capacity for migration across and within discourses is a significant issue to take up. By drawing on theorizings of metaphor and metaphorical readings, it has been possible to make space to identify and examine alternative means for their migrations and persuasiveness. The third trail focused on the detail of pathos. This appears to be a significant aspect of the work of rhetoric within policy descriptions and thus important to consider.

These have been nomadic theorizings within which I have articulated the politics of my activity and emphasized fragmentation and incompleteness in efforts to bring to the fore the locatedness of my work as a condition of its practice. As nomad, as displaced and located subjectivity, I have travelled discontinuous trails of theorization and exploration that have not begun at any predetermined beginnings nor continued in directions that I had previously conceived. I have often ended up in spaces other than I anticipated and with the desire to continue my travels. These travellings have been possible through a specific Foucauldian 'point of attack' (1996: 359) or, as I have called it, point of departure, and through the various theorizings of rules of exclusion and of rhetoric, which I have picked up and put to use in my journeys. They are critical approaches that I suggest are political and active enough in my own terms. Although they do not offer alternative frameworks for policy to take up and deploy, they do not simply contest meanings, but suggest how engaging in the practices of meaning-making is central to engagement in policy.

Discursive and rhetorical approaches may be positioned as inoffensive or submissive forms of solely critique, which can 'do' nothing. I take up this point because of the implication that my own explorations may be politically inactive, or at least not active enough: However, discourse is never passive, in particular when it purports to be. What I hope to have demonstrated in contributing to critical work is the material work of policy texts. The material work of policy texts is fabricated through discursive and rhetorical practices. Alternative formulations need to give more attention to their own such framings if they wish to be a/effective. Policy texts are important actors in policy processes, both condensing and opening possibilities for meaning, often based upon implicit writing and reading practices.

The art of governance is more than this as we have seen. However, by exploring the activity of rhetoric in specific statements of policy it has been possible to encounter, in some small way, its complicity with vast and complex, interrelated systems of inclusion and exclusion through which policy does political work. This is not then a descriptive critique, or entry into contestation, or defensive stance based on local forms of resistance. It is an artful device. It is designed to insert itself *within* meanings of policy and its study. It is a discursive 'wedge', constructed to interrupt the unity of thought that suggests that description can be reflective of reality, or are solely critique. It is an odious device that politicizes descriptions within policy and its study and, of course, by the same token, its own discourse. It borrows from Foucault (1996), as it is sneaky. It interjects into the very roots of thought the notion that policy statements do work, they act.

And if this is the case, we have to ask ourselves *how* our own descriptions of policy act within policy. Do we, as policy analysts, play unwittingly into the hands of those who reinforce and reinscribe those systems of power in operation? This may be no bad thing, if indeed we do. For without such systems we would surely have no democracy at all. However, where we search for descriptions of truth, we reinforce the notion that this is (all) that we should look for. Such descriptions may already be expected by those who would take them up and incorporate them within existing systems of power. The danger is one of the power and desire within discourses being reinscribed and reinforced by those multinational economies and bureaucratic states, which it has been our intention to avoid, criticize or ameliorate in some way. The dominance of the will to truth, of which Foucault speaks (1996), may be what makes it so difficult to think up alternatives. Attempting this is 'to imagine and to bring into being new schemas of politicization. If "politicization" means falling back on ready-made choices and institutions, then the effort of analysis involved in uncovering the relations of force and mechanisms of power is not worthwhile' (Foucault 1980: 190). To guard against incorporation is to fragment and multiply discourse and construct alternative beginnings that do not rely on the same unities of thought.

The notion of exclusions from discourse points to just such a schema of politicization and it is for this reason that I have taken it as a point of departure for my travellings. If systems external to and within discourses indicate the exercise of power and desire, then it is to that which lies on the margins of discourse, or to that which it has been possible to say in the past, which we must look to for help in reconsidering what has been hitherto intelligible in the present. Foucault examines what has counted as the serious truth statements of the past, not to make them plausible, but to explore the systematic order in their dispersions (Dreyfus and Rabinow 1982). This makes the present intelligible in different ways. We might also consider other systems of discourse entirely. For Foucault's analysis is of Western discourses and of their systematic structure. There may be alternatives through which it might be possible, in much the same way, to find a 'wedge' through which to make discourses intelligible in different ways (Dreyfus and Rabinow 1982). It may also be worth being open to and exploring chance events that may bring about shifts in epistemes. And it may be here that this work offers further of the kind of potential that Peters and Marshall (1996) indicate as necessary for policy analysis to move beyond the merely defensive.

There are points available for counter-attack, or politicization, which emerge for consideration through rhetorical analysis. For example, by exposing the rhetorical strategies at work in the construction of policy statements, one exposes their work in the exercise of power in their attempts to shape up our belief that we know the world in which we live and act in accordance with these descriptions. It raises the question of how this discourse of rhetoric might work in detail as a 'wedge' within discursive relations of power.

Globalization, competition, the knowledge age, society and economy are strongly represented to us within policy and elsewhere as facts of the world, and as the exigencies for action. They are commonly gerrymandered as naturally existing objects of the world. They would not be so persuasive if we reversed this and positioned them as socially constructed and as the work of specific people and groups. Who would be prepared to act to construct flexibility and lifelong learning in order to increasingly globalize, compete, or construct the knowledge age, society or economy? Flexibility and lifelong learning are seen primarily, but not only, as reactive to an already set context – an answer – rather than also being proactive in relation to the desirability of that context – a question. It is an adaptive rather than reflexive form of learning at the heart of this policy (Edwards *et al.* 2002).

It may be that through identifying those locations where rhetorical strategies and rules of inclusion and exclusion operate most densely we may find alternative points of attack. For example, I have explored a certain gerrymandering of the boundary between the natural and the socially constructed. A certain instability in the boundary of inclusion and exclusion of those afforded category entitlement to speak authoritatively on issues of policy for education. A certain control and exclusion from discourse operating through policy mechanisms for reference, consultative review and reporting. These strategies appear to operate most powerfully within contemporary discourses of policy and they offer strategic beginnings from which we can mount productive refusals and elaborations.

The world is described to us through generalized nominalizations and naturalizations, as if we had no part in such constructions. It may therefore be that we can avoid within our own discourses, descriptions that begin from the same place. We can act to avoid these as unities and to expose them as constructions within language and as the activities of specific groups. If we reject them, then policy discourses would not be perhaps so able to persuade others that their exigencies for action flow naturally. For who would want to play potentially into the hands of those multinational and intra-national corporations in the construction of our education systems and societies? Of course, you may well say, we already know that globalization, the knowledge age, economy and society, and competition are socially constructed. This is what policy analysts have already been saying. But rather than reject them as the ideological veils of malign interests, I am suggesting we can engage with them by telling the stories differently, by setting in place alternative practices of truth-telling. This is part of the rhetorical work, in finding metaphors that can be mobilized and in fixing certain facts of the world through which to secure narratives for other forms of action.

It may be that there is a *kieros* and *phronesis* for policy analysts to speak authoritatively and publicly on issues of policy for education. For category entitlement is not fixed for once and for all, but is worked up through the repetitions of authoritative speaking that is found by an audience to lie 'within the true'. We do have such an entitlement, afforded by our positions within the academy. But it may be that we are increasingly unheard, as our students close their ears to 'theory' and 'policy', and as our curricula are increasingly reduced to skills-based knowledge. If education and training institutions are to maintain their position in the construction of new propositions, then it may be that we need to disseminate our own work more knowingly and forcefully in contemporary times. We may need to speak up in the media, in public places and in rhetorical styles that are most suitable to our audiences, and perhaps even in unlikely places on the television where 'sound bites' may be best heard in the living rooms of families. However, it appears that we must be careful about what we say, as there is always the danger that we may act to reinforce existing relations of power, or merely to return to old ones. How do we know how to play this? And would we not just increase uncertainty if our counterarguments were to be persuasive? For certainty is not within our grasp, despite the various forms of fundamentalism that stridently mediate our world.

How might we deal with control and exclusion from discourse? We could perhaps pick up on discourses that are afforded status within policy formulation processes, analyse them for their rhetorical strategies and their content, and for their potential in providing alternative tacks that might be productive. For example, the interest in social cohesion within policy exhortations has not emerged from a void. It resonates well for those of us within education and training contexts. Discourses of economics pay serious attention to the potential of centrifugal forces within economic globalization processes, and international corporations are seen to exacerbate this potential. Increasing regionalization is seen as a potential effect of increasing centrifugal forces. The metaphor is a powerful one, which we perhaps all hold in some form in our cultural memories and thus is already being mobilized in many directions. There may be a timeliness and appropriateness for emphasis within education policy analysis, for elaboration around this theme and insertion of such discourses within policy consultation processes and more widely. What begins to emerge is the potential for very strategic engagements in policy analysis, in relation to the *kieros* and *phronesis* of the statements of utterances, as well as their style and dissemination.

154 *An 'odious' but slender wedge*

In refusing a separation of truth from rhetoric we begin to reveal the operation of desire and power within policy statements. Policy works to build up the truth of its narratives through our acceptance of this separation. It is possible therefore that we must look to those discourses that are excluded from policy and its analysis in order that alternatives may be identified, multiplied and disseminated. That the policy narratives of truth and the consultative processes of policy do attempt to accommodate alternative discourses is perhaps encouraging. This provides space for the play of alternative discourses, even though policy strategies for measurement and discourses of choice and flexibility deployed within the discursive formation may increasingly reduce this space.

Others, such as Stephen Ball, have argued that policy texts do not get read, with the implication that they thus perhaps do no work in relation to audiences. Certainly 12,000 responses does not seem an excessive response to an open appeal for engagement in policy debate across the EU member states. It may imply that few bothered to read the text. However, it is by looking specifically at the rhetorical 'style' of policy texts that their work may be further explored. Style is one of the canons drawn upon within traditional rhetorical theory when looking at persuasive genres (Leach 2000). It sits in a complex relationship between the form and the content of discourse and can relate to the kind of persuasion that can be accomplished. A scientific document, for example, is highly stylized and so too are media representations. They are persuasive in part in relation to 'ritual' conventions, which involve those of interpretation as well as those of writing, speaking and representing. Specific styles of television programme are associated with different times of the evening and forms of presentation. Viewers may well watch and interpret these in differing and ritualized ways. Watching the news while preparing the supper may involve engaging in a programme as entertainment, rather than as information, and this may be in part encouraged by the style of the event. News may be represented as a series of colourful and entertaining or exciting 'clips' of what has gone on in the world, emphasizing pathos and ethos rather than detailed logos. 'These rituals and conventions define boundaries and limits of both the creation of discourse and the reception of discourse' (Leach 2000: 215).

Policy texts may also conform to ritual and conventions of representation and interpretation. We begin to see these rituals in their rhetorical style. They commonly draw upon *forensic* analyses of empirical data to warrant the *exigence* and work up the facticity of the crisis to be addressed. They construct realist descriptions through which they narrate pictures of the world that may be accepted. They invite the audience to enter into a debate and shape up decisions that are made over the future within these narratives. This rhetorical work requires a particular style of engagement. Consider for a moment the kind of policy text that is drawn up by political parties within an election process. The probable fact that few read these texts and the certain fact that few exercise their rights at the voting polls does not negate the significance of these texts and invitations in securing our allegiance that due democratic process has been followed. Audiences may well interpret such invitations in differing and ritualized ways and may watch rather than engage. They may be entertainment for some and they certainly offer a certain style in the rhetorical performance. There may be an equivalence to media 'sound bites' in their overviews and executive summaries. They offer a participation, which is perhaps not far from that of audience participation reality shows on the television. They engage and satisfy us as we are invited in, but may just wish to watch the fun.

A discourse of policy rhetoric, a demonstration that the rhetorical is at play in the construction of truth, may offer a wedge to insert, oh so odiously, between and within discourses and contemporary relations of power. A focus on discourse and rhetorical strategies and the relations of power, which they constitute, support and maintain through their repetitions permits us to language into being a policy analysis that also points to the politics of discourse in policy. The wedge is odious, because it is not immune from that about which it speaks. We need to be 'monsters' on the prowl, which to some extent exist at the edge of discourse and pose a danger to the regular unfolding of the history of knowledge and the stabilized systems of desire and power implicit within it (Foucault 1996). In academic disciplines, monsters are those whose discourses require the reconfiguration of the rules of the discipline if they are to be accepted. It is the rules that determine what is to be counted within the true at any one time. Monsters are most visible when they are rejected for a period of time and then become accepted through various reconfigurations. We have seen this many times, in the rejection of non-linear mathematics in science, for example. Within policy discourses, it has become quite common to attribute madness, power and desire to the speech of particular individuals or groups. For example, the 'spin' of a 'spin doctor'. This indicates the enactment and reinforcement of rules of exclusion, permitting such rejections. It may be, however, through statements that are monsters that we may find alternative beginnings. It may even be that this text represents one such monster, although perhaps only in some small way. The outcome is dependent upon the persuasiveness of the text itself, the extent to which I have successfully positioned the description as within the true and identified and deployed the rhetorical strategies necessary to count this text a felicitous act of truth-telling.

Bibliography

Adnett, N. and Davis, P. (2000) 'Competition and curriculum diversity in local schooling markets: theory and evidence', *Journal of Education Policy*, 15, 2: 157–67.

Agger, B. (1992) *Cultural Studies as Critical Theory*, London: Falmer.

Apple, M. (1996) 'Being popular about national standards: a review of national standards in American education: a citizens' guide', *Education Policy Analysis Archives*, 4,10: 1–6. Available HTTP: <http://epaa.asu.edu/epaa/v4n10.html> (accessed 30 August 2005).

Atkinson, E. (1996) 'Some observations on how the open learning initiative is facilitating change in Australian tertiary education', *Hot Topics*, Australian Council for Educational Administration, 2, November: 15.

Atkinson, P. (1996) *Sociological Readings and Re-readings*, Aldershot: Avebury Press.

Australian Education Council (1991) *Young People's Participation in Post-compulsory Education and Training: Report of the Australian Education Council Review Committee (Finn Report)*, Canberra: AGPS.

Avis, J. (1997) 'Globalization, the learner and post-compulsory education: policy fictions', *Research in Post-Compulsory Education*, 2, 3: 241–59.

Axford, B. and Huggins, R. (Eds) (2001*) New Media and Politics*, London: Sage.

Ball, S. (1990a) *Politics and Policy Making in Education. Explorations in Policy Sociology*, London: Routledge.

Ball, S. (Ed.) (1990b) *Foucault and Education: Disciplines and Knowledge*, London: Routledge.

Ball, S. (1994a) *Education Reform: A Critical and Post-structural Approach*, Buckingham: Open University Press.

Ball, S. (1994b) 'Some reflections on policy theory: a brief response to Hatcher and Troyna', *Journal of Education Policy*, 9, 2: 171–82.

Ball, S. (1998) 'Big policies/small world: an introduction to international perspectives in education policy', *Comparative Education*, 34, 2: 119–30.

Barry, A. (2002) 'In the middle of the network', in J. Law and A. Mol (Eds), *Complexities: Social Studies of Knowledge Practices*, Durham, NC: Duke University Press.

Bartel, A. and Lichtenberg, F. (1987) 'The comparative advantage of educated workers in implementing new technology,' *Review of Economics and Statistics*, 69, 1: 1–11.

Beck, U. (1997) *The Reinvention of Politics: Rethinking Modernity in the Global Social Order*, Cambridge: Polity Press.

Bikhchandani, S., Hirshleifer, D. and Welch, I. (1998) 'Learning from the behaviour of others: conformity, fads and informational cascades', *Journal of Economic Perspectives*, 12, 3: 151–70.

Boshier, R. (2001) 'Lifelong learning as bungy jumping: in New Zealand what goes down doesn't always come up', *International Journal of Lifelong Education*, 20, 5: 361–77.

Bottomley, J. (2000) 'Reconfiguring institutional strategies for flexible learning and delivery', in V. Jakupec and J. Garrick (Eds), *Flexible Learning, Human Resource and Organizational Development: Putting Theory to Work*, London: Routledge.

Bourdieu, P. (1992) 'Thinking about limits', in M. Featherstone (Ed.), *Cultural Theory and Cultural Change*, London: Sage Publications.

Bowe, R., Ball, S. and Gold, A. (1992) *Reforming Education and Changing Schools*, London: Routledge.

Brown, B. (1992) 'Why government's run schools', *Economics of Education Review*, 11, 4: 287–300.

Campion, M. (1991) 'Distance education and the debate about Fordism', *Critical Issues in Distance Education*, Geelong: Deakin University and University of South Australia.

Chibulka, J. (1994) 'Policy analysis and the study of the politics of education', *Politics of Education Association Yearbook*, 105–25.

Chilton, P. (2004) *Analyzing Political Discourse*, London: Routledge.

Codd, J. (1988) 'The construction and deconstruction of educational policy documents', *Journal of Education Policy*, 3, 3: 235–48.

Coffield, F. (2002) 'Breaking the consensus: lifelong learning as social control', in R. Edwards, N. Miller, N. Small and A. Tait (Eds), *Supporting Lifelong Learning, Volume 3: Making Policy Work*, London: Routledge.

Commission of the European Community (1994) *Competitiveness, Employment, Growth*, Luxembourg: Office for Official Publications.

Council of the European Union (2004) *'Education and training 2010': the success of the Lisbon strategy hinges on urgent reforms, Council and Commission Joint interim report on the implementation of the detailed work programme on the follow-up of the objectives of the education and training systems in Europe*. Available HTTP: <http://register.consilium.eu.int/pdf/en/04/st06/st06236.en04.pdf> (accessed 10 October 2005).

Dale, R. (1999) 'Specifying globalization effects on national policy: a focus on the mechanisms', *Journal of Education Policy*, 14, 1: 1–17.

DEETYA (Department of Employment, Education, Training and Youth Affairs) (1997a) *Learning for Life: Review of Higher Education Financing and Policy, a Policy Discussion Paper*, Canberra: DEETYA.

DEETYA (1997b) *Higher Education Review Releases Discussion Paper*. Available HTTP: <http://www.dest.gov.au/archive/highered/hereview/media.html> (accessed 1 August 2005).

DEETYA (1997c) *First Meeting of the Higher Education Review Committee*. Available HTTP: <http://www.dest.gov.au/archive/highered/hereview/media.html> (accessed 1 August 2005).

DEETYA (1998) *Learning for Life: Final Report. Review of Higher Education Financing and Policy*, Canberra: DEETYA.

DfEE (Department for Education and Employment) (1995) *Lifetime Learning: A Consultation Document*, Sheffield: Department for Education and Employment/ Scottish Office/Welsh Office.

DfEE (1998) *The Learning Age: A Renaissance for a New Britain*, London: HM Stationary Office.

DfEE (1999) *Learning to Succeed: A New Framework for Post-16 Learning*, London: Stationery Office.

DfES (Department of Employment and Skills) (2003a) *Developing a National Skills Strategy and Delivery Plan: Underlying Evidence*, London: HM Stationary Office.

DfES (2003b) *21st Century Skills, Realizing Our Potential: Individuals, Employers, Nation*, London: HM Stationary Office.

DfES (2005a) *Skills: Getting On in Business, Getting On at Work*, London: DfES.

DfES (2005b) *14–19: Education and Skills*, London: DfES.

Dreyfus, H. and Rabinow, P. (1982) *Michel Foucault: Beyond Structuralism and Hermeneutics*, New York: Harvester Wheatsheaf.

DTI (Department of Training and Industry) (2002) *The Economic Reform Agenda: Opportunities for Accession Countries*, London: HM Stationary Office. Available HTTP: <http://www.dti.gov.uk/> (accessed 10 October 2005).

DTI (2003) *DTI Strategy – The Analysis, DTI Economics Paper No. 5*, Department of Trade and Industry. Available HTTP: <http://www.dti.gov.uk/> (accessed 20 October 2005).

du Gay, P. (1996a) 'Organizing identity: entrepreneurial governance and public management', in S. Hall and P. du Gay (Eds), *Questions of Cultural Identity*, London: Sage.

du Gay, P. (1996b) *Consumption and Identity at Work*, London: Sage.

Edwards, D. (1997) *Discourse and Cognition*, London: Sage.

Edwards, R. (1991) 'The inevitable future? Post-Fordism and open learning', *Open Learning*, 6, 2: 36–42.

Edwards, R. (1995) 'Different discourses, discourses of difference: globalization, distance education and open learning', *Distance Education*, 16, 2: 241–55.

Edwards, R. (1997) *Changing Places? Flexibility, Lifelong Learning and a Learning Society*, London: Routledge.

Edwards, R. (1999) 'Lifelong (l)earning and a "new age" at work', in P. Oliver (Ed.), *Lifelong and Continuing Education: What is a Learning Society?* Aldershot: Ashgate.

Edwards, R. (2002) 'Mobilizing lifelong learning: governmentality in educational practices', *Journal of Education Policy*, 17, 3: 353–65.

Edwards, R. and Boreham, N. (2003) ' "The centre cannot hold": complexity and difference in European Union policy towards a learning society', *Journal of Education Policy*, 18, 3: 429–43.

Edwards, R. and Nicoll, K. (2001) 'Researching the rhetoric of lifelong learning', *Journal of Education Policy*, 16, 2: 103–12.

Edwards, R. and Tait, A. (1999) 'Forging policies in flexible learning', in V. Jakupec and J. Garrick (Eds), *Flexible Learning, Human Resource and Organizational Development: Putting Theory to Work*, London: Routledge.

Edwards, R., Nicoll, K. and Tait, A. (1999) 'Migrating metaphors: the globalisation of flexibility in policy', *Journal of Education Policy*, 14, 6: 619–30.

Edwards, R., Ranson, S. and Strain, M. (2002) 'Reflexivity: towards a theory of lifelong learning', *International Journal of Lifelong Education*, 525–36.

Employment Skills Formation Council (1992) *The Australian Vocational Certificate Training Program*, Canberra: NBEET.

European Centre for the Development of Vocational Training (CEDEFOP) (2001) *Summary and Analysis of the Feedback from the Member States and EEA Countries as Part of the Consultation on the Commission's Memorandum on Lifelong Learning*, Thessaloniki (Pylea): Cedefop. Available HTTP: <http://europa.eu.int/comm/education/policies/lll/life/communication/cedefop_en.pdf> (accessed 21 October 2005).

European Commission (1993) *Growth, Competitiveness, Employment*, Luxemburg: Office for Official Publications of the European Communities.

European Commission (1996) *Teaching and Learning: Towards a Learning Society*, Luxembourg: Office for Official Publications of the European Communities.

European Commission (2000a) *Commission Staff Working Paper, Memorandum on Lifelong Learning*, Brussels: European Commission.

European Commission (2000b) *Presidency Conclusions, Lisbon European Council*, European Commission. Available HTTP: <http://ue.eu.int/ueDocs/cms_Data/docs/pressData/en/ec/00100-r1.en0.htm.>(accessed 14 October 2005).

European Commission (2001) *Communication from the Commission, Making a European Area of Lifelong Learning a Reality*, European Commission. Available HTTP: <http://eurpoa.eu.int/comm/education/policies/lll/life/communication/ com_en.pdf> (accessed 14 October 2005).

European Commission (2003) *Implementing lifelong learning strategies in Europe: progress report on the follow-up to the Council resolution of 2002, EU and EFTA/EEA countries, European Commission and the European Centre for the Development of Vocational Training (Cedefop)*. Available HTTP: <http://europa.eu.int/comm/education/policies/2010/doc/synthesis_efta_eea_en.pdf> (accessed 14 October 2005).

European Commission (2004a) *Implementation of 'Education & Training 2010' Work Programme, Working Group A, Progress Report*, European Commission.

European Commission (2004b) *Implementation of 'Education & Training 2010' Work Programme, Working Group B, 'Key Competences', Key Competences for Lifelong Learning a European Reference Framework*, European Commission.

European Commission (2005) 'Education and Training 2010: diverse systems, shared goals, Key objectives and areas of cooperation'. Available HTTP: <http://europa.eu.int/comm/education/policies/2010/objectives_en.html#basic> (accessed 13 October 2005).

Evans, T. (1995a) 'Postgraduate research supervision in the emerging "open" universities', *The Australian Universities' Review*, 38, 2: 23–27.

Evans, T. (1995b) 'Globalization, post-Fordism and open and distance education', *Distance Education*, 16, 2: 256–69.

Evers, C. (1988) 'Policy analysis, values and complexity', *Journal of Education Policy* 3, 3: 223–33.

Fairclough, N. (1989) *Language and Power*, London: Longman.

Fairclough, N. (1992) *Discourse and Social Change*, Cambridge: Polity Press.

Fairclough, N. (2000) *New Labour, New Language?* London: Routledge.

Fauconnier, G. (1997) *Mappings in Thought and Language*, Cambridge: Cambridge University Press.

Faure, E., Herrara, F., Kaddoura, A.-R., Lopes, H., Petrovsky, A., Rahnema, M. and Ward, F. (1972) *Learning to Be: The World of Education Today and Tomorrow*, Paris: Harrap/UNESCO.

Field, J. (1994) 'Open learning and consumer culture', *Open Learning*, 9, 2: 3–11.

Field, J. (1995) 'Globalization, consumption and the learning business', *Distance Education*, 16, 2: 270–83.

Field, J. (2000a) 'Governing the ungovernable: why lifelong learning policies promise so much yet deliver so little', *Education Management and Administration*, 28, 3: 249–61.

Field, J. (2000b) *Lifelong Learning and the New Educational Order*, Stoke on Trent: Trentham Books.

Flyvberg, B. (2002) *Making Social Science Matter*, London: Sage.

Foucault, M. (1970) *The Order of Things: An Archaeology of the Human Sciences*, London: Routledge.

Foucault, M. (1972) *The Archaeology of Knowledge*, London: Tavistock.

Foucault, M. (1977) *Discipline and Punish: The Birth of the Prison*, Harmondsworth: Peregrine Books.

Foucault, M. (1980) *Power/knowledge; Selected Interviews and Other Writings 1972–1977*, Brighton: Harvester Press.

Foucault, M. (1996) 'The discourse on language', in R. Kearny and M. Rainwater (Eds), *The Continental Philosophy Reader*, London: Routledge.

Freedman, A. and Medway, P. (Eds) (1994) *Genre and the New Rhetoric*, London: Taylor & Francis.

Friedman, M. (1955) 'The role of government in education', in R. Solo (Ed.) *Economics and the Public Interest*, New Brunswick: Rutgers University Press.

Fuwa, K. (2001) 'Lifelong education in Japan, a highly school-centred society: educational opportunities and practical educational activities for adults', *International Journal of Lifelong Education*, 20, 1/2: 127–36.

Giddens, A. (2000) *The Third Way and Its Critics*, Cambridge: Polity Press.

Giere, U. and Piet, M. (1997) *Adult Learning in a World at Risk: Emerging Policies and Strategies*, Hamburg: UNESCO Institute for Education.

Gill, R. (2000) 'Discourse analysis', in M. Bauer and G. Gaskell (Eds), *Qualitative Researching with Text, Image and Sound: A Practical Handbook*, London: Sage.

Griffin, C. (1999a) 'Lifelong learning and social democracy', *International Journal of Lifelong Education*, 18: 329–42.

Griffin, C. (1999b) 'Lifelong learning and welfare reform', *International Journal of Lifelong Education*, 18, 6: 431–52.

Group of Eight (1999) *Koln Charter: Aims and Ambitions for Lifelong Learning, 18 June 1999*, Cologne: Group of Eight.

Hake, B. (1999) 'Lifelong learning policies in the European Union: developments and issues',*Compare*, 29, 1: 53–69.

Harvey, D. (1990) *The Condition of Postmodernity*. Oxford: Basil Blackwell.

Hatcher, R. and Troyner, B. (1994) 'The "policy cycle": A ball by Ball account', *Journal of Educational Policy*, 9, 2: 155–70.

Hawkridge, D. (2000) 'Using media and technologies for flexible workplace learning', in V. Jakupec and J. Garrick (Eds), *Flexible Learning, Human Resource and Organizational Development: Putting Theory to Work*, London: Routledge.

Howarth, D. (2000) *Discourse*, Buckingham: Open University Press.

Hughes, C. and Tight, M. (1995) 'The myth of the learning society', *British Journal of Educational Studies*, 43, 3: 290–304.

Humes, W. and Bryce, T. (2003) 'Post-structuralism and policy research in education', *Journal of Education Policy*, 18, 2: 175–87.

Hursh, D. and Martina, C. A. (2003) 'Neoliberalism and schooling in the U.S. How state and federal government education policies perpetuate inequality', *Journal of Critical Education Policy Sociology*, 1, 2: 47–59.

Jakupec, V. and Garrick, J. (Eds) (2000) *Flexible Learning, Human Resource and Organizational Development: Putting Theory to Work*, London: Routledge.

Jakupec, V. and Nicoll, K. (1994a) 'Crises in Australian distance education', *Higher Education Review*, 26, 2: 7–32.

Jakupec, V. and Nicoll, K. (1994b) 'Legitimizing policy analysis as research in open and distance education', in T. Evans and D. Murphy (Eds), *Research in Distance Education 3*, Geelong: Deakin University Press.

Journal of Education Policy (1997) *The Concept of the Learning Society Explored*, 12, 6.

Keating, P. (1994) *Working Nation – Policies and Programs*, Canberra: AGPS.

Keep, E. and Rainbird, H. (2002) 'Towards the learning organization', in F. Reeve, M. Cartwright and R. Edwards (Eds), *Supporting Lifelong Learning: Volume 2*, London: Routledge.

Kennedy, H. (1997) *Learning Works: Widening Participation in Further Education*, Coventry: FEFC.

Kenway, J. (1990) *Gender and Education Policy: A Call for New Directions*, Geelong: Deakin University Press.

King, B. (2000) 'Managing institutional change and the pressures for new approaches to teaching and learning', in V. Jakupec and J. Garrick (Eds), *Flexible Learning, Human Resource and Organizational Development: Putting Theory to Work*, London: Routledge.

Kirkpatrick, D. (1997) 'Becoming flexible: contested territory', *Studies in Continuing Education*, 19, 2: 160–73.

Kumar, K. (1995) *From Post-Industrial to Post-Modern Society: New Theories of the Contemporary World*, Oxford: Blackwell.

Laclau, E. and Mouffe, C. (1985) *Hegemony and Socialist Strategy*, London: Verso.

Lakoff, G. and Johnson, M. (1980) *Metaphors We Live By*, Chicago: University of Chicago Press.

Latour, B. and Wolgar, S. (1979) *Laboratory Life: The Construction of Scientific Facts*, Beverley Hills: Sage.

Lawson, K. (1982) 'Lifelong education: concept or policy?', *International Journal of Lifelong Education*, 1, 2: 97–108.

Lea, M. and Nicoll, K. (Eds) (2002) *Distributed Learning: Social and Cultural Approaches to Practice*, London: Routledge.

Leach, J. (2000) 'Rhetorical analysis', in M. Bauer and G. Gaskell (Eds), *Qualitative Researching With Text, Image and Sound. A Practical Handbook*, London: Sage Publications.

Leith, D. and Myerson, G. (1989) *The Power of Address: Explorations in Rhetoric*, London: Routledge.

Levin, B. (1998) 'An epidemic of education policy: (what) can we learn from each other?', *Comparative Education*, 34, 2: 131–41.

Lingard, B. (1996) 'Educational policy making in a postmodern state: On Stephen J. Ball's education reform: a critical and poststructural approach', *Australian Educational Researcher*, 23, 1: 65–91.

Lingard, B. and Rawolle, S. (2004) 'Mediatizing educational policy: the journalistic field, science policy, and cross-field effects', *Journal of Education Policy*, 19, 361–80.

Lingard, B. and Rizvi, F. (1998) 'Globalization, the OECD, and Australian higher education', in J. Currie and J. Newson (Eds), *Universities and Globalisation: Critical Perspectives*, Thousand Oaks, CA: Sage.

Lyotard, J.-F. (1984) *The Postmodern Condition: A Report on Knowledge*, G. Bennington and B. Massumi (Trans.), Manchester: Manchester University Press.

McCright, A. and Dunlap, R. (2003) 'Defeating Kyoto: The conservative movement's impact on U.S. climate change policy', *Social Problems*, 50, 3: 348–73. Available HTTP: <http://stephenschneider.stanford.edu/Publications/PDF_ Papers/McCrightDunlap2003.pdf>(accessed 11 August 2005).

Macdonell, D. (1986) *Theories of Discourse: An Introduction*, Oxford: Basil Blackwell.

MacLure, M. (2003) *Discourse in Educational and Social Research*, London: Sage.

MacMillan, K. (2002) 'Narratives of social disruption: education news in the British tabloid press', *Discourse*, 23,1: 27–38.

Marginson, S. (1993) *Education and Public Policy in Australia*, Cambridge: Cambridge University Press.

Marginson, S. (1997) *Educating Australia: Government, Economy and Citizen Since 1960*, Cambridge: Cambridge University Press.

Marshall, C. and Anderson, G. (1994) 'Rethinking the public and private spheres: feminist and cultural studies perspectives on the politics of education', *Politics of Education Association Yearbook*, 169–82.

Miller, P. and Rose, N. (1993) 'Governing economic life', in M.Gane and T. Johnson (Eds), *Foucault's New Domains*, London: Routledge.

Murray, A. (2004) *Scorecard IV The Status of Economic Reform in the Enlarging EU*, *Centre for European Reform, Working Paper*, Centre for European Reform. Available HTTP: <http://www.cer.org.uk/pdf/wp505_lisbon_iv.pdf> (accessed 13 September 2005).

NAGCELL (National Advisory Group for Continuing Education and Lifelong Learning) (1997) *Learning for the Twenty-first Century, First report of the National Advisory Group for Continuing Education and Lifelong Learning*, Sheffield: DfEE.

NAGCELL (1999) *Creating Learning Cultures: Next Steps in Achieving the Learning Age, Second report of the National Advisory Group for Continuing Education and Lifelong Learning*, Sheffield: DfEE.

NCIHE (National Committee of Inquiry into Higher Education) (1997) *Higher Education in the Learning Society: Summary Report*, Norwich: HMSO.

Nelson, J. (1987) 'Stories of Science and Politics', in J. Nelson, A. Megill, and D. McCloskey (Eds), *The Rhetoric of the Human Sciences: Language and Argument in Scholarship and Public Affairs*, Madison, WI: The University of Wisconsin Press.

Nelson, J., Megill, A. and McCloskey, D. (Eds) (1987) *The Rhetoric of the Human Sciences: Language and Argument in Scholarship and Public Affairs*, Madison, WI: The University of Winsconsin Press.

Nelson, R. and Phelps, E. (1966) 'Investment in humans, technological diffusion and economic growth,' *American Economic Review*, May, 69–75.

NIACE (2001) *A Memorandum on Lifelong Learning, Response to the Consultations from UK NGOs working in the Field of Adult Learning*, NIACE. Available HTTP: <http://www.niace.org.uk/Organisation/advocacy/memorandum/Response.pdf> (accessed 20 October 2005).

Nicoll, K. (1997) ' "Flexible learning" – unsettling practices', *Studies in Continuing Education*, 19, 2: 100–11.

Nicoll, K. (1998) ' "Fixing" the "facts": flexible learning as policy invention', *Higher Education Research and Development*, 17, 3: 291–304.

Nicoll, K. and Chappell, C. (1996) 'Policy effects: "flexibility" and "vocationalisation" in tertiary education', *Studies in Continuing Education*, 20, 1: 39–50

Nicoll, K. and Edwards, R. (1997) 'Open learning and the demise of discipline', *Open Learning*, 12, 3: 14–24.

Nicoll, K. and Edwards, R. (2000) 'Reading policy texts: lifelong learning as metaphor', *International Journal of Lifelong Education*, 19, 5: 459–69.

Nicoll, K. and Edwards, R. (2004) 'Lifelong learning and the sultans of spin', *Journal of Education Policy*, 19, 1: 43–55.

Nunan, T. (2000) 'Exploring the concept of flexibility', in V. Jakupec and J. Garrick (Eds), *Flexible Learning, Human Resource and Organizational Development: Putting Theory to Work*, London: Routledge.

OECD (1996) *Lifelong Learning for All: Meeting of the Education Committee at Ministerial Level, 16/17 January 1996*, Paris: Organization for Economic Co-operation and Development.

OECD (2005) *Progress and Output Results of the Programme of Work 2002 to 2004)*, *Meeting of OECD Education Chief Executives*, Copenhagen: OECD. Available HTTP: <www.oecd.org/dataoecd/17/17/35378941.pdf> (accessed 20 October 2005).

Olssen, M. and Peters, M. (2005) 'Neoliberalism, higher education and the knowledge economy: from the free market to knowledge capitalism', *Journal of Education Policy*, 20, 3: 313–45.

Onman, C. (1996) *The Policy Challenges of Globalization and Regionalization, Policy Brief No. 11*, OECD Development Centre. Available HTTP: <http://www.oecd.org/> (accessed 20 October 2005).

Osborne, D. and Gaebler, T. (1993) *Rethinking Government*, New York: Plume Books.

O'Shaughnessy, N. D., (2004) *Politics and Propaganda: Weapons of Mass Seduction*, Manchester: Manchester University Press.

Oxford English Dictionary (1989) Volume XIII, Oxford: Clarendon Press.

Parker, S. (1997) *Reflective Teaching in the Postmodern World: A Manifesto for Education in Postmodernity*, Buckingham: Open University Press.

Perry, N. (1998) *Hyperreality and Global Culture*, London: Routledge.

Peters, M. (1996) *Poststructuralism, Politics and Education, Critical Studies in Education and Culture Series*, H. Giroux and P. Freire (Eds) Connecticut and London: Bergin and Garvey.

Peters, M. (2003) 'Education policy in the age of knowledge capitalism', *Policy Futures in Education*, 1, 2: 361–79.

Peters, M. and Humes, W. (2003) 'Editorial: the reception of post-structuralism in educational research and policy', *Journal of Education Policy*, 18, 2: 109–113.

Peters, M. and Marshall, J. (1996) *Individualism and Community: Education and Social Policy in the Postmodern Condition*, London: Falmer Press.

Potter, J. (1996) *Representing Reality: Discourse, Rhetoric and Social Construction*, London: Sage.

Power, S. (1992) 'Researching the impact of education policy: difficulties and discontinuities', *Journal of Education Policy*, 7, 5: 493–500.

Pusey, M. (1991) *Economic Rationalism in Canberra: A Nation-Building State Changes its Mind*, Cambridge: Cambridge University Press.

Raggatt, P., Edwards, R. and Small, N. (Eds) (1996) *The Learning Society: Challenges and Trends*, London: Routledge with The Open University.

Ransom, J. (1997) *Foucault's Discipline: The Politics of Subjectivity*, Durham: Duke University Press.

Rein, M. (1983) *From Policy to Practice*, London: Macmillan.

Rizvi, F. and Kemmis, S. (1987) *Dilemmas of Reform*, Geelong: Deakin Institute for Studies in Education.

Rose, N. (1988) *Inventing Our Selves. Psychology, Power and Personhood*. Cambridge: Cambridge University Press.

Rose, N. (1999) *Powers of Freedom: Reframing Political Thought*, Cambridge: Polity Press.

Rubenson, K. (1999) 'Adult education and training: the poor cousin. An analysis of OECD reviews of national policies for education', *Scottish Journal of Adult and Continuing Education*, 5, 2: 5–32.

Rumble, G. (1995) 'Labour market theories and distance education 1: industrialization and distance education', *Open Learning*, 10, 1: 10–19.

Ryan, A. (2005) 'New labour and higher education', *Oxford Review of Education*, 31, 1: 87–100.

Scheurich, J. (1994) 'Policy archaeology: a new policy studies methodology', *Journal of Education Policy*, 9, 4: 297–316.

Schon, D. (1979) 'Generative metaphor: a perspective on problem-setting in metaphor', in A. Ortony (Ed.), *Metaphor and Thought*, Cambridge: Cambridge University Press, 254–83.

Schuller, T. (1998) 'Three steps towards a learning society', *Studies in the Education of Adults*, 30, 1: 11–20.

Scottish Office (1998) *Opportunity Scotland*, Edinburgh: The Stationery Office.

Seddon, T. (1996) 'The principle of choice in policy research', *Journal of Education Policy*, 11, 2: 197–214.

Seddon, T. and Angus, L. (1999) 'Steering futures: practices and possibilities of institutional redesign in Australian education and training', *Journal of Education Policy*, 14, 5: 491–506.

Shapiro, M. (Ed.) (1984a) *Language and Politics*, Oxford: Basil Blackwell.

Shapiro, M. (1984b) 'Literary production as a politicizing practice', in M. Shapiro (Ed.), *Language and Politics*. Oxford: Basil Blackwell.

Shapiro, M. (1989) 'Representing world politics: the sport/war intertext', in J. Der Derian and M. Shapiro (Eds), *International/Intertextual Relations*. Lexington, MA: Lexington Books.

Shorter Oxford English Dictionary on Historical Principles (1992) Volume 2, Oxford: Clarendon Press.

Simons, H. (1990) 'Introduction: the rhetoric of inquiry as an intellectual movement', in H. Simons (Ed.), *The Rhetorical Turn: Invention and Persuasion in the Conduct of Inquiry*, Chicago, IL: University of Chicago Press.

Straehle, C., Weiss, G., Wodak, R., Muntigl, P. and Sedlak, M. (1999) 'Struggle as metaphor in European Union discourses on unemployment', *Discourse and Society*, 10, 1: 67–99.

Strain, M. (1998) 'Towards an economy of lifelong learning: reconceptualizing relations between learning and life', *British Journal of Educational Studies*, 40, 3: 264–77.

Strain, M. and Field, J. (1997) 'On the myth of the learning society', *British Journal of Education Studies*, 45, 2: 141–55.

Stronach, I. and MacLure, M. (1997) *Educational Research Undone: The Postmodern Embrace*, Buckingham: Open University Press.

Swales, J. (1990) *Genre Analysis*, Cambridge: Cambridge University Press.

Tait, A. (1996) 'Open and distance learning policy in the European Union 1985–1995', *Higher Education Policy*, 9, 3: 221–38.

Taylor, P. (1995) 'Postgraduate education and open learning: anticipating a new order?', *The Australian Universities' Review*, 38, 2: 28–31.

Taylor, P. (1997) 'Creating contexts conducive to flexibility', *Studies in Continuing Education*, 19, 2: 112–23.

Taylor, S. (1997) 'Critical policy analysis: exploring contexts, texts and consequences', *Discourse*, 18, 1: 23–35.

Taylor, S., Rizvi, F., Lingard, B. and Henry, M. (1997) *Educational Policy and the Politics of Change*, London: Routledge.

Thorpe, M. (2000) 'Pedagogical implications of flexible learning', in V. Jakupec and J. Garrick (Eds), *Flexible Learning, Human Resource and Organizational Development: Putting Theory to Work*, London: Routledge.

Tight, M. (1998) 'Education, education, education! The vision of lifelong learning in the Kennedy, Dearing and Fryer reports', *Oxford Review of Education*, 24, 4: 473–85.

Tikly, L. (2003) 'Governmentality and the study of education policy in South Africa', *Journal of Education Policy*, 18, 2: 161–74.

Tobias, R. (2004) 'Lifelong learning policies and discourses: critical reflections from Aotearoa, New Zealand', *International Journal of Lifelong Education*, 23(6), 569–88.

Torfing, J. (1999) *New Theories of Discourse: Laclau, Mouffe and Zizek*, Oxford: Blackwell.

Trood, C. and Gale, T. (2001) 'The diffusion of policy in contexts of practice: flexible delivery in Australian vocational education and training', *Journal of Vocational Education and Training*, 53, 1: 161–74.

UNESCO (1996) *Learning: The Treasure Within, Report to UNESCO of the International Commission on Education for the Twenty-first Century*, Paris: UNESCO.

UNESCO (1997) *Open and Distance Learning: Prospects and Policy Considerations*, Paris: UNESCO.

Urry, J. (2000) *Sociology Beyond Societies: Mobilities for the Twenty-first Century*, London: Routledge.

Usher, R., Bryant, I. and Johnston, R. (1997) *Adult Education and the Postmodern Challenge: Learning Beyond the Limits*, London: Routledge.

Wain, K. (2000) 'The learning society: postmodern politics', *International Journal of Lifelong Education*, 19, 1: 36–53.

Walters, S. and Watters, K. (2001) 'Twenty years of adult education in Southern Africa', *International Journal of Lifelong Education*, 20, 1/2: 100–113.

Webster, F. (1995) *Theories of the Information Society*, London: Routledge.

Welsh, P. and Frost, D. (2000) 'Understanding the reorganization of secondary schooling: a political games approach', *Journal of Education Policy*, 15, 2: 217–35.

West, R. (1998) Copy of letter presenting the Review Report to David Kemp from the then Minister for Employment, Education Training and Youth Affairs, in

DEETYA (1998) *Learning for Life, Final Report: Review of Higher Education Financing and Policy*, Canberra: DEETYA.

Wilson, J. D. (2001) 'Lifelong learning in Japan – a lifeline for a "maturing" society?', *International Journal of Lifelong Education*, 20, 4: 297–313.

Wodak, R. (2000) 'Recontextualization and the transformation of meanings: a critical discourse analysis of decision making in European Union meetings about employment policies', in S. Sarangi and M. Coulthard (Eds), *Discourse and Social Life*, Harlow: Pearson Education.

Yeatman, A. (1994) *Postmodern Revisionings of the Political*, London: Routledge.

Index

Poststructuralist Marxisms 46
Poststructuralist theorizings of policy
texts 48–55; discursive and
non-discursive practices 51–52;
pure description, of discursive
events 53; serious speech act 53
Power and desire 55, 58–59, 70,
83, 87, 139, 141, 143, 145,
150–51, 155
Power-knowledge 6
Productive point of departure *see*
Foucault, Michael, systems of
exclusion

Rarefaction, principles of 57–60, 143
Reflexivity 47–48, 64
Reification 111–12, 118, 121
Rhetorical analyst, role of 4
Rhetorical strategies: ironizing 112;
narrative structure as 73–77;
reification 111–12, 118, 121
Rhetorical work: analysis 4–5, 7, 12,
14, 43, 55, 61, 63, 78, 113, 135–37,
148–49, 152; fellowships, role of 87;
genres of 11, *see also* Genre;
rhetoric, notion of 4, 6–7; rhetorical
strategies 66
Ritual 55, 58, 60, 113, 142–44, 154;
see also Doctrine; Fellowship
Rules of exclusion 10, 58, 59, 60,
63–64, 84, 144–45, 150, 155

Schemas of politicization *see*
Politicization, schemas of
Social Darwinian system 104–05
Speech acts 53–55
Spin 3, 4, 14, 111–12, 123, 136,
148–49, 155
Stake 14, 30, 67–68, 78, 81, 87, 111,
125, 128, 142, 144; management of
69–70, 74, 120

Statement 13, 52–55, 60–61,
63–64, 66–67, 73, 83–85, 89,
91, 113–14, 116, 120, 123,
129–30, 132–34, 137–45,
150–55
Subjectivity 12, 49, 68, 150
System of metaphors 86, 93, 103,
146–47
Systems of exclusion 55; division of
madness 56; prohibited words
55–56; will to truth 55

TAFE Institutes *see* Australia, TAFE
sector in
Taylorist organizational
structures 29
Theorizings, trails of 5, 12, 140;
see also Poststructuralist theorizings
of policy texts
Theory 5, 11–12, 140; mobility of
100–01
Third Way thinking 113
Trails 5, 12, 140

Ultimate uncertainty 78
UNESCO 8

Vassalage 93, 95
VET, *see* Vocational education and
training teachers
Vocational education and training
teachers 18

Warranting 68–70, 74, 85, 89,
119, 127
Welfare state forms, of governance 2
West Report 10, 66, 70, 77, 79,
87, 115, 117, 120, 126,
142, 146
White Papers 113, 119, 122
Will to truth 55–58, 138, 151